'In *Sándor Ferenczi's Confusion of Tongues Theory of Trauma*, Arnold Rachman and Clara Mucci take us into the origin and genius of Ferenczi's concept of the "Confusion of Tongues," Ferenczi's insight into the trauma of child sexual abuse in the origins of psychopathology, and Freud's campaign against Ferenczi's ideas. The book is a rich, erudite, and close-up view into Ferenczi's contributions and the intellectual climate of that era.'

—**Beatrice Beebe**, *New York State Psychiatric Institute, Columbia University Medical Center*

'Rachman and Mucci pull together in this slim heavy-hitting volume a masterful account of the complicated intense relationship between Sándor Ferenczi and Sigmund Freud. They show how Ferenczi, with his 'confusion of tongues paradigm' – an all-embracing term for dissociation and splitting defenses, that takes account of the disturbingly large number of adults who suffered abuse/trauma perpetrated against them by adults when they were children. Freud knew all of this in the 1890s when his 'affect/trauma model' of psychopathology was advanced. But Freud moved on and modified his own ideas in the direction of codifying the principle of psychosexual development and children's incest wishes, turning his back on patients' actual traumatic experiences. Ferenczi in the early 1920s essentially, and increasingly, feuded with Freud, or rather Freud feuded with Ferenczi who told Freud more-or-less, '*you did your best work 25 years ago, prior to you taking a dreadful wrong turn into the psychosexual stages, and advancement of the oedipal complex as a core influence upon the child.*' For Freud, this was a threat to his authority, and Ferenczi was cast by Freud as a 'pathological liar' while Ferenczi perceived Freud as given to 'emotional blindness' with respect to the actual high level of experiences of child sexual, physical and emotional abuse among patients seeking treatment. Children are often targets of incestuous attacks, but children arguably do NOT have incestuous wishes. This painful but important chapter in the history of psychoanalysis has been reported on by others before, but Rachman and Mucci achieve a masterful integration of sources to articulate a clinical view of trauma that resonates deeply with our contemporary world. Diverse case histories and explorations into literature (e.g. Kafka) add substance to this important volume. Social workers, counsellors, psychologists, and psychoanalysts wishing to fine tune their trauma-informed understanding will be well-served by reading this volume.'

—**Howard Steele** *is Professor of Psychology, Director of Graduate Studies, and Co-Director (with Miriam Steele) of the Center for Attachment Research at the New School for Social Research, New York*

'This far reaching and deep exploration of Ferenczi's classic paper, "Confusion of Tongues," brings scholarship and understanding of this contribution to psychoanalysis to a new level of detail and specificity. A powerful addition to our appreciation of what Ferenczi has meant to psychoanalysis, and to the crucial role of trauma in character formation and development.'

—**Adrienne Harris**, *faculty and supervisor at both New York University and the Psychoanalytic Institute of Northern California*

Ferenczi's Confusion of Tongues Theory of Trauma

Arnold Wm. Rachman and Clara Mucci provide a detailed examination of the significance of Sándor Ferenczi's paradigm shifting theory of trauma, the Confusion of Tongues, and confirm its relevance for the psychoanalytic theory and analysis of trauma today.

As the first alternative to Freud's theory of the Oedipal complex, Ferenczi's Confusion of Tongues theory expanded the theoretical and clinical boundaries of psychoanalysis to establish that psychological trauma as a result of childhood sexual abuse and trauma experiences are a significant contributing factor to the development of psychological disorders. The authors address the lack of attention paid to the significance of sexual abuse trauma to understanding psychological ill health in psychoanalysis, and integrate the latest research on neurobiology to demonstrate how Ferenczi's theory is meaningful to understanding many aspects of human behavior today.

This work will be formative to psychoanalysts and psychotherapists both in training and in practice and provide renewed insight into the treatment of childhood sexual abuse and psychological trauma.

Arnold Wm. Rachman, PhD, is a clinical psychologist and relational psychoanalyst who has contributed to the recovery of the life and work of Sándor Ferenczi and the Budapest School of Psychoanalysis.

Clara Mucci, PhD, received a doctorate on Shakespeare and Psychoanalysis from Emory University, USA, and a psychology degree specializing in psychoanalytic psychotherapy (University of Chieti; SIPP, Milan). Professor of Psychodynamic Psychology at the University of Bergamo, Italy, she is the author of several books on Shakespeare, psychoanalysis, trauma, and personality disorders.

Psychoanalytic Inquiry Book Series

Joseph D. Lichtenberg
Series Editor

Like its counterpart, *Psychoanalytic Inquiry: A Topical Journal for Mental Health Professionals*, the Psychoanalytic Inquiry Book Series presents a diversity of subjects within a diversity of approaches to those subjects. Under the editorship of Joseph Lichtenberg, in collaboration with Melvin Bornstein and the editorial board of *Psychoanalytic Inquiry*, the volumes in this series strike a balance between research, theory, and clinical application. We are honored to have published the works of various innovators in psychoanalysis, including Frank Lachmann, James Fosshage, Robert Stolorow, Donna Orange, Louis Sander, Léon Wurmser, James Grotstein, Joseph Jones, Doris Brothers, Fredric Busch, and Joseph Lichtenberg, among others.

The series includes books and monographs on mainline psychoanalytic topics, such as sexuality, narcissism, trauma, homosexuality, jealousy, envy, and varied aspects of analytic process and technique. In our efforts to broaden the field of analytic interest, the series has incorporated and embraced innovative discoveries in infant research, self psychology, intersubjectivity, motivational systems, affects as process, responses to cancer, borderline states, contextualism, postmodernism, attachment research and theory, medication, and mentalization. As further investigations in psychoanalysis come to fruition, we seek to present them in readable, easily comprehensible writing.

After more than 25 years, the core vision of this series remains the investigation, analysis and discussion of developments on the cutting edge of the psychoanalytic field, inspired by a boundless spirit of inquiry. A full list of all the titles available in the *Psychoanalytic Inquiry* Book Series is available at www.routledge.com/Psychoanalytic-Inquiry-Book-Series/book-series/LEAPIBS.

Recent Books in the Series:

An Experience-based Vision of Psychoanalytic Theory and Practice
by Joseph D. Lichtenberg, Frank M. Lachmann, James L Fosshage

Peace Building Through Women's Health: Psychoanalytic, Sociopsychological, and Community Perspectives on the Israeli-Palestinian Conflict
Edited By Norbert Goldfield

The Self-Restorative Power of Music
A Psychological Perspective
by Frank M. Lachmann

Psychoanalysis and Society's Neglect of the Sexual Abuse of Children, Youth and Adults
Re-addressing Freud's Original Theory of Sexual Abuse and Trauma
by Arnold Wm. Rachman

Leadership, Psychoanalysis and Society
by Edited Michael Maccoby and Mauricio Cortina

Freud, Dora, and the Confusion of Tongues
by Arnold Wm. Rachman and Paul Mattick

Ferenczi's Confusion of Tongues Theory of Trauma

A Relational Neurobiological Perspective

Arnold Wm. Rachman
and Clara Mucci

Routledge
Taylor & Francis Group

LONDON AND NEW YORK

Designed cover image: Confusion of Tongues Collage by Arnold Wm. Rachman, 06/2022.

First published 2024
by Routledge
4 Park Square, Milton Park, Abingdon, Oxon OX14 4RN

and by Routledge
605 Third Avenue, New York, NY 10158

Routledge is an imprint of the Taylor & Francis Group, an informa business

© 2024 Arnold Wm. Rachman and Clara Mucci

The right of Arnold Wm. Rachman and Clara Mucci to be identified as authors of this work has been asserted in accordance with sections 77 and 78 of the Copyright, Designs and Patents Act 1988.

British Library Cataloguing-in-Publication Data
A catalogue record for this book is available from the British Library

Library of Congress Cataloging-in-Publication Data
Names: Rachman, Arnold Wm., author. | Mucci, Clara, author.
Title: Ferenczi's confusion of tongues theory of trauma : a
    relational neurobiological perspective / Arnold Wm. Rachman,
    Ph.D. and Clara Mucci, Ph.D. — Provided by publisher.
Identifiers: LCCN 2023010503 (print) | LCCN 2023010504 (ebook) |
    ISBN 9781032207469 (hbk) | ISBN 9781032207476 (pbk) |
    ISBN 9781003265030 (ebk)
Subjects: LCSH: Psychoanalysis. | Child sexual abuse—
    Psychological aspects. | Ferenczi, Sándor, 1873–1933.
Classification: LCC BF173 .R135 2024 (print) | LCC BF173
    (ebook) | DDC 150.19/5—dc23/eng/20230510
LC record available at https://lccn.loc.gov/2023010503
LC ebook record available at https://lccn.loc.gov/2023010504

ISBN: 9781032207469 (hbk)
ISBN: 9781032207476 (pbk)
ISBN: 9781003265030 (ebk)

DOI: 10.4324/9781003265030

Typeset in Times New Roman
by Apex CoVantage, LLC

On May 2021, Joe Lichtenberg, M.D. died at 95 years old, and the psychoanalytic community, and I (AWR), lost a very special person. He was a beloved, respected, modern pioneer of psychoanalysis. Everyone who knew him respected his intellect, sophistication, and humanness. From the moment I met Joe, I felt his positive presence. He was intellectually stimulating and engaging, responsive, friendly, and kind. He was one of the theoretical leaders in self psychology as well as in the wider analytic community, the innovative editor of Psychoanalytic Inquiry, a sought-after supervisor and seminar leader and well-beloved human being. We shared an interest and respect for the contributions of Sándor Ferenczi to psychoanalysis. Joe's analyst had been analyzed by Ferenczi. Joe encouraged me to present papers at the self psychology conferences and asked me to produce three issues of Psychoanalytic Inquiry. I am grateful and indebted to him for becoming a mentor by accepting and nourishing seven books of mine, in his position as Editor-in-Chief of the Psychoanalytic Inquiry Book Series at Routledge Press. I was also honored when he joined me as a discussant at the Elizabeth Severn Symposium to celebrate the founding of the Elizabeth Severn Section of the Freud Archives at the Library of Congress, Washington, D.C., in June 2014.

For thirty years, I have been privileged to know one of the great psychoanalysts in the modern period of psychoanalysis as a mentor, colleague, and friend. Joe was, as my grandmother, Bertha Metsch Beispiel would say, "A terre ganze Mensch." I would translate this from the Yiddish to mean – "Joe was for me, a precious, total human being."

Contents

Acknowledgments

There have been three primary colleagues and friends who have helped me (AWR) share my voice about the significance of the contributions of Sándor Ferenczi and the Budapest School of Psychoanalysis. The late Esther Menaker, Ph.D., served as a mentor, role model, revered colleague, and friend. Her courageous journey from an analysand of Anna Freud to her research on Otto Rank to embracing self psychology, affirmed my journey from client-centered psychotherapy to discovering Sándor Ferenczi and the Budapest School of Psychoanalysis to finding a contemporary intellectual and clinical home in the relational psychoanalysis perspective. Esther's affirmation of my scholarship and her warm embrace as a friend lit my path as I journeyed into the darkness that was Sándor Ferenczi's forgotten world.

The late Paul Roazen, Ph.D., writings, such as Freud and His Followers opened a window into the scholarly critical studies of Freud and psychoanalysis. As a scholar and friend, he gave me the support and intellectual strength to believe in my ideas about Ferenczi's importance to psychoanalysis and his subsequent suppression. His affirmation as a scholar and friend was essential to my professional growth.

Jeffrey Moussaieff Masson, Ph.D., has been a scholar and friend who has been an inspiration. His pioneering intellectual research and findings about Sándor Ferenczi and Elizabeth Severn has provided the impetus to explore new territory in psychoanalytic history. His voice has been silenced in psychoanalysis as was Ferenczi's. I admire his intellectual courage and emotional capacity to tell the truth to the psychoanalytic establishment. He continues to inspire me to express my own idea about the establishment's deliberate silencing of Ferenczi and the harm it has done to psychoanalysis.

We wish to express our appreciation to Georgina Clutterbuck, Editorial Assistant, Routledge Press, for her skill, prompt responsiveness, and interpersonal warmth in her interaction in helping with the technical aspects of publishing this book.

Cassidy McKenna was invaluable in helping create a typed manuscript of the material given to her.

And, as always, Kate Hawes, Senior Publisher, Routledge Press, guided a proposal into a published book, for which we are very grateful.

Arnold Wm. Rachman and Clara Mucci

Our Collaboration

I wish to pay tribute to the experience of collaborating in writing this book with Clara Mucci. Meeting Clara at the Sándor Ferenczi Summer Seminar in Florence, Italy, developed and organized by Carlo Bonomi, in his capacity as president of the International Sándor Ferenczi Community, in July of 2017, has become a significant personal and professional event. We both gave seminars, Clara on trauma disorders and myself on the discovery of the contributions of Elizabeth Severn (Ferenczi's famous analysand). I was both personally and professionally moved by Clara's presentation. Her description of her analysis of the trauma suffered by a holocaust survivor was so emotionally moving, it brought me to tears. Her humanity as a psychoanalyst illuminated her scholarly understanding of the theory and clinical treatment of trauma. When she finished her presentation, I approached her, telling her how moved I was by her presentation. She expressed a similar experience with my seminar. Then we enjoyed a wonderful lunch together. Since then we have become collaborating colleagues and close friends.

Arnold Wm. Rachman

The Origin of Ferenczi's Confusion of Tongues Concept in the Biblical Narrative of the Tower of Babel

The Tower of Babel

Ferenczi used the Jewish Bible's narrative of the Tower of Babel and the "talking in tongues" as described in the Book of Genesis, Verses 1–9, in the Old Testament (Werblowsky & Wigoder, 1997, p. 701), as the fundamental reference for his Confusion of Tongues paradigm. The Confusion of Tongues is the initial fragmentation of human languages described in Genesis 11: 1–9, as a result of the construction of the Tower of Babel (Berlin & Bretter, 2004, p. 29). The Jewish-Roman historian Flavius Josephus, in his antiquities of the Jews, wrote that it was Nimrod who had the tower built. He was a tyrant who tried to turn the people away from God. Rather than destroying the people, they were confused because annihilation with a flood had not taught them to be godly. The Tower of Babel was erected by the inhabitants of Sinar (Babylonia) to reach heaven. The name Babel is attributed to the Hebrew verb balal, which means to confuse or confound (Werblowsky & Wigoder, 1997).

The description of the Tower of Babel and the Confusion of Tongues experience as referenced in the Bible can be described as follows:

> Tower Babel, a structure erected after the Flood by the inhabitants of Sindar (Babylonia) for the purpose of reaching heaven . . . looking down upon the builders and finding their purpose ill conceived, God is said to have confounded their speech and scattered them over the earth. . . . The origin of the literary motif of the confusion of tongues and the subsequent division and dispersal of humankind into nations and all over the earth . . . the central motif of the "confounding" of tongues was the result of the rivalry between God and humans.
>
> (Werblowsky & Wigoder, 1997, p. 701 – Genesis 11: 1–9)

DOI: 10.4324/9781003265030-1

Reading the text of the Tower of Babel in Genesis 11: 1–9, one can interpret the events described. The issue with the tower was the sin: the people thinking they could build a tower that could reach God in heaven; by their own strength they also wanted to make a name for themselves; and to preserve vanity for themselves. God came down to see the city and the tower. The text described God's concern for the growing pride of the human race. If people are allowed to build this immense tower, it will mean they will do whatever they want to do in the future. If God does not intervene, they will become too powerful. He must intervene. He does two specific things: he confuses their speech, and he scattered them abroad. The conclusion is that pride is the enemy. God humbled the people by confusing their language and scattering them among the different lands.

Confusion of Tongues

There are several themes that can be discerned in the Tower of Babel narrative: The sin of people believing they could reach God by building a stairway to heaven; people wanting to compete with God; people becoming prideful and losing their humility; people being dispersed throughout the land; people's speech being confused. Of all the themes in the Tower of Babel, we believe Ferenczi was interested in the idea that people who were demonstrating unacceptable behavior would be victims of not being able to speak or relate to one another in a meaningful way. Speaking in incompatible languages and confused ways of relating created a crisis between an authority and an individual, which struck a chord in Ferenczi's thinking and feeling. Did this phenomenon described in biblical times remind Ferenczi of an experience with which he was familiar? This is possible in the description and analysis of Ferenczi's own childhood sexual trauma (Rachman, 2018). The familiarity with the personal experience of sexual trauma was enhanced by significant observation in his growing clinical interaction with sexual trauma survivors which he chronicled in his Clinical Diary (Ferenczi, 1988). This indicated a fundamental issue in human behavior that as a psychoanalyst he was struggling to understand and describe. His clinical work with analysands, who were abused by their parents, demonstrated that the child and parent were functioning in different worlds, speaking different languages. The child enters a relationship with a parent, who is an authority, an individual who has power, control and status over them. Let us not forget children see their parents as godlike figures. This parent can use their authority to get what they need from the child. Without the child's permission, they initiate a traumatic experience. The parent approaches the child, as if they are going to fulfill the child's needs, which encourages the child to feel they are being loved. But because the parental authority is interested in their own self-fulfillment, they are aggressing against the child. They are not loving. The child senses the discrepancy between love and exploitation, reacting with confusion and a host of psychological defense mechanisms.

Ferenczi used the Babel narrative where the ultimate authority (God), imposed a punishment on the people who he believed were behaving in an ill-conceived way, by <u>confounding their speech</u>. This motif of a person(s) behaving in a negative manner is a characteristic of the authority's use of language and behavior to exploit another, which leads to the disturbance of confusion.

In formulating the Confusion of Tongues idea, as a way to conceptualize what Ferenczi was observing in his clinical interaction, he was communicating to psychoanalysis that he was concerned with several important issues:

1. The sexual abuse of children was occurring in middle-class families, as in the reports of abuse by his analysands. This verified Freud's original finding in The Seduction Hypothesis (Freud, 1954), which changed the notion that sexual abuse of children was perpetrated by criminal or lower class individuals. Ferenczi's observations pointed to a modern view that sexual abuse of children in upstanding family interaction was an issue which needed attention but had been neglected.
2. Child sexual abuse was an important psychodynamic in the development of psychopathology. In particular, child sexual abuse leads to a trauma disorder. This was the introduction of a new category of psychological disorder, which was in contrast to Freudian view of neurosis whose origin was in the Oedipus complex.
3. Locating psychological disorder in the actual interaction in the parental/child relationship contributed an added dimension to the psychodynamics that psychoanalysis needed to consider. Ferenczi realized that

real experiences in familial relationships were harmful to psychological development and could encourage a psychological disorder.

4. When individuals within a family start speaking different languages and act as if they are living in different universes, they are not empathically connected to one another. The possibility of trauma enters their relationship, as one of the dyad does not understand or respond to the needs of the other.

5. Developing a two-person psychoanalysis was necessary. The authority, the analyst, expands the analytic encounter to invite the analysand to be a responsive partner in the analytic relationship. The clinical philosophy of a two-person analytic experience is that the relationship is mutual and democratic. The analysand is seen as an individual who is encouraged to contribute to the analysis as he/she is invited to share their ideas about the therapeutic process, the analytic relationship, and any changes in the process that may be necessary.

The Confusion of Tongues idea which Ferenczi developed focused psychoanalysis as the narrative of the relationship between the parent and child and analyst and analysand. His new idea was intended to expand the clinical perspective to include actual as well as unconscious factors in the development of psychological disorders. His so-called difficult cases were not analysands who were struggling with unconscious Oedipal conflicts who developed neurotic traits, but were individuals who suffered from parental abuse who were struggling with real trauma. The Oedipally conflicted analysands needed interpretation to help uncover their unconscious thoughts and feelings to develop insight into their Oedipal conflicts. Ferenczi's analysands, he observed, needed empathy so they could feel affirmed that their abuse was real and was the cause of their emotional disorder. Empathy would allow them to accept, retrieve and confront their childhood trauma. Empathizing with the subjective experience of the analysand allowed Ferenczi to concentrate on the analysand's experience rather than to interpret his version of the analysand's experience. With concentration directed on the analysand's subjective experience, it was possible to hear the emotional needs of the analysand rather than the analyst offering his/her wisdom. The Confusion of Tongues idea translated the analytic encounter from a one-person to a two-person experience (see Mucci, Chapter 13, this volume, Rachman, 1989a, 1989b, 1997, 2003, 2018).

References

Berlin, A. and Bretter, M.Z. (Eds.) (2004). *The Jewish Study Bible*. New York: Oxford University.

Ferenczi, S. (1988). *The Clinical Diary of Sándor Ferenczi* (J. Dupont, Ed., M. Balint and N.Z. Jackson, Trans.). Cambridge, MA: Harvard University Press.

Freud, S. (1954). *The Origins of Psychoanalysis: Letters to Wilhelm Fliess, Drafts and Notes, 1887–1902* (M. Bonaparte, A. Freud and E. Kris, Eds., Mosbacker and J. Strachey, Trans.). New York: Basic Books.

Rachman, A.W. (1989a). Confusion of Tongues: The Ferenczian metaphor for childhood seduction and emotional trauma. *Journal of the American Academy of Psychoanalysis*. 17(2), 182–205.

Rachman, A.W. (1989b). Ferenczi's contributions to the evolution of a self psychology framework in psychoanalysis. In Detrick, D.W. and Detrick, S.P. (Eds.) *Self Psychology: Comparison and Contrast*. Hillsdale, NJ: Analytic Press, pp. 81–100.

Rachman, A.W. (1997). *Sándor Ferenczi: The Psychotherapist of Tenderness and Passion*. Northvale, NJ: Jason Aronson.

Rachman, A.W. (2003). *Psychotherapy of Difficult Cases: Flexibility and Responsiveness in Clinical Practice*. Madison, CT: Psychosocial Press.

Rachman, A.W. (2018). *Elizabeth Severn: The "Evil Genius" of Psychoanalysis*. London: Routledge.

Werblowsky, R.J.Z. and Wigoder, G. (Eds.) (1997). *The Oxford Dictionary of the Jewish Religion*. New York: Oxford University Press.

Chapter 2

Ferenczi's Presentation of the Confusion of Tongues Paper

The 12th International Psychoanalytic Congress, Wiesbaden, Germany, September 4, 1932

The 12th International Psychoanalytic Congress was held at the Hotel Rose, at the Street George-August-Linn-Strauss, Landeshauptstadt, Wiesbaden, Germany. Hotel Rose is situated on the eastern edge of Kochbrunnenplatz. Its name goes back to 1523, where a complaint of failure to pay rent was filed against Margrethe Zur Rose, who was, at that time, the lessee. In 1896, the owner was finally permitted to tear down the building. The hotel had 200 rooms, a large bathing facility, and an indoor tennis court; in its prime it welcomed many prominent guests (www.wiesbaden. HotelRose). The town of Wiesbaden in southern Germany was famous as a resort. During the 18th and 19th centuries it was frequented by J.W. von Goethe, Johannes Brahms, Fydor Dostoyevksy, as well as various members of royal families. Wiesbaden with 27 hot, saline springs, mild climate, its park-like setting and other amenities made it a popular resort and conference center (www.wiesbaden/HotelRose).

The 12th Psychoanalytic Congress was scheduled from September 4–7, 1932, held at the Small Assembly Hall of the Kurhaus at the Hotel Rose. The officers of the congress, who sponsored the congress meeting were Max Eitingon, M.D. President; Anna Freud, Secretary; J.H.W. Van Ophuijsen, treasurer; Sándor Ferenczi, M.D., and Ernest Jones, M.D. Vice President (Freud, 1933). Anna Freud reported that there was a concern that the time and place of the congress was questionable. Further, she noted that attendance was down; 119 members were in attendance, which included 59 members of the association and 60 guests. The president of the congress, Max Eitingon, as did Anna Freud, pointed out that the congress was being held in spite of difficult times. Apparently, both were referring to the gathering storm of the Nazi regime in Germany and

DOI: 10.4324/9781003265030-2

the number of Jewish individuals who were psychoanalysts who were traveling to Wiesbaden. Nevertheless, Anna Freud thought the meeting was a success.

   Though desperately ill in the terminal phase of pernicious anemia, a then untreatable disease, Ferenczi managed to deliver his most famous paper: "The Confusion of Tongues between adults and children: The language of tenderness and passion" (Ferenczi, 1933). An additional burden was the emotional crisis from which Ferenczi was suffering. Ferenczi was given the honor of being the first presenter at the congress, giving his paper to open up the meeting on Sunday, September 4 at 9:00 am. One would not have predicted the 12th Congress would celebrate the Confusion of Tongues Paper, after the negative reaction Freud expressed in late August, just prior to the congress, when Ferenczi presented this paper to him for his approval. Ferenczi, who never gave up hope that Freud would affirm his trauma theory unfortunately suffered a trauma experience as a result of Freud's reaction to hearing Ferenczi's personal presentation of his paper. Freud not only completely rejected the paper but rejected Ferenczi (Fromm, 1959; see Chapter Four). Freud was so angry at Ferenczi's Confusion of Tongues paper that when Ferenczi anxiously waited for a word of affirmation at the ending, Freud did not shake his hand goodbye and turned his back on him as he left the room. Ferenczi was emotionally devastated by Freud's hostility and rejection (Fromm, 1959). Those close to Ferenczi believed he never recovered from Freud's abusive treatment (Rachman, 2018). The emotional burden that Ferenczi carried with him during the Confusion of Tongues presentation was the trauma Freud rejected him because he was presenting his own ideas against Freud's wishes.

   To understand the trauma Ferenczi suffered from Freud's negative reaction to his presentation of the Confusion of Tongues paper, Ferenczi reported this interaction:

> When I visited the Professor I told him of my latest technical ideas . . . empirically based on my work with patients . . . I have . . . endeavored through empathy to imagine what kind of loving care . . . the patient needs a different experience of tender, supporting care. . . . This process is one of trial and error . . . and must be pursued . . . with all skill and tact and loving kindness, and fearlessly. It must be absolutely honest and genuine.

The Professor listened to my exposition with increasing impatience and finally warned me that I was treading on dangerous ground and departing fundamentally from traditional actions and techniques of psycho-analysis . . . the Professor said, [it] might easily lead to sexual indulgence rather than an expression of parental devotion.

The warning ended the interview, I held out my hand in affectionate adieu. The Professor turned his back on me and walked out of his room.

(Fromm, 1959, f3, p. 65 Personal Communication from Izette de Forest to Eric Fromm)

Freud, in telling Ferenczi not to present this paper, was clearly denouncing the ideas that actual sexual abuse of children was not a meaningful psychodynamic for psychoanalysis to consider. Ferenczi was not introducing a dangerous idea, but trying to expand the boundaries of psychoanalysis to include trauma disorders (Rachman, 2018). The courageousness of Ferenczi in going ahead with his presentation in the light of his physical and emotional difficulties can be seen as a gift to psychoanalysis that was not appreciated at the time it was delivered or fully appreciated in contemporary psychoanalysis (Rachman, 2022).

Ferenczi's presentation was the first scientific session of the congress, with Ernest Jones, M.D. as chairman. The presentation was described as follows:

I. Dr. Sándor Ferenczi: The Emotions of Adults and Their Influence on the Development of the Sexual Life and Character of Children.

Previous analytic experience considered and amplified by illustrations throwing a deeper light on the subject. Influence of these findings on our views of the pathogenesis of the neurosis and possibly on certain points in the theory of sexuality.

(Freud, 1933, p. 142)

The brief description of the talk by Ferenczi masked the dramatic meaning and significance of Ferenczi's paper. It was Ferenczi's last presentation given at a time when he was considered by Freud and his followers as an unwelcomed dissident. He had isolated himself in Budapest with his Hungarian colleagues while he enjoyed the status of being the founder and president of the Hungarian Psychoanalytic Society. Also, he was a foremost teacher and supervisor, while providing the theoretical perspective for the Budapest School of Psychoanalysis (Rachman, 2016). If one examines the proceedings of the 12th Congress, it is clear that the Orthodox analytic community did not invite Ferenczi into the inner workings of the International Psychoanalytic Association, matching Ferenczi's own withdrawal from participation (Rachman, 1997a). One could characterize Ferenczi's participation at the 12th Congress as being a shadow figure of his previous stature as Freud's <u>favorite son and Grand Vizier</u>. Psychoanalytic dissidents, as bold and innovative as Ferenczi have been paid a serious price for their willingness to create an alternate theory and method to Freud's tradition. His Confusion of Tongues paper was considered so shockingly deviant that the assembled psychoanalysts became outraged at Ferenczi, fueling a Totschweigen campaign to suppress his ideas (Rachman, 1999; see Chapter Four) The reaction of the analysts attending the presentation were described as follows:

> many of the leading analysts of the time were there: Anna Freud, Federn, Alexander, Jekels, Jones, de Groot, Brunswich, Simmel, Harnik, Bonaparte, Sterba, Balint, Deutsch, Rado, Weiss, Odier, Glones, Roheim, Menniger, de Saussure [Freud did not attend because he was ill]. <u>The senior analysts,</u> the "bearers of the ring" <u>were of the opinion that views such as those expressed in the paper should not be circulated more widely than was absolutely necessary, that the dissemination of such views constituted a danger to society.</u>
>
> (*Masson, 1984, p. 151*)

There needs to be an amendment to the view described in Masson's description of the negative response to Ferenczi's Confusion of Tongues paper at the 12th International Psychoanalytic Congress. Michel Balint, Ferenczi's analysand and student who was a congress attendee was an advocate for Ferenczi's Confusion of Tongues. First, he translated this paper from German to English because Jones and Freud did not want to publish it in English (Rachman, 1997a, 1997b). Most psychoanalysts, at that time, did not know German and had no access to the journals that were not translated into English (Masson, 1984). Although it took from 1933 to 1949, Balint published the Confusion of Tongues paper into English in the International Psychoanalytic Journal (Balint, 1949; Ferenczi, 1933). Balint's courageous activity saved Ferenczi's landmark paper for the psychoanalytic community. Secondly, Balint used Ferenczi's Confusion of Tongues idea to be the first psychoanalyst within mainstream psychoanalysis to accept and promulgate Ferenczi's theory. But he went further than that when he expanded Ferenczi's idea of childhood sexual abuse as a psychodynamic in the development of a trauma disorder. Balint's view contributed to the idea that the nature of the emotional interaction between parent and child was fundamental to the development of trauma. The search for <u>primary object love</u> was Balint's expansion of the Confusion of Tongues idea. The search for primary love was Balint's fundamental concept for understanding human behavior:

> I consider . . . primitive or archaic, object love . . . to be the fone et origo [source and origin] of human libido development. The original and everlasting aim of all object relations is the primitive wish: <u>I must be loved without and expectation of return from me</u> . . . the desire to be loved always, everywhere, in every way, my whole body – is the primary tendency.
>
> *(Balint, 1965, pp. 50, 233)*

Interaction is necessary for fully analyzing personal issues and moving towards change. <u>The other can observe and illuminate an individual's functioning.</u>

References

Balint, M. (Ed.) (1949). Sándor Ferenczi number. *International Journal of Psycho-Analysis*. 30(4).

Balint, M. (1965). *Primary Love and Psychoanalytic Technique*. London: Tavistock (Original work published 1952).

Ferenczi, S. (1933). Sprachverwirring zwischen Erwachsenen und Kind: Die Sprache der Zärtlichkeit und der Leidenschaft (Confusion of Tongues between Adults and the Child: The Language of Tenderness and Passion). *Internationale Zeitshcrift für Psychoanalyse*. XIX(1–2): 5–15 [not printed in English until 1949, Balint, M. (1949). Sándor Ferenczi Number. *International Journal or Psycho-analysis*. 30(4)].

Freud, A. (1933). Report of the twelfth international psycho-analytic congress. *Bulletin of the International Psycho-Analytic Association*. 14: 138–140.

Freud, S. (1900). The interpretation of dreams. *Standard Edition*. 4(1): 8 (London: Hogarth Press, 1953).

Fromm, E. (1959). *Sigmund Freud's Mission*. New York: Harper & Row.

Masson, J.M. (1984). *The Assault on Truth*. New York: Farrar, Straus, and Giroux.

Rachman, A.W. (1997a). *Sándor Ferenczi: The Psychotherapist of Tenderness and Passion*. Northvale, NJ: Jason Aronson.

Rachman, A.W. (1997b). The suppression and censorship of Ferenczi's Confusion of Tongues paper. *Psychoanalytic Inquiry* (*Psychoanalysis' Favorite Son: The Legacy of Sándor Ferenczi*). 17(4): 459–485.

Rachman, A.W. (1999). Death by silence (Totschweigen): The traditional method of silencing the dissident in psychoanalysis. In Prince, R.M. (Ed.) *The Death of Psychoanalysis: Murder, Suicide, or Rumor Greatly Exaggerated?* Northvale, NJ: Jason Aronson, pp. 154–164.

Rachman, A.W. (2016). *The Budapest School of Psychoanalysis*. London: Routledge.

Rachman, A.W. (2018). *Elizabeth Severn: The "Evil Genius" of Psychoanalysis*. London: Routledge.

Rachman, A.W. (2022). *Psychoanalysis and Society's Neglect of Sexual Abuse of Children, Youth, and Adults: Reassessing Freud's Original Theory of Sexual Abuse and Trauma*. London: Routledge Press.

Chapter 3

Freud's Diagnosis of Sándor Ferenczi as Having a Pseudologia Fantastica Disorder

Pathological lying is a behavior of habitual or compulsive lying (Griffith et al., 2005). It was described in the medical literature in 1891 by Anton Delbruck, the German physician, when he observed that some of his patients told lies that were so abnormal and out of proportion that they deserved a special category. He subsequently described the lies as pseuodologia fantastica (Dike, 2008). Pathological lying is a rare phenomenon and a controversial topic. There is no consensus in the psychiatric community on its definition. Such telling of falsehoods is apparently characterized by a long history (maybe lifelong) of frequent and repeated lying under which no apparent psychological motive of external benefit can be discerned. The stories told tend towards presenting the liar favorably. The liar tells stories as the hero of the victim; for example, as being fantastically brave, as knowing or being related to famous people or as having great power, position, or wealth (Healy-Tenney & Healy, 2004). This discussion about pseudologia fantastica is by means of amplifying Freud's accusation about Ferenczi's controversial analysand, Elizabeth Severn, who Freud did not like or respect (Rachman, 2018). Freud's mean-spirited accusation about Ferenczi was that

> She [E.S.] seems to have produced in him a pseudologia fantastica since he believed her accounts of the most strange childhood traumas, which he then defended against us. In these disorders was snuffed out his was so brilliant intelligence. But let us preserve his sad exit as a secret among ourselves.
>
> (Letter from Sigmund Freud to Ernest Jones, May 29, 1933)

Freud accused Ferenczi of being a pathological liar because he believed Severn's lies about her trauma. In other words, she confabulated these

DOI: 10.4324/9781003265030-3

traumatic experiences (with no explanation by Freud about what motivated Severn's behavior). Ferenczi, he also believed, was emotionally unstable during the period he was treating her because he allowed Severn to influence his thinking and feeling in such a nontraditional, pathological way. This accusation is remarkably mean-spirited and entirely false. This position can be made because previously unknown papers by Elizabeth Severn were unearthed (Rachman, 2016). These materials were unpublished manuscripts, published books, notes, photographs, and certain personal possessions which she left to her daughter, Margaret upon her death in 1959. These materials, as well as Ferenczi's <u>Clinical Diary</u> (Ferenczi, 1988), Kurt Eissler's interview of Elizabeth Severn (Eissler, 1952), Michael Balint's book (Balint, 1968), as well as Rachman's book (Rachman, 2018), contain the most comprehensive data regarding the trauma analysis between Ferenczi and Severn. There is no data to indicate that Ferenczi was emotionally unstable during his analysis with Severn (Rachman, 2018). Freud and Jones influenced the traditional psychoanalytic community through initiating a Totschweigen campaign to silence and remove Ferenczi's and Severn's ideas from mainstream psychoanalysis (Rachman, 2018). They confabulated that Ferenczi and Severn developed a folie à deux; that they shared a kind of delusion that Ferenczi was convinced to believe Severn because of his need for love from his analysand; used unconventional methods which crossed the boundaries of analytic methodology; the research (Rachman, 2018) indicated that Severn's horrific childhood traumas were retrieved through a co-created process, where Severn contributed her <u>Subjective or Trance State Technique</u> (Severn, 1916), which allowed her to <u>therapeutically regress</u> to periods of her childhood trauma. Ferenczi integrated Severn's method into his active and empathic analytic method to retrieve the horrific childhood traumas that were reported in Ferenczi's <u>Clinical Diary</u> (Ferenczi, 1988). What was so important about the trauma analysis process that Ferenczi and Severn developed to retrieve, confront and analyze her childhood traumas was that Ferenczi was empathically attuned to Severn's subjective experience of trauma. The trauma became part of the analytic encounter, thereby integrating these active abusive experiences into the analysis. <u>Ferenczi because he did not think Severn was lying about her childhood trauma</u> was able to pioneer the analysis of trauma (Rachman, 2014). What is more, Ferenczi's capacity for empathy enabled him to not only revive Freud's original concept of sexual abuse trauma within the family as an important psychodynamic, but also allowed him to establish trauma as a meaningful new psychological disorder and develop a new methodology for treating it, namely trauma analysis (Rachman, 2018).

We need to ask the important question: Why was Freud so antagonistic to Ferenczi's Confusion of Tongues idea that abusive behavior by parental interaction with their own children was an important dimension of human psychodynamics and psychopathology and can contribute to a revision of psychoanalytic theory and method? There are, at least, two important ideas to consider. First, Freud's repression of his own childhood sexual trauma, making such experiences unavailable to his intellectual and emotional functioning. Freud could not conceptualize or really understand the idea that adults like himself and his analytic colleagues could be abusers of children, causing them to develop a psychological disorder. He could not tolerate that he possessed a darkness within his own psyche that needed to be analyzed. Freud's belief and dedication to his self-analysis, in combination with his not allowing anyone in the analytic community to analyze him, did not allow him to entertain an alternative to his own intellectual ideas and emotional experiences. As Fromm (1959) pointed out, Freud believed only his ideas and methods should become the standard in psychoanalysis. Freud stated that real psychological functioning occurs in the unconscious, not in the reality of the interpersonal interaction. What is more, the conscious dimension of humans is an imperfect source of data (Freud, 1900).

Ferenczi's introduction of clinical empathy, as a primary dimension of the analytic encounter, was not fully accepted by Freud. The Confusion of Tongues paradigm grew out of Ferenczi's clinical thinking about empathy which was influenced by Elizabeth Severn from their eight year psychoanalysis (Ferenczi, 1928, 1929, 1931, 1933). Ferenczi had the capacity to listen and believe Severn's self-reports of sexual, physical, and emotional trauma and respond with empathy. He did not interpret the self-reports as lies or resistances. Ferenczi was deviating from interpretation as the road to the unconscious, believing, with Severn's help, that her childhood abuse was a result of actual relational interaction that needed affirmation. Survivors of abuse, as we now understand, need the analyst to be a witness to their trauma (Mucci, 2013). The survivor needs to feel the empathic presence of the analyst when they share their trauma so they will not blame themselves for the harm they suffered. They also need the therapeutic relationship to be the container for safety and repair, detoxifying the poison of abuse. Ferenczi understood this need and was able to create an analytic encounter where Severn experienced his empathy and affirmation of her real trauma.

Originally, Freud was welcoming when Ferenczi introduced clinical empathy into psychoanalysis (Rachman, 1997a), even admitting that his original recommendations for clinical practice had a negative connotation. He told clinicians what not to do rather than what they should do (Rachman, 1989, 1997a). During that initial time of the introduction of clinical empathy, Freud seemed to welcome Ferenczi's pioneering effort to introduce a two-person psychology into psychoanalysis. But when Freud began to hear the rumors spread by Clara Thompson about Ferenczi's participation in the so-called kissing technique with her, Freud became angry and critical of Ferenczi. He was so angry that he, once again, made outlandish accusations. He said Ferenczi was acting out sexually with his analysands, which is contained in the now famous kissing letter (Rachman, 2018, 2022). Freud exaggerated the statement that Clara Thompson circulated among the analytic community that she could kiss Ferenczi anytime she wanted. It was true that Thompson initiated kissing Ferenczi in a session. Actually, as Ferenczi reported in his Clinical Diary, he felt annoyed by this because he felt Thompson was taking advantage of his empathic approach (Ferenczi, 1988). What is more, it can also be seen as acting out of her erotic transference to Ferenczi that he reported as her childhood sexual experience with her father. He allowed her to act out because he felt it would help her express her dissociated experience of her childhood sexual trauma in the safety of an empathic analytic experience. This was only the beginning of this therapeutic process, but this trauma was never fully worked through in her analysis (Rachman, 2018).

Freud never contacted Ferenczi when he heard about Thompson's claim that she was kissing Ferenczi to discuss Ferenczi's rationale for the non-traditional clinical behavior. This seems to indicate he readily accepted that Ferenczi was acting out sexually. It was a prejudicial response that was contained in the kissing letter. Freud had concluded Ferenczi's trauma analysis was indicative of acting out behavior because his dissident therapeutic method, he thought, was based upon deteriorating emotional functioning, influenced by a severely disturbed analysand. If Freud could have continued to be loving towards Ferenczi by showing empathy instead of condemnation, he would have seen that his pupil was making a meaningful, pioneering attempt to expand the boundaries of psychoanalysis to treat trauma disorders. Ferenczi had no interest in being a rival to Freud by beginning a new form of psychoanalysis. He would not have visited Freud before his Confusion of Tongues presentation to read his paper if he were a rival of Freud's. His visit was predicated on receiving Freud's approval so that the Confusion of Tongues paradigm could be integrated into mainstream psychoanalysis (Rachman, 1997b). It is now totally clear that <u>Ferenczi was not suffering from a pseudologia fanastica disorder</u>. He was an intellectual and clinical visionary. Ferenczi predicted the importance of sexual trauma disorder as a significant issue in clinical psychoanalysis and society (Rachman, 2018, 2022). Here are some of the contemporary data to support Ferenczi's assertions in 1932–1933 about the presence of sexual abuse in families:

1. Offenders are more likely to be relatives or acquaintances of their victim than strangers (Fergusson et al., 1996).
2. Research has indicated that more than 70 percent of abusers are immediate family members or someone very close to the family (Finkelhor, 1979, 1986).
3. The global prevalence of childhood sexual abuse has been estimated at 19.7 percent for females and 7.9 percent for males (Pereda et al., 2009).
4. Childhood sexual abuse can result in both short-term and long-term harm, including psychopathology in later life (Dinwiddie et al., 2000). Psychological effects of child sexual abuse include depression (Roosa et al., 1999); eating disorders and poor self-esteem (Walsh & Dilillo, 2011) somatization (Arnow, 2004); sleep disturbances (Noll et al., 2006); dissociative and anxiety disorders, including post-traumatic stress disorder (Widom, 1999; Arehart-Treichel, 2005).

<u>If the mother-child bond is unsatisfactory from the start, the remainder of the individual's life will be spent seeking reparation from the missing primary love object. What is more, the enactment of this deficiency will occur in the interpersonal interaction of the psychoanalytic situation.</u>

References

Arehart-Treichel, J. (2005). Dissociation often precedes PTSD in sexually abused children. *Psychiatric News American Psychiatric Association.* 40(15): 34.

Arnow, B.A. (2004). Relationship between childhood maltreatment, adult health and psychiatric outcome and medical utilization. *Journal of Clinical Psychiatry.* 65(12): 10–15.

Balint, M. (1968). The disagreement between Freud and Ferenczi and its repercussions. In *The Basic Fault: Therapeutic Aspects of Regression.* London: Tavistock Publications, pp. 149–156.

Dike, C.C. (2008). Pathological lying: Symptom or disease? *Psychiatric Times.* 25: 7.

Dinwiddie, S., Heath, A.C., Dunne, M.P., et al. (2000). Early sexual abuse and lifetime psychopathology: A co-twin control study. *Psychological Medicine.* 30(1): 41–52.

Eissler, K. (1952). *Interview with Dr. Elizabeth Severn. December 20, 1952. Container 121. Sigmund Freud Papers.* Washington, DC: Manuscript Division, Library of Congress.

Ferenczi, S. (1928). The elasticity of psychoanalytic technique. In Balint, M. (Ed.) *Final Contributions to the Problems and Methods of Psychoanalysis. Vol. III.* New York: Bruner/Mazel, 1980, pp. 87–102.

Ferenczi, S. (1929). The principle of relaxation and neocatharsis. In Balint, M. (Ed.) *Final Contributions to the Problems and Methods of Psychoanalysis, Vol. III.* New York: Bruner/Mazel, 1980, pp. 108–125.

Ferenczi, S. (1931). Child analysis in the analysis of the adult. In Balint, M. (Ed.) *Final Contribution to the Problem and Methods of Psychoanalysis. Vol. III.* New York: Bruner/Mazel, 1980, pp. 126–142.

Ferenczi, S. (1933). The confusion of tongues between adults and children: The language of tenderness and passion. In Balint, M. (Ed.) *Final Contributions to the Problems and Methods of Psychoanalysis* (E. Moscher, Trans.). New York: Bruner/Mazel, 1980, pp. 156–167.

Ferenczi, S. (1988). *The Clinical Diary of Sándor Ferenczi* (J. Dupont, Ed., M. Balint and N.Z. Jackson, Trans.). Cambridge, MA: Harvard University Press.

Fergusson, D.M., Lynskey, M.T. and Harwood, L.J. (1996). Childhood sexual abuse and psychiatric disorder in young adulthood: Prevalence of sexual abuse and factors associated with sexual abuse. *Journal of the American Academy of Child and Adolescence Psychiatry.* 35(10): 1355–1364.

Finkelhor, D. (1979). *Sexually Victimized Children.* New York: Free Press.

Finkelhor, D. (1986). *A Sourcebook of Child Sexual Abuse.* Thousand Oaks, CA: SAGE.

Freud, S. (1900). The interpretation of dreams. *Standard Edition.* 4(1): 8 (London: Hogarth Press, 1953).

Fromm, E. (1959). *Sigmund Freud's Mission.* New York: Harper & Row.

Griffith, E.H., Baranoski, M. and Dike, C.C. (2005). Pathological lying revisited. *American Academy of Psychiatry and Law*. 33(3): 342–349.

Healy-Tenney, M. and Healy, W. (2004). *Pathological Lying, Association and Swindling: A Study in Forensic Psychology*. Whitefish, MT: Kessinger.

Mucci, C. (2013). *Beyond Individual and Collective Trauma: Intergenerational Transmission, Psychoanalytic Treatment, and the Dynamics of Forgiveness*. London: Karnac Books.

Noll, J.G., Truckett, P.K., Susman, E.J. and Putnam, F.W. (2006). Sleep disturbances and childhood sexual abuse. *Journal of Pediatric Psychology*. 31(5): 469–480.

Pereda, N., Guilera, G., Forms, M. and Gómez-Benito, J. (2009). The prevalence of childhood sexual abuse in community and student samples: A meta analysis. *Clinical Psychology Review*. 29(4): 328–338.

Rachman, A.W. (1989). Confusion of tongues: The Ferenczian metaphor for childhood seduction and emotional trauma. *Journal of the American Academy of Psychoanalysis*. 17(2): 182–205.

Rachman, A.W. (1997a). *Sándor Ferenczi: The Psychotherapist of Tenderness and Passion*. Northvale, NJ: Jason Aronson.

Rachman, A.W. (1997b). The suppression and censorship of Ferenczi's Confusion of Tongues paper. *Psychoanalytic Inquiry (Psychoanalysis' Favorite Son: The Legacy of Sándor Ferenczi)*. 17(4): 459–485.

Rachman, A.W. (2014) Sándor Ferenczi's analysis with Elizabeth Severn: "Wild analysis" or pioneering study of the incest trauma (Sándor Ferenczi's contributions to the evolution of the theory and technique in psychoanalysis). *Psychoanalytic Inquiry*. 34(2): 145–168.

Rachman, A.W. (2016). *The Acquisition, Restoration and Donation of the Elizabeth Severn Papers: A Lost Legacy of Psychoanalysis* (Unpublished).

Rachman, A.W. (2018). *Elizabeth Severn: The "Evil Genius" of Psychoanalysis*. London: Routledge.

Rachman, A.W. (2022). *Psychoanalysis and Society's Neglect of Sexual Abuse of Children, Youth, and Adults: Reassessing Freud's Original Theory of Sexual Abuse and Trauma*. London: Routledge Press.

Roosa, M.W., Reinholtz, C. and Angelini, P.J. (1999). The relation of child sexual abuse and depression in young women: Comparisons across four ethnic groups. *Journal of Abnormal Child Psychology*. 27(1): 65–76.

Severn, E. (1916). "Dictated in a subjective or trance state." *Friday Morning*, January 14. In Rachman, A.W. (Ed.) *Elizabeth Severn, The "Evil Genius" of Psychoanalysis*. London: Routledge, 2018, pp. 246–248.

Walsh, K. and Dilillo, D. (2011). Child sexual abuse and adolescent sexual assault and revictimization. In Paludi, A. (Ed.) *The Psychology of Teen Violence and Victimization*. Santa Barbara, CA: A. Praeger, pp. 203–216.

Widom, C.S. (1999). Post traumatic stress disorder in abused and neglected children grown up. *The American Journal of Psychiatry*. 156(8), 1223–1229.

Chapter 4

Freud's Denunciation of Ferenczi and the Confusion of Tongues

His Self-Analysis, "Emotional Blindness," and Pathologizing of Ferenczi

Freud's Self-Analysis and Childhood Sexual Trauma

It is generally accepted that Freud's self-analysis was an intellectual achievement of heroic proportions. Ernest Jones stated this for the traditional analytic community:

> In the summer of 1897, Freud undertook his most heroic feat – a psychoanalysis of his own unconscious. It is hard for us nowadays to imagine how momentous this achievement was, that difficultly being the fate of most pioneering exploits. Yet the uniqueness of the feat remains. Once done it is done forever. For no one again can be the first to explore those depths.
>
> (Jones, 1953, p. 319)

In contrast to Jones's hero worshiping comments on Freud's self-analysis, Anzieu (1986) offered a comprehensive examination of Freud's special endeavor. Anzieu avoided classic biography, such as Jones's contribution, in order to apply the psychoanalytic method to its creator. This examination of Freud's work is supported by a thorough chronological inventory of the documents of the self-analysis (dreams, screen memories, slips of the tongue, instances of forgetting and parapraxes) from 1895 to 1902, the date of the break with Wilhelm Fliess and the founding of the Psychoanalytic Society of Vienna. The central focus of Anzieu's book is essentially an investigation into the subjective conditions that led Freud to create psychoanalysis, such as creativity, masochism, his mother's favorite, active attitude in relation to the primal scene, the creative subject's heroic identifications and castration anxiety. Anzieu also contributed

DOI: 10.4324/9781003265030-4

the understanding that Wilheim Fliess to whom Freud wrote about his self-analysis, played a supportive role in that analysis. He believed there is no serious self-analysis if it is not spoken to someone (Anzieu, 1986). Talking to someone in the form of exchanging letters is a sufficient form of speaking to someone about your experiences or feelings. But Freud's self-analysis suffered from the lack of actual presence of a significant other. Analysis must include an actual interaction with a significant other.

The lack of a significant other in Freud's self-psychoanalysis related to the neglect of his integrating his childhood sexual trauma into his understanding of his personality as well as integrating childhood trauma into his theory. Freud's self-analysis, as special as an intellectual achievement it may have been, was seriously limited emotionally and interpersonally. Any therapeutic experience must be conducted in a dyadic or group relationship. Human beings develop their emotional/interpersonal problems in relationships, and therefore, need to explore and work through these same problems in a relationship. Freud's personal functioning and his theoretical therapeutic attitude favored what can be considered a one-person experience, an authority, such as an analyst who offers his/her wisdom to an analysand. What is missing in a one-person experience is the contribution of a significant other to the therapeutic treatment of an individual.

There were two psychoanalysts who had the courage and analytic talent to offer Freud an analytic experience. Jung, Freud and Ferenczi on their trip to America to attend the 20th anniversary celebration of Clark University in Worcester Massachusetts would while away their time on the sea voyage by telling each other their dreams. It was assumed that the experience would contain mutuality, each of the three analysts telling each other their dreams and then taking turns being the analyst, interpreting the dream. Jung was offered an opportunity to be the analyst to Freud, but it was refused. During one of these dream sharing sessions, Jung asked Freud to associate with his dream. Freud refused. Roazen (1975) quotes Jung as saying:

And so, when Freud told me his dream in which his wife and his sister played important parts I asked Freud to tell me some of his personal associations with the dream. He looked at me with bitterness and said, "I could tell you more, but I cannot risk my authority." That, of course finished my attempt to deal with his dreams.

(Roazen, 1975, pp. 246, f17)

Freud would not let anyone analyze him, even though Jung was held in high esteem by the original analytic community, and they believed his intellect was on Freud's level. Needing to be the only authority hampered Freud from benefiting from the opportunity to expand his self-analysis with the richness of an interaction with a significant other.

Ferenczi also offered to analyze Freud in February of 1926 (Falzeder et al., 2000). Kramer (2003), has said that Ferenczi's offer to analyze Freud was absurd. Yet Mėszaros (2014) has said that Ferenczi once reminded Freud:

> Don't forget for years I have been occupied with nothing but the products of your intellect and I have always felt the man behind every sentence of your works and made him my confidant.
>
> (Brabant et al., 1993, p. 219)

Ferenczi's analysis of Freud, if it would have taken place, would present the possibility of reaching a deep emotional level, since Ferenczi was becoming the analyst of difficult cases (Rachman, 1997a). This new kind of psychoanalysis is exactly what Freud needed because he needed an analysis which reached the depths of his childhood sexual trauma (Rachman, 2016). As has been suggested, Freud's inability to confront and analyze his childhood sexual trauma with his nursemaid, Resi Witteck, made him emotionally blind to the importance of childhood sexual trauma as an important dimension of psychological disorder (Rachman, 2018, 2022). Ferenczi, the analyst of difficult cases (Rachman, 1997a) and the inventor of trauma analysis (Rachman, 2018) would have been able to create a therapeutic atmosphere where Freud's childhood sexual trauma could have been explored. The most important question, however, is would Freud have allowed himself to be emotionally vulnerable to Ferenczi, so that a two-person relational therapeutic experience could develop? It is unlikely since it was not only Freud's intellectual insistence on a binary theory of psychoanalysis (Rachman & Mattick, 2012), but also his need to be in charge of his psychoanalysis (Fromm, 1959).

Freud's "Emotional Blindness" to Sexual Trauma

Freud's formulation of the seduction hypothesis asserted that the origin of psychoneurosis in adults (the so-called hysteria, and obsessive compulsive neuroses and possibly some functional psychosis like paranoia) are the result of the reactivation of repressed memories of actual sexual abuse within familial interaction during the childhood years (Freud, 1896a, 1896b). Such an assertion was revolutionary in human thought. Until modern times, it was widely assumed that a child sexual molester was a single male who could be easily identified by his unsavory looks and unshaven appearance. He would lurk in the shadows of a dark alley and grab children one by one. Many families believed they could protect their children by teaching them not to talk to strangers. Freud's clinical experience and astute observations changed this widely held belief. He made the intellectual connection between adult trauma victims and their childhood sexual abuse by parental figures. The psychopathology they manifested as adult patients in their analysis was a result of parent abuse. This discovery was a courageous intellectual disclosure as it added and identified the middle-and upper-class Viennese families as the source of sexual abuse of children. In this observation Freud identified the community of physicians, scientists and scholars to which he belonged. This must have alienated and angered his peers. By not identifying himself as a sexual abuse survivor, after he created the seduction hypothesis, he also alienated himself from the incest survivors who existed in his lifetime, to whom he could have helped. Furthermore, because he could not confront and integrate his own childhood sexual trauma, he could not help society fully understand the importance of childhood sexual trauma.

One would have expected Freud to have welcomed his favorite pupil, Sándor Ferenczi's attempt to reverse and verify the seduction hypothesis in the development of the Confusion of Tongues paradigm. As has been mentioned, Freud was actually angered by Ferenczi's theory and clinical innovations which focused on sexual trauma (Rachman, 1997a, 1997b).

An explanation for Freud's anger can be understood to emanate from, at least, two primary sources, one personal and one professional. The personal dimension of Freud's anger can be considered to have developed from his repression of his own childhood sexual trauma. In the same letters that Freud wrote to Wilheim Fliess, announcing the intellectual discovery of childhood sexual seduction, he revealed his own seduction with his nursemaid, Resi Wittek (Freud, 1954). The descriptions of the childhood sexual traumas are so revealing that it seems mysterious why Freud never went on to elucidate their influence in his personality development or the development of his theory of psychoanalysis (Rachman, 2016) The descriptions are as follows:

> She was my instructioness in sexual matters, and chided me for being clumsy and not being able to do anything. . . . Also, she washed me in the reddish water which she had previously washed herself (not difficult to interpret; I find nothing of the kind in my chain of memories, and so I take it for a genuine rediscovery)."
>
> (Freud, 1954, p. 220. – Letter from Freud to Fliess,
> October 4, 1897)

Marianne Krüll, a German sociologist investigated the history of Freud's family as well as his childhood. She first presented the results of her investigations in a German edition of her book in 1984, then in an English translation in 1986 (Krüll, 1986). Krüll identified Freud's nursemaid as Resi Wittek on the basis of discovering an entry in the list of visitors to a spa, which included the names of Freud's mother, himself as a child, and his nursemaid (Krüll, 1986, p. 119). After Freud recovered his repressed childhood memory of his sexual seduction, he asked his mother if his memories of his nursemaid we real or imagined. He reported:

> I have succeeded in finding a number of real points of reference. I ask my mother whether she remembered my nurse. "of course", she said, "an elderly woman, very shrewd indeed.
>
> (Freud, 1954, p. 22 – Letter from Freud to Fliess,
> October 15, 1897)

Besides the sexual trauma suffered by Freud, his relationship with Resi Wittek also produced an abandonment trauma. Freud's mother also told him that his nursemaid was a thief and was sent to jail:

> all the shiny Kreuzers and Zehnrs and toys that had been given you were found among her things. Your Philipp went himself to fetch the policeman, and she got ten months.
>
> (Freud, 1954, pp. 221–222 – Letters from Freud
> to Fliess, October 15, 1897)

Freud verified that his nurse was taken away from him, when he cited a screen memory of a cupboard which haunted him:

> I feared she [Freud's mother] <u>must have vanished like my nurse</u> not long before. I must have heard that the old woman had been locked . . . up. The fact that I turned to him [Freud's brother Philipp] shows that I was well aware of his part in my nurse's disappearance.
>
> (Freud, 1954, p. 223 – Letter from Freud to Fliess, October 15, 1897 [the screen memory of the cupboard was used in Freud's, The Psychopathology of Everyday Life])

Freud's disclosures from the self-analysis and in his letters to Fliess clearly indicated he was the victim of childhood trauma, for example, sexual and abandonment traumas. Discussion of Freud's childhood traumas, after sharing them with Fliess, seem to disappear from his writings. His self-analysis started in the mid 1890s and reached its zenith in 1895 and 1900. This is described in two of his main books, *The Interpretation of Dreams* (Freud, 1900) and *The Psychopathology of Everyday Life* (Freud, 1990). *The Interpretation of Dreams* provides a host of Freud's dreams which he used to discover the Oedipus complex and dream interpretation. For the first time it asserted that dreams are the disguised fulfillment of unconscious wishes. *The Psychopathology of Everyday Life* represents Freud's transfer from the clinical to normal life; it proves neurotic features are present not only in sickness but also in health. The difference does not lie in quality but in quantity. It is the first time in the history of psychopathology that Freud overruled the difference between pathology and health that makes it possible to apply psychoanalysis to so-called normal life.

In a surprising moment, in Eissler's hero-worshiping description of Freud's personal functioning, he raised the question of whether Freud was sufficiently analyzed. First, he concluded:

> The charge that Freud was not sufficiently analyzed is correct.
>
> (Eissler, 2001, p. 37)

But, not surprisingly, Eissler walked back his conclusion when he discussed that in science the issue is <u>not to be right</u>, but <u>to be right enough</u>. Eissler further concluded:

> Freud was analyzed "enough for the time" . . . whatever the depth of his self-knowledge. The misfortune of the present-day analysts is

that we have been better analyzed than Freud was, but none of us was "analyzed enough for the time"

(Eissler, 2001, pp. 37–38)

Freud's self-analysis was an emotional courageous event in the history of psychoanalysis, as well as in the history of human behavior. It should be considered an intellectual tour de force. There are, however, inherent limitations in conducting a self-analysis, which Freud did not seem to recognize. There are several indications of emotional blindness in his behavior, of which the results of his self-analysis are one. As has been mentioned, self-analysis is inherently limited by the absence of a <u>therapeutic other</u>. Human beings are so created that they need to <u>presence of an other</u> to enter into a therapeutic relationship. <u>The presence of the other</u> allows attachment, empathy, caring, and responsiveness to become essential dimensions of the therapeutic encounter (Rachman, 2012, 2018). Emotional and interpersonal interaction is necessary for fully analyzing personal issues and moving towards change. <u>The other can observe and illuminate an individual's functioning</u>.

References

Anzieu, D. (1986). *Freud's Self Analysis* (P. Graham, Trans.). Madison, CT: International Universities Press.

Brabant, E., Falzeder, E. and Giampieri-Deutsch, P. (Eds.) (1993). *The Correspondence of Sigmund Freud and Sándor Ferenczi, Vol. I., 1908–1914*. Cambridge, MA: Harvard University Press.

Eissler, K. (2001). *Freud and the Seduction Theory*. New York: International Universities Press.

Falzeder, E., Brabant, E. and Giampieri-Deutsch, P. (Eds.) (2000). *The Correspondence of Sigmund Freud and Sándor Ferenczi, Vol III, 1920–1933*. Cambridge, MA: Harvard University Press.

Freud, S. (1896a). Heredity and the aetiology of the neuroses. *Standard Edition*. 3: 143–156 (London: Hogarth Press, 1962).

Freud, S. (1896b). The aetiology of hysteria. *Standard Edition*. 3: 191–221 (London: Hogarth Press, 1962).

Freud, S. (1900). The interpretation of dreams. *Standard Edition*. 4(1): 8 (London: Hogarth Press, 1953).

Freud, S. (1954). *The Origins of Psychoanalysis: Letters to Wilhelm Fliess, Drafts and Notes, 1887–1902* (M. Bonaparte, A. Freud and E. Kris, Eds., Mosbacker and J. Strachey, Trans.). New York: Basic Books.

Freud, S. (1990). *The Psychopathology of Everyday Life*. New York: W.W. Norton & Co., Inc.

Fromm, E. (1959). *Sigmund Freud's Mission*. New York: Harper & Row.

Jones, E. (1953). *The Life and Work of Sigmund Freud, Vol I.: The Formative Years and Great Discoveries*. New York: Basic Books.

Kramer, R. (2003). Why did Ferenczi & Rank conclude that Freud had no more emotional intelligence than a pre-oedipal child? In Babre, C., Ulanov, B. and Roland, L. (Eds.) *Creative Dissent: Psychoanalysis in Evolution*. Madison, CT: Praeger, pp. 23–36.

Krüll, M. (1986). *Freud and His Father*. New York: W. W. Norton & Company.

Mèszaros, J. (2014). *Ferenczi and Beyond: Exile of the Budapest School and Solidarity in the Psychoanalytic Movement During the Nazi Years*. London: Routledge

Rachman, A.W. (1997a). *Sándor Ferenczi: The Psychotherapist of Tenderness and Passion*. Northvale, NJ: Jason Aronson.

Rachman, A.W. (1997b). The suppression and censorship of Ferenczi's Confusion of Tongues paper. *Psychoanalytic Inquiry (Psychoanalysis' Favorite Son: The Legacy of Sándor Ferenczi)*. 17(4): 459–485.

Rachman, A.W. (2012). Confusion of tongues between Sándor Ferenczi and Elizabeth Severn. *Presentation. International Sándor Ferenczi Congress – "Faces of Trauma."* Budapest, June 3.

Rachman, A.W. (2014) Sándor Ferenczi's analysis with Elizabeth Severn: "Wild analysis" or pioneering study of the incest trauma (Sándor Ferenczi's contributions to the evolution of the theory and technique in psychoanalysis). *Psychoanalytic Inquiry*. 34(2): 145–168.

Rachman, A.W. (2016). *The Budapest School of Psychoanalysis*. London: Routledge.

Rachman, A.W. (2018). *Elizabeth Severn: The "Evil Genius" of Psychoanalysis*. London: Routledge.

Rachman, A.W. (2022). *Psychoanalysis and Society's Neglect of Sexual Abuse of Children, Youth, and Adults: Reassessing Freud's Original Theory of Sexual Abuse and Trauma*. London: Routledge Press.

Rachman, A.W. and Mattick, P. (2012). The confusion of tongues in the psychoanalytic relationship. *Psychoanalytic Social Work*. 19(1–2): 167–190.

Roazen, P. (1975). *Freud and His Followers*. New York: Alfred A. Knopf.

Chapter 5

Traditional Psychoanalysis's Totschweigen Campaign to Silence the Confusion of Tongues Paper

The Confusion of Tongues Paper could have ushered in a new era in psychoanalysis in September of 1932 when Ferenczi delivered it. But Freud and his followers did not welcome his ideas; instead they initiated a *Totschweigen*, death by silence, campaign to remove its existence from mainstream psychoanalysis (Rachman, 1999). The campaign to silence Ferenczi and remove his theoretical and clinical paradigm shifts can be considered one of the darkest moments in the history of psychoanalysis. Freud, Jones, members of the Society of Rings and his orthodox followers reacted with anger, denunciation, and personal attacks towards Ferenczi, his ideas, and clinical techniques. First, we need to examine Freud's negative reaction to Ferenczi, and then his successful attempt to silence the Confusion of Tongues contributions. After Ferenczi introduced clinical empathy into psychoanalysis (Ferenczi, 1928), his theoretical and clinical focus became organized on trauma analysis. In particular, he was very involved with the analysis of Elizabeth Severn (Rachman, 2018a). The period of that analysis, 1925 to 1933, became the changing point in the personal and professional relationship between Freud and Ferenczi, as Freud began to voice his objection to Ferenczi's clinical experiments with treating a severe trauma disorder. Freud's objection was fueled by the behavior of Clara Thompson who let it be known to the analytic community of the 1930s that "I am allowed to kiss Papa Ferenczi, as often as I like" (Dupont, 1988, pp. 2–3n).

When Freud heard about Thompson's statement about Ferenczi's so-called deviant clinical behavior with an analysand, he became alarmed and angry. He sent a letter to Ferenczi that has been characterized as The kissing technique letter (December 13, 1931 – see Rachman 1997b). It is a misnomer to call this document a letter. It was more of a document of

DOI: 10.4324/9781003265030-5

condemnation by Freud. He assumed from Thompson's public statement of Ferenczi's so-called sexual acting out with her during their analytic sessions was accurate. It is not known if Freud communicated with Ferenczi about his so-called kissing technique. The letter gives the impression that Freud believed Thompson's so-called statement of sexual behavior since he accused him of continuing a pattern of erotic engagement that was present earlier in his clinical behavior (Rachman, 1997a). This Ferenczi/Thompson interaction has been discussed in previous publications, offering an understanding that Ferenczi's behavior was actually an empathic intervention. Ferenczi allowed Thompson to kiss him to help her express the underlying sexual trauma which was a meaningful aspect of the analysis. However, there was no such methodology as the kissing technique in Ferenczi's clinical technique. He did not employ erotic touching of the analysand as a methodology (Rachman, 1993, 1997a, 2018a, 2022). In fact, the Confusion of Tongues paradigm specifies that the analysis of sexual trauma must not contain conscious erotic behavior by the analyst. Counter transference analysis is used to work through unanalyzed erotic feelings. Conscious sexual behavior, verbal or physical, by the analyst is absolutely prohibited. A focus on countertransference analysis of erotic feelings is essential (Rachman, 2018a). It is very clear from the Confusion of Tongues paradigm that trauma analysis must be performed in an erotic-free therapeutic atmosphere in order to prevent retraumatization (Rachman, 2018b, 2022) An analyst who introduces sexual behavior isn't performing an analysis of trauma. Such behavior can be considered emotional abuse and is not therapeutic.

The vehement attempt to suppress and remove the Confusion of Tongues paradigm from psychoanalysis followed in the negative direction that Freud had expressed in his confabulation of Ferenczi's kissing technique. Prior to Ferenczi presenting his paper, Freud tried to stop Ferenczi:

> He must be prevented from reading his essay [Confusion of Tongues paper]. Either he will present another, or none at all . . . Our behavior will depend first on his acceptance of the cancellation [of reading his paper] and then the impression you all have of him in Wiesbaden.
>
> (Sylwan, 1984, p. 104 – Unpublished letter to Freud from Eitingon, August 29, 1932)

Freud wanted to enlist the entire psychoanalytic community in preventing Ferenczi from reading his paper at the congress at Weisbaden. Freud intensified his Totschweigen campaign against Ferenczi, a few days before Ferenczi's scheduled congress presentation, as Freud confronted Ferenczi directly. The personal attempt to silence Ferenczi escalated a few days later at a dramatic meeting between Freud and Ferenczi, which became an emotional blow to Ferenczi's personal and professional life, from which he would never recover. On this fateful day in August 1932, just before his Confusion of Tongues presentation, Ferenczi went to Freud in Vienna to fulfill the standard that had developed between the Society of Rings members. Freud's inner circle of pioneering analysts would present their ideas to the Master, first in order to get his blessings as well as his intellectual input on their ideas. It was a meeting filled with anxiety and trepidation for Ferenczi because the shadow of Freud and the orthodox analytic community's Totschweigen campaign was ever present. He did not expect a lively endorsement of the Confusion of Tongues paper, but perhaps, Freud would erase his prohibition against Ferenczi presenting his paper. The emotional details of this meeting were told to Ferenczi's student and analysand, Izette De Forest, who became one of the foremost purveyors of his theory (De Forest, 1942, 1954). When she was in analysis with Eric Fromm, she told him the story of Ferenczi's experience over the Confusion of Tongues paper with Freud, over 20 years after it happened:

> I [Ferenczi] told him [Freud] of my latest technical ideas . . . empirically based on my work with my patients. I have tried to discover from my patients told history, from their association of ideas, from the way they behave even in detailed respects and especially towards one – from the frustrations which arouse their anger or depression, . . . from the content – both conscious and unconscious – of their desires and longings, the manner in which they suffered rejection at the mothers or their parents or surrogates. And I have also endeavored through empathy to imagine what kind of loving care . . . the patient really needed at that early age – a loving care and nurture which would have allowed his self confidence, his self-enjoyment to develop wholesomely. . . . It is possible to sense when I am on the right track, for the patient immediately unconsciously gives the signal by a number of slight changes in mood and behavior. Even his dreams show a response to the new and beneficial treatment. All this should be confided to the patient-the analyst's new understanding of his needs, his ensuing change of relationship to the patient and his expression of this, and the patient's own evident response. Whenever mistakes are made by the

analyst, the patient again gives the signal by becoming angry or despondent. And this can be elicited from the patient and explained to him. It must be honest and genuine.

(Izette De Forest personal communication to Erich Fromm – Fromm, 1959, pp. 63–64)

In this remarkably clear and compelling statement, Ferenczi shared his clinical experiences with traumatized individuals with his analysand, Izette De Forest. He was telling Freud that traumatized individuals have a different psychodynamic than Oedipal conflicted analysands and needed to be clinically treated in a new way. It is not that the Oedipal conflict theory wasn't relevant, rather it is necessary to expand psychoanalysis beyond the Oedipal idea to the presence of trauma and trauma disorders. Ferenczi was not moving away from psychoanalysis as Freud believed, but asking to expand the boundaries of psychoanalysis to include the diagnosis and treatment of trauma disorders. The irony of this meeting which preceded Ferenczi's presentation was that it became an opportunity to intensify the Totschweigen campaign against him for his pioneering ideas about the existence of trauma disorders and specifically, the trauma of sexual abuse. These ideas were not intended to diminish psychoanalysis but expand its knowledge and treatment boundaries. We can now understand what Ferenczi was trying to tell psychoanalysis and society. In the last 89 years, since Ferenczi announced his groundbreaking ideas on sexual trauma and abuse, we have observed how prophetic, important and prevalent sexual trauma exists in human society (Rachman, 2022).

The termination of the meeting between Freud and Ferenczi drew a dark curtain around their relationship and the analytic community. Here is what Ferenczi told Izette De Forest about Freud's reaction to his Confusion of Tongues paper:

The Professor listened to my exposition with increasing impatience and finally warned me that I was treading on dangerous ground and departing fundamentally from the traditional customs and techniques of psychoanalysis. Such yielding to the patient's longings and desires – no matter how genuine – would increase his dependence on the analyst. Such dependence can only be destroyed by the emotional withdrawal of the analyst. In the hands of unskilled analysts, my method, the Professor said, might easily lead to sexual indulgence rather than an expression of parental devotion. This warning ended the interview. I held out my hand in affectionate adieu. The Professor turned his back on me and walked out of the room.

(Sándor Ferenczi's personal conversation with
Izette De Forest – Fromm, 1959, pp. 64–65, f3)

This description of a historically tragic moment in psychoanalysis clearly escalated the Totschweigen campaign to suppress and silence Ferenczi's Confusion of Tongues paper and its ideas from mainstream psychoanalysis. Freud accelerated the political process of the Totschweigen campaign by sending a damning letter to his daughter, Anna, demolishing Ferenczi's attempt to expand his original idea that sexual abuse of children by parental and authority figures is a significant factor in the origin of psychological disorder:

Without any further question of greeting be began: I want to read you my lecture. This he did and I listened thunderstruck. He was totally regressed to the etiological views I believed in and gave up 35 years ago, that the gross sexual traumas of childhood are the regular cause of neurosis, says it in almost the same words I used then. No word about the technique by which he obtains this material, in the middle of it all remarks about the hostility of patients and the necessity of accepting their criticism and admitting one's errors to them. The consequence of this confused, torturously contrived. The whole thing is actually stupid of it seems so since it is so devious and incomplete.

(Letter from Sigmund Freud to Anna Freud,
March 9, 1932 – Molnar, 1992, p. 131)

It is a remarkable document that Freud sends his daughter, Anna, regarding Ferenczi's Confusion of Tongues contribution, since it aimed at destroying Ferenczi's professional credibility within the analytical community. In essence, Freud said that the Confusion of Tongues contribution has no value as a psychoanalytic contribution. What is more, Freud expanded his Totschweigen campaign to colleagues and the greater analytic community as witness of the following event. On Friday, September 2, 1932, Freud sent the following telegram to Eitingon, condemning the Confusion of Tongues paper.

Ferenczi read me his paper. Harmless. Stupid. Another way [for Ferenczi] to be unreachable. Disagreeable impression.

(Sylwan, 1984, p. 109 – Telegram from Freud
to Eitingon, September 2, 1932 – [Unpublished])

The analytic community accelerated their participation in the Totschweigen campaign against Ferenczi and the Confusion of Tongues paper with Freud's approval. Joan Rivière wrote a hostile letter about Ferenczi's contribution:

> Its scientific contentions and it statements about analytic practice are just a tissue of delusions which can only discredit psychoanalysis and give credit to its opponents. It cannot be supposed that all Journal readers will appreciate the mental condition of the writer, and in this respect, one has to think of posterity, too.
>
> (Masson, 1984, p. 152 – Letter from Joan Rivière to Ernest Jones, Jones Archive, London [Unpublished])

Rivière's letter to Jones, who was characterized as Ferenczi's political assassin (Roazen, 1975), was on the level of Jones's intent to destroy Ferenczi's personal and professional reputation. She tears apart Ferenczi's Confusion of Tongues ideas, calling them delusional, clearly joining Jones's campaign to prevent the Confusion of Tongues paper from being published in the analytic community's foremost journal, *The International Journal of Psychoanalysis*. Rivière was declaring to the analytic community that the paper should not be published in the English language. Jones, with Freud's approval, became the primary Totschweigen campaigner to prevent the Confusion of Tongues from being published in *The International* (Rachman, 1997a, 1997b, 2018b, 2022). Jones betrayed Ferenczi in his promise to publish the paper in *The International*. First, Jones told Ferenczi

> that he had translated the paper into English, and that it would appear in the International Journal of Psycho-Analysis.
>
> (Masson, 1984, p. 151)

Ferenczi verified Jones's promise of publication:

> I thank you for wanting to publish my Congress paper in the English Journal.
>
> (Masson, 1984, pp. 151–152 – Letter from Sándor Ferenczi to Ernest Jones, March 22, 1933 [Unpublished letter])

About three months after Ferenczi is joyous about Jones's promise to publish the Confusion of Tongues paper in English, Jones reneged on this promise. In a little less than a month after Ferenczi's death, on May 22, 1933, Jones wrote a letter finalizing the suppression of the Confusion of Tongues paper:

> To please him I had already printed his Congress paper, which appeared in the Zeitschrift [German Journal], for the July number of the Journal, but now, after consultation with Freud, have decided not to publish it. It would certainly not have done his reputation any good.
>
> (Masson, 1984, pp. 151–152 – Letter from Ernest Jones to Abraham Arden Brill, June 20, 1933, Jones Archive, London)

Freud, Jones, Rivière, Brill, Eitingon, and other members of the orthodox analytic community declared they were protecting Ferenczi's personal and professional reputation by suppressing his Confusion of Tongues paper, but the reverse actually happened. They ruined his reputation as a psychoanalyst and person with their accusations that he was emotionally disturbed, delusional, intellectually discredited and doing harm to psychoanalysis. After Ferenczi's death in 1933, the Totschweigen campaign intensified to totally remove Ferenczi's ideas and clinical functioning from psychoanalysis. The tragedy for psychoanalysis, psychotherapy, the mental health professions, and society is that their Totschweigen campaign was totally successful. Ferenczi's Confusion of Tongues Paper was not published in English until Ferenczi's student Michael Balint published the paper in English 17 years later, in *The International* (Balint, 1949). The Confusion of Tongues ideas continued to be silenced. Ferenczi's work was removed from study in traditional psychoanalytic institutes, and no courses or case studies were offered on Ferenczi's theory. The Budapest School of Psychoanalysis, which Ferenczi founded and helped verify, maintain, expand and contribute to the evolution of psychoanalysis was also not formally recognized or integrated into course work, supervision, presentation, invited lectures or seminars in traditional psychoanalytic institutes. The experience of one of this book's authors (AWR), completely verifies the success of the Totschweigen campaign that silenced and removed Ferenczi's work from what was called mainstream psychoanalysis at the time of the 1960s in the United States. All through six years training at a psychoanalytic institute which was considered to be of an eclectic orientation, represented by ego psychology, eclectic, interpersonal, humanistic, and contemporary Freudian perspectives, no mention of Ferenczi was made. The institute also was considered to have a flexible, contemporary, progressive and open attitude towards psychoanalysis. What is more, the institute's founder and primary force in setting the institute's analytic perceptive was trained at the William Alanson White Institute, the founding community for the interpersonal psychoanalytic perspective. In addition, the founder and head of the institute was analyzed by Clara Thompson, Ferenczi's analysand, student and follower. With these considerations in mind, during the aforementioned six-year training program at what can be considered an analytic institute, no reference was ever made to Sándor Ferenczi or the Budapest School of Psychoanalysis in any course, presentation, seminar, invited lecture, case study, supervision session, or informal interaction, by any psychoanalyst whether they be a teacher, supervisor, training analyst, administration, invited scholar or analytic candidate. The first time any reference was made to Ferenczi was when Arnold Wm. Rachman was invited to give a lecture at a course given by Bill Meaders, Ph.D., who had heard through the grapevine of Rachman's interest and research in Ferenczi. Meaders was, at that time, a junior, but courageous member of the institute's faculty. The reception of the analytic candidates to this first exposure was very positive. The institute's candidates and younger analysts showed interest in Ferenczi by inviting Rachman to give lectures on Ferenczi at the institute's Friday evening ongoing invited lecture series. It was the first time in the institute's history founded in the late 1940s, when Ferenczi was ever studied. The audience for the first presentation was made up of the younger community of analysts at the institute. They had never heard anything about Ferenczi during their analytic training. They were so pleased with the first presentation they asked for a second talk about Ferenczi. It became clear from these presentations that there was a new openness to being responsive to Ferenczi and The Budapest School of Psychoanalysis' ideas and methods in contemporary psychoanalysts.

It must be understood that the suppression and silencing of the Confusion of Tongues paper was very successful because it led to the removal of the importance of considering trauma as a significant psychodynamic in psychological disorder as well as introducing new measures for treating this newly considered emotional disorder. These ideas were removed from psychoanalysis, and they remained absent from psychoanalysis because the psychoanalytic establishment encouraged a negative view of Ferenczi personally and professionally (Rachman, 2022). The establishment acted as if Ferenczi never existed, never contributed to the evolution of psychoanalysis, left no heritage of important ideas and techniques for psychoanalysis to study and pass down to generations of psychoanalysts, did not contribute a paradigm shift in thinking and clinical practice that changed the nature of thinking about psychological disorder, who was a seriously disturbed individual, who was not a theoretical and clinical genius and deserved to be forgotten and removed from study in any psychoanalytic institute, conference, course, or interaction.

Michael Balint, who was a witness to the presentation of the Confusion of Tongues paper as well as the Totschweigen campaign to remove it from psychoanalysis and society, noted the traumatic effect that the disagreement that ensued around the Confusion of Tongues and trauma analysis had on the psychoanalytic community:

> The tragic disagreement between Freud and Ferenczi which caused both of them so much pain, and considerably delayed the development of our analytic technique, . . . [and] acted as a trauma on the psychoanalytic world. Whether one assumed . . . [that] the two most prominent psychoanalysts, were not able to understand and evaluate each other's clinical findings, observations, and theoretical ideas, the shock was highly disturbing and extremely painful.
>
> (Balint, 1968, pp. 152–153)

References

Balint, M. (Ed.) (1949). Sándor Ferenczi number. *International Journal of Psycho-Analysis*. 30(4).

Balint, M. (1968). The disagreement between Freud and Ferenczi and its repercussions. In *The Basic Fault: Therapeutic Aspects of Regression*. London: Tavistock Publications, pp. 149–156.

De Forest, I. (1942). The therapeutic technique of Sándor Ferenczi. *International Journal of Psycho-analysis*. 23(1): 121–139.

De Forest, I. (1954). *The Leaven of Love: A Development of the Psychoanalytic Theory and Technique of Sándor Ferenczi*. New York; Cambridge, MA: Harvard University Press.

Dupont, J. (Ed.) (1988). *The Clinical Diary of Sándor Ferenczi*. Cambridge, MA: Harvard University Press.

Eissler, K. (2001). *Freud and the Seduction Theory*. New York: International Universities Press.

Ferenczi, S. (1928). The elasticity of psychoanalytic technique. In Balint, M. (Ed.) *Final Contributions to the Problems and Methods of Psychoanalysis. Vol. III*. New York: Bruner/Mazel, 1980, pp. 87–102.

Fromm, E. (1959). *Sigmund Freud's Mission*. New York: Harper & Row.

Masson, J.M. (1984). *The Assault on Truth*. New York: Farrar, Straus, and Giroux.

Molnar, M. (1992). *The Diary of Sigmund Freud: 1929–1939, A Record of the Final Decade*. New York: Charles Scribner's Sons.

Rachman, A.W. (1993). Ferenczi and sexuality. In Aron, L. and Harris, A. (Eds.) *The Theoretical and Clinical Contributions of Sándor Ferenczi*. Hillsdale, NJ: Analytic Press, pp. 81–100.

Rachman, A.W. (1997a). *Sándor Ferenczi: The Psychotherapist of Tenderness and Passion*. Northvale, NJ: Jason Aronson.

Rachman, A.W. (1997b). The suppression and censorship of Ferenczi's Confusion of Tongues paper. *Psychoanalytic Inquiry (Psychoanalysis' Favorite Son: The Legacy of Sándor Ferenczi)*. 17(4): 459–485.

Rachman, A.W. (1999). Death by silence (Totschweigen): The traditional method of silencing the dissident in psychoanalysis. In Prince, R.M. (Ed.) *The Death of Psychoanalysis: Murder, Suicide, or Rumor Greatly Exaggerated?* Northvale, NJ: Jason Aronson, pp. 154–164.

Rachman, A.W. (2018a). *Elizabeth Severn: The "Evil Genius" of Psychoanalysis*. London: Routledge.

Rachman, A.W. (2018b). Ferenczi's confusion of tongues: A regressive idea conceived by a madman or one of the most important papers in the history of psychoanalysis. *Proposal. International Sándor Ferenczi Conference*. Florence, May 2–6.

Rachman, A.W. (2022). *Psychoanalysis and Society's Neglect of Sexual Abuse of Children, Youth, and Adults: Reassessing Freud's Original Theory of Sexual Abuse and Trauma*. London: Routledge Press.

Roazen, P. (1975). *Freud and His Followers*. New York: Alfred A. Knopf.

Sylwan, B. (1984). An untoward event: Òu la guerre du trauma de Breuer à Freud de Jones à Ferenczi. *Cahiers Confrontation*. 12: 101–122 (About the trauma wars between, Breuer, Freud, Jones, and Ferenczi) [Translated by Sylvie Teicher].

Chapter 6

The Confusion of Tongues Between Freud and Ferenczi

A confusion of tongues experience requires understanding in terms of a two-person psychology. Ferenczi's original formulation of the Confusion of Tongues identified the two parties as the abusing parent and the child victim. But one can extend this clinical paradigm to include the functioning of any authority figure with a subordinate, or more clearly stated, any relationship where there is an imbalance of status, power, and control (Rachman & Mattick, 2012). They can be applied to the relationship between Freud and Ferenczi. The analytic and personal relations between these two were eventually marked by trauma, confusion, and double-blind communication. Analysis of the relationship between these two giants of psychoanalysis had generally favored Freud. Ferenczi, as has been discussed, was typically described as an emotionally immature, dependent, ambivalent, and neurotic individual who had disturbed relationships with Freud and others (Jones, 1953, 1955, 1957). There is a host of commentaries on Ferenczi's disturbed personality (Gedo, 1997; Grünberger, 1980; Nemes, 1988), and sometimes seen as psychotic (Jones, 1957). Why has there been such a relative silence about Freud's neurotic personality and the link between his personality and the development of his clinical approach? In particular, why isn't Freud's behavior placed under the same scrutiny that Ferenczi's has endured when the relationship between the two is discussed? Traditional psychoanalysis has silenced scholarship and research on issues that threaten the Freud mystique, the view of Freud as an exemplar of personal and professional functioning. What is more, the practice of Totschweigen views dissidents who threaten this traditional view as unacceptable to mainstream psychoanalysis. This behavior can be compared to an adult's injunction to an abused child not to speak of what has happened. This silencing is itself a further abuse and attempt to

DOI: 10.4324/9781003265030-6

block the mobilization of psychic (and social) resources to deal with traumatic experience. In Dora's story (see Chapter Eleven) as we shall see, the same pattern appears in Freud's insistence on an Oedipal interpretation of Dora's problems, an attempt to silence her expression of sexual trauma and a need for parental tenderness.

In lifting the injunction on the practice of Totschweigen in discussing the Freud-Ferenczi relationship, we need to discuss the contributions of both men to their Confusion of Tongues experience. Freud acted neurotically in several instances. On the now famous trip the two took to Sicily in 1910, Freud's behavior in reality was quite different from the authorized version of the story told in the Jones biography and approved by Anna Freud as representative of the Freud family (Masson, 1984). According to Phyllis Grosskurth's account, Freud may have led Ferenczi to believe that they would spend a portion of their vacation in Sicily writing a joint paper (Grosskurth, 1991). Ferenczi was ecstatic about the prospect of collaborating with the master. However, Freud's message about the collaboration was a confused one. When Ferenczi entered Freud's room to begin their joint work, Freud asked him to take dictation on the Schreiber case, sending the message, "I am your superior." Ferenczi became angry and stormed out of the room. Once could view Ferenczi's behavior as neurotic in that his anger and departure from the scene did not help resolve their differences. Perhaps, his behavior indicated that at this early point in the relationship he could neither create a more equal role with his mentor nor accept that his mentor did not view him as a peer. Freud clearly contributed to this difficulty by the mixed emotional message he offered to Ferenczi. He disguised the language of authority in the language of collaboration. This was a Confusion of Tongues, a dynamic made possible because of Freud's actual dominance (like that of adult over a child) in relation to Ferenczi. Ferenczi wanted mutuality but was offered subordination. Was Ferenczi's expectation of mutuality neurotic? Freud wanted a particular kind of relationship with colleagues. Although he was friendly, responsive, and encouraging, he always wanted to retain the role of the master (Fromm, 1959). Ferenczi, like Jung before him, could never accept this limitation in their relationship. Freud struggled with the issue of mutuality but could not bend in this direction; perhaps he never recovered fully from the feeling that Wilheim Fliess had betrayed their relationship and never again allowed himself to be completely open to a colleague (Rachman, 2022).

Erich Fromm's study of Freud's authoritarianism in *Sigmund Freud's Mission* (Fromm, 1959) suggests that Freud played the role of an infallible leader. He surrounded himself, as in the group of close followers called the Society of Rings, with what Fromm called "company men," the most dramatic example of which was Ernest Jones. Jones was totally devoted to Freud as a person and as the founder of psychoanalysis. It was he who suggested the formation of the Society of Rings to protect Freud and the psychoanalytic community from criticism from the outside world. It is this kind of thinking, of us vs. them, that Freud embraced, if not initiated himself. It created the notion of a movement (more than a science) which must be protected from criticism and dissidence. Freud never lost the notion of being an embattled pioneer, a political leader who needed to protect his movement, continuing to fight the battle even though it had long been won. It is this sort of parochial thinking and functioning that Freud applied to silence Ferenczi's dissident voice. Ferenczi took seriously the notion of psychoanalysis as a science, which needed to be open to revision of its ideas and methods on the basis of clinical experience. What is more, he took it seriously as a method of treatment, aiming at the relief of pain. He was devoted to healing (Rachman, 2003), requiring above all, responsiveness to the experience of patients. Ferenczi had no political ambitions, turning down the presidency of the International Psychoanalytic Association to concentrate on the development of his Confusion of Tongues theory and method of curing trauma.

It is this background of authoritarianism, parochialism, and orthodoxy that led Freud to conclude erroneously that Ferenczi was trying to break away from his mentor and leave the fold of mainstream psychoanalysis. Freud can be seen as paranoid in his belief that Ferenczi's Confusion of Tongues theory and the clinical experimentation with trauma analysis were attempts to break away from psychoanalysis. In fact, Ferenczi never intended to break away from Freud (though Clara Thompson, for one, believed he should have done so). There were important personal and clinical differences between Freud and Ferenczi. By Freud's own admission, he could not be the "mother in the transference," nor could he work in the zone of regression (Balint, 1968), nor tolerate the emotional vicissitudes of the kind of "difficult cases" Ferenczi worked with. He did not see himself primarily as a healer (Roazen, 1975). His motivation was to build a comprehensive theory of human behavior and to establish that theory – psychoanalysis – as the foundation of scientific psychology. Ferenczi's primary motivation, in contrast, was to be a healer, extend the boundaries of psychoanalytic therapy to include the treatment of trauma, and to raise awareness of the psychodynamic of sexual abuse. Freud did not understand the positive meaning of dissidence in science – that it aids the development of science. He believed that loyalty and conformity to standard procedure were paramount. Ferenczi came within a hair's breadth of being expelled from the psychoanalytic community. Freud could not embrace a loving son who wanted to examine and change his theory and method. In the terms of his own theory, Freud had an Oedipal problem with Ferenczi (as Ferenczi did with Freud). Freud did not let the son challenge the father, in order to find his own sense of self. Ferenczi, for his part, could not break away from Freud to give full expression to his ideas and clinical methods. He needed the constant approval of the father. Freud also could neither accept nor understand Ferenczi's clinical genius or his passion to heal emotional and trauma disorder. Freud sexualized Ferenczi's clinical experimentation with trauma survivors when he heard through the grapevine that Clara Thompson boasted of her so-called sexualized contact with Ferenczi. Freud assumed Ferenczi was having sexual contact with his analysands. Freud's willingness to believe this may have been connected to an earlier issue, which was the "Elma affair" (Rachman, 1993). Ferenczi fell in love with Elma Palos after she began her analysis with him. She had come to him on the advice of her mother, Gizella, who was Ferenczi's mistress. The letters Ferenczi had written to Freud during the time of her analysis with him reveal a mutual romantic interest. But careful investigation of the letters indicated no actual sexual contact between them. Ferenczi sent Elma to Freud for analysis when his romantic interest developed with Elma. Ferenczi ended their relationship, and Elma left analysis. Elma eventually moved to the United States and married. Ferenczi married Gizella, Elma's mother, which was obviously a complicated sexual matter. The situation was traumatic for Elma and Ferenczi. Unfortunately, Freud used this difficult experience to condemn Ferenczi for his sexually acting out (Rachman, 1993). After hearing of Thompson's remark, Freud wrote Ferenczi what has become known as the "kissing letter" on December 5, 1931:

> I see that differences between us come to a head in a technical detail . . . You have not made a secret of the fact that you kiss your patients and let them kiss you . . . Why stop at a kiss? Which after all

does not make a baby. And then bolder ones will come along, which will go further to peeping and showing . . . and petting parties . . . . The younger of our colleagues will find it hard to stop at the point they originally intended, and God the Father Ferenczi, gazing at the lively scene he has created, will perhaps say to himself: <u>Maybe after all I should have halted in my technique of motherly affection before the kiss</u>.

(Jones, 1957, p. 197)

Masson who read the original letter in German said that Jones's translation had significant omissions, such as:

According to my memory, the tendency to sexual playing about with patients (Ferenczi's romance with Elma) was not foreign to you in the pre-analytic times, so that it is possible to bring the new technique into relation with old misdemeanors.

(Masson, 1984, pp. 159–160)

Ferenczi was wounded by the accusation of sexual acting out. He replied to Freud on December 27, 1931, in an unpublished letter Masson discovered at Maresfield Gardens in Freud's desk:

I consider your fear that I will develop into a second Stekel. [Stekel was noted for a tendency to invent case histories; he resigned from the psychoanalytic society in 1912, to Freud's evident relief.] The sins of youth, misdemeanors, if they are overcome and analytically worked through, can make a man wiser and more cautious than people who never even went through such storms. . . . Now, I believe, I am capable of creating a mild, passion-free atmosphere, suitable for bringing forth even that which has been previously hidden.

(Masson, 1984, p. 160)

By 1932, when Ferenczi presented the Confusion of Tongues paper, he had been a practicing analyst for 20 years, without any sexual incident with a patient. The Confusion of Tongues idea states that seductive behavior on the part of an analyst, even if unintentional, is a retraumatization for the patient. Ferenczi's letter indicates that he had analytically worked through his erotic feelings for Elma, someone he had wanted to marry. The Elma experience may have contributed to the formation and understanding of the Confusion of Tongues. Ferenczi, in formulating a theory of sexual trauma was integrating his own clinical and professional experiences.

Ferenczi's willingness to practice therapeutic touch with Clara Thompson was fueled not by an unresolved neurotic need to have physical contact with and analysand, but rather a realization that incest survivors suffer from severe physical and emotional deprivation. In certain instances, such as in Thompson's case, limited nonerotic physical contact can contribute to the curative process. As Judith Dupont had observed, Freud misunderstood Ferenczi's behavior: "Contrary to the rumor, Ferenczi did not kiss his patients. The story is based on a misunderstanding between Ferenczi and Freud, created by one of Ferenczi's patients (Clara Thompson) and which his *Clinical Diary* clarified" (Dupont, 1989, p. 255). It is worth noting that a colleague who had ongoing contact with Thompson while she was in analysis with Ferenczi reported that his clinical work with her produced significant positive results (Hidas, 1991). Ferenczi certainly seems to have gone beyond the bounds of therapeutic affection in the case of Elma, allowing himself to engage in a romantic crush, no doubt with sexual overtones. Freud's insistence that Ferenczi had actually had sexual contact with Elma, however, suggests an indictment of his former student. He believed, as Ferenczi studied and treated the most difficult analytic cases, such as Elizabeth Severn, had become an acting out, nonpsychoanalytic clinician. Freud was so bound to his Oedipal theory and interpretation method that he was <u>intellectually and emotionally blinded</u> to Ferenczi's courageous, creative, and landmark theory and method to understand and treat trauma disorder (Rachman, 2018, 2022).

References

Balint, M. (1968). The disagreement between Freud and Ferenczi and its repercussions. In *The Basic Fault: Therapeutic Aspects of Regression*. London: Tavistock Publications, pp. 149–156.

Dupont, J. (Ed.) (1988). *The Clinical Diary of Sándor Ferenczi*. Cambridge, MA: Harvard University Press.

Dupont, J. (1989). Ferenczi's madness. *Contemporary Psychoanalysis*. 24(2): 250–261.

Fromm, E. (1959). *Sigmund Freud's Mission*. New York: Harper & Row.

Gedo, J. E. (1997) Ferenzi as the orthodox vizier. In Rachman, A.W. (Ed.) *The Legacy of Sándor Ferenczi Psychoanalytic Inquiry*. 17(4): 28–436.

Grosskurth, P. (1991). *The Secret Ring: Freud's Inner Circle and the Politics of Psychoanalysis*. New York: Addison-Wesley.

Grünberger, B. (1980). From the "active technique" to the "Confusion of Tongues": On Ferenczi's deviations. In Lebovici, S. and Widlöcher, D. (Eds.) *Psychoanalysis in France*. New York: International Universities Press.

Hidas, G. (1991). Elma and Ferenczi (Personal Communication).

Jones, E. (1953). *The Life and Work of Sigmund Freud, Vol I.: The Formative Years and Great Discoveries*. New York: Basic Books.

Jones, E. (1955). *The Life and Work of Sigmund Freud, Vol II.: Years of Maturity. 1901–1919*. New York: Basic Books.

Jones, E. (1957). *The Life and Work of Sigmund Freud, Vol. III: The Last Phase 1919–1939*. New York: Basic Books.

Masson, J.M. (1984). *The Assault on Truth*. New York: Farrar, Straus, and Giroux.

Nemes, L.C. (1988). Freud and Ferenczi: A possible interpretation of their relationship. *Contemporary Psychoanalysis*. 24(2): 240–249.

Rachman, A.W. (1993). Ferenczi and sexuality. In Aron, L. and Harris, A. (Eds.) *The Theoretical and Clinical Contributions of Sándor Ferenczi*. Hillsdale, NJ: Analytic Press, pp. 81–100.

Rachman, A.W. (1997a). *Sándor Ferenczi: The Psychotherapist of Tenderness and Passion*. Northvale, NJ: Jason Aronson.

Rachman, A.W. (1997b). The suppression and censorship of Ferenczi's Confusion of Tongues paper. *Psychoanalytic Inquiry (Psychoanalysis' Favorite Son: The Legacy of Sándor Ferenczi)*. 17(4): 459–485.

Rachman, A.W. (2003). *Psychotherapy of Difficult Cases: Flexibility and Responsiveness in Clinical Practice*. Madison, CT: Psychosocial Press.

Rachman, A.W. (2018). *Elizabeth Severn: The "Evil Genius" of Psychoanalysis*. London: Routledge.

Rachman, A.W. (2022). *Psychoanalysis and Society's Neglect of Sexual Abuse of Children, Youth, and Adults: Reassessing Freud's Original Theory of Sexual Abuse and Trauma*. London: Routledge Press.

Rachman, A.W. and Mattick, P. (2012). The confusion of tongues in the psychoanalytic relationship. *Psychoanalytic Social Work*. 19(1–2): 167–190.

Roazen, P. (1975). *Freud and His Followers*. New York: Alfred A. Knopf.

Chapter 7

Ferenczi's Alternative Confusion of Tongues Theory to Freud's Oedipal Complex Theory

Expanding the Psychoanalytical Perspective to Include Trauma

On Sunday morning, September 4, 1932, at about 9:00 am, a stocky, balding man with a sweet face, walked up to the podium in the small assembly hall at the Hotel Rose in the town of Wiesbaden, in Southern Germany. In the gathering storm of Nazi Germany, traveling to Germany for Jews was becoming problematic. Europe was on the verge of totalitarianism. Freud could not attend the 12th International Psychoanalytic Congress because of illness. His mouth cancer was progressing and taking its toll on his mind and body. Ferenczi was also ill in body and spirit. Physically he was suffering from the impending collapse of his body due to pernicious anemia. What is more, Ferenczi's presentation was also overshadowed by the growing personal and professional conflict between himself and Freud (Rachman, 1997).

The presentation that held the coveted place of opening the congress belonged to Ferenczi and was his last appearance before an analytic congress. Ferenczi delivered what was thereafter, considered by Orthodox psychoanalysts as his infamous, but what should be now considered, his most famous paper. Originally it was titled, "The Passions of Adults and Their Influence on the Sexual Character Development of Children." This original title for what later became the "Confusion of Tongues" paper, best described the intention of Ferenczi's theoretical and clinical contribution to the study and treatment of trauma. He was focusing on the adult's passion and sexual activity with children. This actual (not symbolic) experience was also considered to have a significant effect on the development of psychological disorders both in childhood and later in life. Not only did Ferenczi verify Freud's original finding that childhood sexual trauma was a significant factor in the development of psychological disorder (Freud, 1954), but he also was the first analyst to describe and outline

DOI: 10.4324/9781003265030-7

the psychodynamics of this kind of traumatic experience. He outlined, in empathic terms, the child's inner struggle as well as the interpersonal encounter with family and adult authority to maintain a sense of self cohesion in the face of sexual seduction. Ferenczi's original contribution of the Confusion of Tongues has been expanded over the last 80 years and made relevant: to the study and analysis of trauma; development of a relational perspective in psychoanalysis; a two-person philosophy of clinical interaction; expanding the psychodynamics of the Oedipal findings of Freud of the significance of child sexual abuse as a psychodynamic in the development of psychological disorder and personality development; and as a tool in understanding human behavior (Rachman, 2022).

Parental Sexual Seduction

Ferenczi's Confusion of Tongues paradigm outlines the process that ensues when a child is traumatized by parental sexual abuse. The child has natural development needs for nurturance, love, affection, and tenderness from parental caretakers. This is the fundamental empathic and affectionate experience to which all children are emotionally entitled. It is this essential interaction with a parent that promotes emotional growth. When a child is unfortunate to have a parent with serious psychological problems which leads to sexual abuse, Ferenczi identified the psychological process that overtakes a child when sexual trauma ensues. Parental sexual abuse is mostly perpetrated by fathers (Herman, 1981), but Ferenczi identified mothers, siblings, relatives, family friends, and strangers as perpetrators (Ferenczi, 1933, 1988). A father misinterprets the daughter's natural need for affection, physical contact, and love as lust, which is his own projection onto the child. Sexual innocence does not mean sexual feelings are absent. There does exist a developmentally sequenced phase/appropriate element of sexuality, which is embedded within the relational context of the parent/child interaction. But such sensuality must be kept at the level of fantasy. When the father or other abusing adult or adolescent, under the pressure of his/her own narcissistic needs, distorts the total motivation of the child, reducing it to a predominantly sexual one, the stage is set for pathological, incestuous, acting out with the child.

The parent confuses the natural, phase appropriate longings for tenderness, sensuality, affection, and psychosocial play by the child for sexuality, thereby reducing the complexity of normal attachment strivings for merely one of its components. The parent initiates a part-object relationship and uses the child as a discharge object rather than as a whole object in which the capacity for nonerotic affection predominates. The particular example that Ferenczi used was the remarkable discrepancy between sexuality and affection; for example, the disturbing experience when a child yearns for tenderness and receives sexuality. It is not only that the child is confused by the adult's responding to its need for affection with sex. Molesting the child is really overpowering the child. It is actually aggressing against the child. Therefore, there are, at least two unrealities, for example, distortion of reality in the experience (Jacobson, 1994; Modell, 1990). It is sex and aggression that the adult is communicating in the interpersonal contact with the child. It is not tenderness the abusing adult gives the child. The narcissistic and unempathic parent (or parental surrogate) expresses his/her affection in the form of passion, sexuality. This is a disguised and distorted form of tenderness. The sexual seduction can vary from seductive verbal interaction to erotic touching or go as far as actual intercourse. The child yearning for tenderness and love succumbs to the abuser, entering into an unholy alliance that can be paraphrased as the child saying: "I will give you the sex you want because I need the affection or love you say you will give me." The adult seducer exercises power and control over the child by threats of physical or emotional abuse. As mentioned, the sexual contact between parent and child disrupts the intrapsychic fantasy process. The seduction intrudes upon the child's developmental needs to have a fantasy romance with a parent, not a real romance. The fantasy experience is not intended to be a real experience. When it becomes a real experience, it encourages the idea of the child as a sexual object for the need fulfillment of the parent. Fundamentally, at the deepest level of the child's subjective experience, the seduction is a rape of the body and soul (Shengold, 1989). The adult seducer is also in a state of confusion, not able to distinguish his/her narcissistic, aggressive needs for passion from the tenderness for which the child really yearns.

A Profound Sense of Confusion

A series of psychological mechanisms develop that enable the child to cope with sexual trauma. One of the most fundamental mechanisms is an overwhelming sense of emotional and intellectual confusion. The seduced child is confused (traumatized) as a result of the adult's betrayal, intrusiveness, manipulation, aggression, and unempathetic violation of their relationship. The perpetrator can also be confused since he/she can use denial and dissociation to distance themselves from the abusive act. The child developmentally expects erotic-free tenderness and affection in the form of emotional and physical nurturance. The child wants and should receive tenderness, not sexual passion. A child needs the physical and affectionate embrace of a parent. There is a fundamental need to distinguish between touching as nurturance and touching as erotic. Most parents intuitively know this difference. It is the narcissistic and emotionally disturbed parent who can't (or won't) distinguish between the two. Therefore the child who has been sexually seduced confuses passion for tenderness. A child, because of his/her need for parental affection, responsiveness, and caring becomes emotionally programmed in the future because of the trauma, to yield to an adult, to give an adult what he/she wants.

Alteration in the Child's Sense of Reality

The child's sense of reality can be seriously altered by the Confusion of Tongues experience with an adult. The parent's reality overshadows the child's because the child is in an emotionally vulnerable position. Usually a child needs the parent's response more than the parent needs the child's response. A child's sense of self is more easily threatened than the adult. What is more, the child is in a lowered position of status, control, and power, easily dominated by the parent. Parental narcissism interferes with the child's ability to understand what has happened. This is especially true when the adult denies the reality of the seductive experience. The adult's denial and unresponsiveness attempts to convince the child that a different or a nontraumatic experience has taken place. In the case of sexual seduction, the parent attempts to convince the child that a loving experience has occurred. In the case of emotional unresponsiveness, neglect, or abuse, the child also feels abandoned to their own feelings, without parental acknowledgment or affirmation of the reality of the abusive interaction. Under these emotionally vulnerable circumstances, the child becomes confused about the reality of his/her experience. What is more, a child can actually deny their own subjective experience while adapting to the parent's version of reality. The parent's version of reality is a distorted one. The child is left in a confused state, which once dissociated, remains essentially the same. Because the sexual experience is traumatic, the child spits off the thoughts and feelings of the traumatic experience, including the image of her/himself at that time. The child feels victimized, helpless, overwhelmed, frightened, angry, and confused. Once repressed this dissociated state fails to change, becomes semi-autonomous and continues to unconsciously influence the adult personality. It exerts an ego-weakening disruptive effect on healthy adult functioning, especially in the area of mature object relations.

The parental seducer can influence the child's sense of reality because the child's sense of reality testing is still in the process of formation. A child's sense of reality can easily be destabilized when trauma and associated reactive fantasies intrude. In the experience of sexual trauma, the child's intrapsychic functioning is flooded with intrusive fantasies as a reaction to parental sexual abuse. Such intrusive fantasies are more characteristic of the Confusion of Tongues experience because they are a result of disturbance in the interpersonal relationship between the parental abuser and the child victim. Oedipal theory posited a biologically driven child/ parent fantasy occurring intrapsychically as part of human development. The child's subjective experience of the seduction can be characterized as, "This happened to me because I am bad. I feel guilty and need to be punished. There is something wrong with me." The child is developmentally inclined to believe the parent's presentation of reality because acceptance of parental authority is associated with love, protection, and object attachment. Seduction fosters a profound sense of betrayal and the capacity to perceive reality accurately. This then engenders a serious difficulty in trusting one's perceptions. Manifestations of this difficulty appear in masochistic patients who repeatedly enter into abusive relationships from which they are unable to protect or extract themselves. The child assumes the reality of the parent, denying its own. This is an essential development of psychopathology. When the child denies its own subjective experience, denies it is being intruded upon or aggressed against, it is not being given love, it is not being molested, and wounded, the child assumes the parental view of the seduction as being an act of love. Such a psychological process places the child in a precarious position, vulnerable to the serious influence of another and on the edge of distinguishing reality.

Being Tongue-Tied

Parental authority also prevents the child from speaking about their sense of confusion. The child is confused intellectually, interpersonally, and emotionally. At some level of awareness the child realizes that their disturbed experience emanates from the parent. The child becomes tongue-tied, which can be considered as a form of elective mutism. The child cannot give voice to the difference between their definition of seduction and the parent's definition, since it is associated with the danger of loss of parental love, retaliation, and abandonment. This is further compounded by the fact that, at this immature level of cognitive and emotional development, the child actually needs the parent to help him/her to understand and verbalize what has happened. This requires truthful explanation given in context of emotional support, something which the abusive parent is quite unable to do. Emotional support cannot come from a parent who is in a narcissistic experience intruding on the needs of a child. Because the child is not helped to understand and verbalize the effects of the seduction, a pathological split-off nucleus of traumatic affect, self-image, and relational interaction develops and becomes the basis for later psychopathology. This affects all subsequent developmental stages, including the ego functions of reality testing, self-regulation and object relations.

Invariably the abused child, if he/she is able to talk, is criticized as being a hysterical liar. Often the child victim is blamed for the seduction because the nonabusing parent does not want to confront the reality of the evil in his/her spouse, friend, cleric, teacher, neighbor, or older child. The parental or adult bystander does not want to be forced to act, which may compromise the tenuous emotional and interpersonal equilibrium that has been established with their partner. The adult seducer also does not speak of the seduction: "The guilt that the parent or parental surrogate ought to feel but does not is then introjected by the child. The act is perceived as wrong, but there is nobody else to take responsibility for it except the child victim" (Masson, 1984, pp. 148–149). Often the adult becomes violent towards the child-victim, denying his/her aggression towards the child or that the sexual seduction was harmful. The evil of the act is projected onto the child, emotionally cleansing the adult of responsibility and negative intent. The child is left during and after the seduction in a disrupted intellectual, interpersonal and emotional state. The child has internalized an introject that disrupts reality-oriented thinking and prohibits thinking about what actually occurred. Consequently, the child and subsequently the adult doubts his/her own perceptions of reality, and is often unable to perceive actual abuse in later abusive relationships to which he/she masochistically clings.

Becoming an "Automata": Denial, Detachment, Dissociation, and Splitting

Ferenczi described the process of the child's psychological adaptation to the seduction trauma as becoming the emotional prisoner of the abuser:

> These children feel physically and morally helpless, their personalities are not sufficiently consolidated in order to be able to protest, even if only in thought, for the overpowering force and authority of the adult makes them dumb and can rob them of their senses. The same anxiety, however, if it reaches a certain maximum, compels them to subordinate themselves like automata to the will of the aggressor, to divine each one of his desires and to gratify these completely oblivious of themselves, they identify themselves with the aggressor.
>
> (Ferenczi, 1933, p. 162)

Splitting occurs because the child is unable to integrate the extremes of the parent's actual disturbed behavior from nonseductive to suddenly seductive, invasive, intrusive, and massively overstimulating. The splitting is related to the actual quality of the parent's behavior and not based predominantly on the child's fantasies and distortions of reality. The parent's real behavior is so extreme and unexpected that the child's ego is unable to integrate such a split. This is a lack of integration of self and object in the child's personality development. The capacity to integrate develops in about the three-year-old period when object constancy occurs (Jacobson, 1964; Mahler et al., 1973).

The intensity of trauma and the painful affects that ensue are so great that it disrupts and impedes the synthetic and integrative functions of the child's ego (Rachman, 1989, 1994; Rachman & Klett, 2015). This results in the persistence of a developmental lack of integration, which is referred to as splitting. It is manifested as the person shifting from one extreme state to another, in which the images of the self or the other are extreme opposites, which are not integrated into a whole balanced composite. There is a self-image that remains either good or bad. But, to view this phenomenon merely as a defense against aggression misses the earlier developmental interference with normal integration caused by the parent's seductive behavior. The earlier the sexual trauma, the greater the capacity to integrate is arrested. If the seduction occurs before the age of three, it is likely the child will remain emotionally arrested, in a state of severe fragmentation, in which the self and object world and other important aspects of reality functioning will be experienced with massive discontinuities, irregularities, and bewildering confusion.

Detachment is a defense against getting re-attached to an abusive object and re-experiencing the trauma. Psychologically it is removing oneself from an interpersonal field and from one's painful feelings. Dissociation is a phenomenon in which the split-off parts of the individual's experience becomes quasi-autonomous and take on a life of their own, dominating the individual's consciousness and behavior. An individual will then have internal objects and split-off parts of the self which exist as pathologically motivational systems in which the original trauma is repeatedly reenacted and replayed. Freud's ego psychology did emphasize the attempt to achieve mastery over the earlier trauma by repeating it, but missed the need to remain attached to earlier abusive objects, despite conscious aversion to those objects.

Another consequence of the adaptation to the incest trauma would be blunted affect. This mechanism is the habituation of detachment and also the manifestation of feeling dead inside (Bollas, 1983). The child feels he/she has been psychologically murdered (Shengold, 1989). Incest survivors talk about being murdered by their abusers. They feel that the trusting, affectionate, loving child-self in them has been murdered. They no longer have access to a wide range of feelings which are associated with vulnerability, pain, abuse, and betrayal.

Out of Body Experience

Out of body experiences which have been reported by incest survivors are dramatic examples of the process of detachment and dissociation which have their origin in childhood incest trauma. A female analysand had a childhood history of severe sexual abuse by relatives. An uncle and his 19-year-old son would abuse her as a child every time they visited her home, which included forced fellatio and vaginal and anal penetration. After these repeated sexual attacks, she developed an intense form of the Confusion of Tongues trauma to cope with what she felt was the impending fragmentation of her core self. During a session focused upon the recall of early childhood memories of incest, she recalled a horrific scene of sexual abuse in which a severe dissociative experience had developed:

> My uncle and his son came into the bathroom while I was taking a bath. I could not believe it, they locked the door, took off their clothes and got into the tub with me. They started playing a game called Suck the Popsicle! This time I was angry and didn't want to do it. I was also afraid, but, for the first time, I said, 'No!' They pushed my head on their cocks. I swallowed water, I thought I was drowning, going to die.
>
> Then, all of a sudden, I was floating in the air, moving toward the ceiling, I stayed there for a while. While I was on the ceiling I was looking down on the scene. I saw this little beautiful child choking with a cock in her mouth. For a while I thought the child would die. Then, something again happened. I said this little girl doesn't want to die. I began to float back down from the ceiling. All of a sudden, I was back in the water choking. I spit out the water, pushed the hand away from my head, and stood up. I went out of the bathroom screaming.

This description of the individual's out of body experience was both a meaningful phenomenological description of a severe dissociative experience, but also an emotional breakthrough in the unfolding analysis of the incest trauma.

"Helplessly Binding a Child to an Adult": Psychodynamics of Victimization

There are methods in the Confusion of Tongues experience of trauma which form psychodynamics of helplessly binding the child to an adult. These three mechanisms are passionate love, passionate punishment, and terrorism of suffering (Ferenczi, 1933 pp. 165–66).

1. Passionate Love and Identification with the Aggressor

In the dynamics of passionate or erotic love, the seduction emerges from the erotic love of the child by a parent. In the nonpathologic form, the parent's love is the psycho-biological human natural affectionate bond to a child. The child may nurse the fantasy of taking the role of the parent to the adult. There is a very important distinction between Freudian and Ferenczian views of childhood erotic fantasies, which became one of the intellectual ideas which began to distinguish The Budapest School from the Viennese School of Psychoanalysis. This fantasy play can assume an erotic form but remains on the level that Ferenczi terms "tenderness" not passion. The child can approach the parent in a way which may contain a seductive quality that is the unconscious feelings of the Oedipal drama. But the adult who responds with actual sexual behavior is a predator. Ferenczi's idea is that tenderness is maintained at a nonerotic level. This is akin to the love of a mother for a child (Rachman, 2018, 2022). The child is not the seducer; the parent contaminates the child's needs. Such adults are expressing a lack of impulse control and pathologic narcissism in their sexual desires for the child, whether it be by virtue of their own childhood trauma, psychological disorder, or alcohol or drug addiction. Abusing adults use the affectionate play of a child as an excuse to express their desires, as if the child was an adult. Fabricating the interaction as if they were involved with a peer, they believe they are not responsible for the damage they are contributing to the child.

In a statement which reflects his extensive clinical work with trauma cases which he reported in his Clinical Diary, Ferenczi described the spectrum of sexual abuse he observed in trauma cases:

> The real rape of girls who have hardly grown out of the age of infants, similar sexual acts of mature women with boys, and also enforced homosexual acts, are more frequent occurrences than has hitherto been assumed.
>
> (Ferenczi, 1988, pp. 161–162)

This observation, written in 1932, shows how prophetic Ferenczi's observations were, as we now take into account contemporary incidence of sexual abuse (Rachman, 2022, Rachman & Klett, 2015).

2. "Passionate Punishment"

The adult abuser has to deal with his/her feelings of anger, remorse, and shame for the seduction. However, the abuser behaves as if the sexual seduction has never taken place, consoling him/herself with the confabulation that a child does not know or remember the abuse. The seducer subsequently can be moralistic and religious, attempting, "to save the soul of the child by severity" (Ferenczi, 1988, pp. 162–163).

3. "Terrorism by Suffering"

All children have a developmentally phase-appropriate compulsion to take the blame for the abuse rather than believe it is their parents who are causing them harm. A parent who constantly complains to her child about her miserable life can create, "a nurse for life out of her child" (Ferenczi, 1988, p. 166). The child victim is caught in the bind of being terrorized by parental emotional abuse and identifies with the aggressor, taking on characteristics of the abuser. By so doing the child attempts to maintain the emotional fiction of parental love and tenderness. Ferenczi's concept of terrorism of suffering shows a similarity with Harold Searles, "The patient as a therapist to his analyst" (Searless, 1979). As the child attempts to cure the parent of his/her difficulties, the patient attempts to help the analyst with his/her emotional issues.

Identification with the Aggressor

Ferenczi developed this concept to understand the perverse bond that can be created between the abuser and the sexual victim. He observed how an intense emotional bond can develop with the very person who has abused him/her. Incorrectly, this method of coping with the sexual trauma had been credited to Anna Freud, which she supposedly introduced in her book, *The Ego and the Mechanisms of Defense* (Freud, 1936). But chronology of discovery favors Ferenczi. Anna Freud attended Ferenczi's Confusion of Tongues presentation at the 12th International Psychoanalytic Congress in Weisbaden in 1932. In fact, she reported on the presentation in the official publication of the IPA (Freud, 1933). The term identification with the aggressor appears for the first time in the original publication of The Confusion of Tongues paper:

> The same anxiety . . . compels them to subordinate themselves like automata to the will of the aggressor, to divine each one of his desires and to gratify these; completely oblivious of themselves they identify themselves with the aggressor.

> (Ferenczi, 1933, p. 162)

The child forms a masochistic bond with the abuser. Rather than reject-ing or rebelling against the abusive authority, the child attaches itself to the parental seducer. It is a desperate but effective way to gain or continue an affectionate tie with the parent, maintaining the fiction (delusion, if you wish) that the seduction is actually an act of love and tenderness. By intro-jecting the bad object, the child's attempts to master the trauma by becom-ing like the oppressor. Identification with the aggressor is a child's way to cope with the overpowering trauma of incest, which constitutes an exer-cise in power, control, and aggression by an authority over a subordinate.

There is an inherent communicative function or effort in identification with the aggressor. It can be seen as an effort to convey the child's internal state to another person. In a more dramatic fashion, it is the child's way to force an adult to feel what they feel. Contained in the concept of projective identification is this idea of putting your own internal state into the other person in such a way as to induce in the other person what you are feeling so that they will know your experience. Essentially, the child is signaling its distress about the trauma by causing the other person to feel it (Ogden, 1979).

Resilience in Recovery from Trauma

The Confusion of Tongues paper also includes a pioneering statement about the much neglected issue of an individual's capacity to recover from trauma. In this book's prologue this concept was mentioned. It is now important to pay full attention to what Ferenczi developed as a pioneering idea about the natural capacity to recover from trauma:

> It is . . . remarkable . . . a mechanism can be observed, . . . of the exist-ence of which I, for one, have had but little knowledge. I mean the sudden, surprising rise of new faculties after a trauma, like a miracle that occurs upon the wave of a magic wand, or like that of the fakirs [bird] who are said to rise from a tiny seed, before our very eyes, a plant, leaves and flowers. Great need, and more especially mortal anxiety, seem to possess the power to waken up suddenly and to put into operation latent dispositions which, un-cathected, waited in deep-est quiet for their development.
>
> When subjected to a sexual attack, under the pressure of a trau-matic urgency, the child can develop instantaneously all of the emo-tions of a mature adult and all the potential qualities dormant in him

that normally belong to marriage, maternity and fatherhood. One is justified – in contradistinction to the familiar regression – to speak of a traumatic progression, of a precocious maturity of the fruit that was injured by a bird or insect. Not only emotionally, but also intellectually can the trauma bring to maturity a part of the person.

(Ferenczi, 1933, p. 165)

As Ferenczi described in the quotation presented, as part of the Confusion of Tongues paradigm, his observation is clearly a landmark contribution to understanding human behavior in its darkest moment of trauma to its capacity to triumph over harm. In his contribution to understanding human trauma and the psychoanalytic understanding and treatment of it, he addressed a topic not previously recognized. In nature, there is a phenomenon observed, which Ferenczi used to symbolize resilience which can occur after childhood sexual abuse. Ferenczi used the example of a fakir bird. Their beak strikes a plant seed, opening it up, which prematurely allows the flower to grow out of the seed. Premature, in this instance, refers to the attack of the bird on the seed which prematurely opens the seed to allow it to flower. If left alone, the seed would mature and flower in its normal time sequence. Ferenczi used this observation from nature to compare what he called "traumatic progression" or "precocious maturity." This is the phenomenon that occurs when a child is sexually abused and under the urgency of this trauma, the child can develop instantaneously all of the emotions of a mature adult. The child can take on the identity and functioning, as if he/she were a parent. Rather than regress as an injured individual as a result of sexual trauma, the child becomes a precocious adult survivor. In an ironic way, sexual trauma, in the instance, produces a premature positive effect. It is similar to the phenomena of a parentified child, that is to say, a child who suffered from inadequate or disturbed parenting can, in response, become the parent in the family.

A Traumatized Analysand with Resilience

There is a contemporary example of an individual who suffered childhood trauma and developed into a survivor who demonstrated resilience. A female analysand in mid-age began analysis in order to understand and receive answers as to the meaning of her very disturbed childhood trauma experience. According to her report, she finally found the correct doctor who was helpful. Previous doctors wanted to take care of her but didn't answer her questions. This individual had a significant intelligence which she relied upon to maintain her emotional equilibrium and understand her traumatic experiences. She particularly had a series of questions about her mother's psychopathology. Both parents had serious psychological problems; the mother was a severe borderline individual with dissociative features, and the father suffered from bipolar (manic-depressive) disorder all his life. This individual, whom we shall call Erika, reported a lifetime of struggling with trauma when she entered analysis. The father was hospitalized in a psychiatric facility for over a decade for alcoholism. He was hospitalized because he could not stop drinking. He would create a trauma experience by his obsessive, frightening, and uncontrollable behavior. At one point, during adolescence, she moved out of her parents' apartment and moved in with a childhood friend. She felt empathy for her father's uncontrollable never-ending emotional struggles. She loved and respected him. He felt that same way about her. The father's emotional illness absented him, but when he was well, he was emotionally present. He would always apologize for his behavior. Erika's mother was an even more complex issue to unpack. She was described as an individual who had two different faces she presented to the world of relatives, friends, and the public. To the world, the mother appeared to be an intelligent, likable, functional person. People did not understand that her mother was emotionally disturbed, interpersonally difficult, or at times, intellectually limited. But with her daughter, she demonstrated a completely different experience. Erika described this experience with her mother as, "a life of trauma." As Erika described her emotional experiences with her mother, it became clear her mother suffered from a borderline personality disorder with dissociative features. Psychotic-like episodes appeared on occasion. She did not understand her mother's disturbed behavior. Importantly, she felt all alone in the experience of coping with the harm she was experiencing.

A classical traumatic experience of childhood involved the mother's dissociative behavior. The mother, on a consistent basis, would fail to pick up Erika after school was finished for the day. During her grammar school years, it was the mother's responsibility to be at the school mid-afternoon to meet her daughter to bring her home after school closed. Often, Erika reported her mother would not be there when school was over for the day. In fact, Erika had constant anxiety that she never knew when, or if, her mother would come to the school to pick her up. There were times when the mother would be hours late. At such times, Erika could no longer sit in the school building because it was closed to everyone, except custodial personnel. At such times it was of some comfort to her that she had the positive attention and concern of the teachers and custodians of the school building. Erika would call her mother on the half hour to see if she was going to be picked up from the school.

The trauma of abandonment, unempathetic understanding, yearning for love and attention, and emotional attachment as well as feelings of hurt and rejection swirled around Erika as she tried to retain her emotional balance. She could not understand, nor explain what her mother was doing during those dissociative experiences. She yearned to make sense of this chaos. Someday, when the traumas subsided, she hoped to find a way with someone's help to unpack her trauma and work through it.

Compounding the relational traumas were Erika's psychological and medical issues. There were the existence of Addison's disease, allergies, and dyslexia, which were detected during adulthood. Addison's disease produced a sense of weakness and being unwell. Her diseases needed constant attention. There were sensitivities to the physical environment, which caused irritations in breathing, skin, nose, and ear difficulties. The discovery of different forms of dyslexia heightened the experience of there being internal as well as external trauma. Some forms of dyslexia produce dysfunction in understanding, remembering, and producing ideas and content. This led to feeling intellectually inadequate, lowered self-esteem, and reduced motivation for intellectual achievement. Erika felt surrounded by familial and personal trauma. Her capacity to deal with a trauma environment is relevant to the discussion of the issue of an individual's capacity for resilience in dealing with psychological disorder and trauma.

Erika's parents had very serious emotional disorders and, consequently, showed serious dysfunction. As mentioned, her father had a formal psychiatric diagnosis of manic-depressive disorder, now described as bi-polar disorder. He was hospitalized at a private psychiatric hospital for severe alcoholism for over a decade. He was treated with psychotherapy and medication while hospitalized, as well as after release. The mother was in private psychotherapy with a psychiatrist for an extended period of time. Erika had questions about her mother's psychotherapist's clinical functioning as well as her professional ethics. The psychotherapist attempted to engage Erika to be her patient, but she refused. She did not feel the psychotherapist had been helpful to her parents. Growing up, Erika had no idea of the psychiatric disorder her mother had or what type of treatment she was receiving. What is more, she had never been helped to understand her disturbed relationship with her mother and how her mother's disorder had affected her. She had a head full of questions about her parent's disturbed personalities, her own emotional functioning, her mother's disturbance, how her mother's emotional disturbance affected her personality development, and what she needed to do as an adult to recover from her childhood traumas.

It became clear as Erika disclosed her childhood traumas, as well as her present functioning, her personality and emotional functioning was very different from her parents. A tentative psychiatric diagnosis for Erika could be considered to be generalized anxiety disorder or post-traumatic personality disorder. She finished her education, despite her handicap of dyslexia. There were a group of school friends with which she has maintained contact all through her adult life. She has administered her family's financial holdings in a meaningful manner as to be able to maintain a high-level lifestyle. The marriage relationship she has maintained for an extended period is enjoyed by her and her husband. She is regularly involved in social causes. Her family, friends, and business associates view her as a well-functioning, outstanding individual whom they turn to in moments of need. How do we account for Erika's capacity to be so functional in the light of her traumatic experiences in childhood as well as her physical and psychological issues? We shall turn to Erika's personal functioning and development and the issue of her capacity for psychological resilience.

There are several important factors that aided Erika's resilient reaction to her childhood traumatic experience so that, at the present time, she leads a meaningful and a relatively happy adult life. A fundamental issue in her psychological resilience is that Erika was not a blood relative of either her father or mother. She is an adopted child and did not, therefore, have any genetic or biological determinates related to her father's biologically-driven mood disorder or her mother's personality disorder. With two parents with severe psychological disorders, she escaped inheriting any predisposition for psychological disorder. She is interested in researching the history and biology of her biological parents with the possibility that she would find her biological parents had characteristics that aided her capacity for psychological resilience.

Erika, from childhood onward, showed an intense curiosity, questioned how things were made, read books on a regular basis, and was interested in public events. Her intellectual achievements were damaged by her childhood traumas, and her undiagnosed dyslexia. Her inability to achieve and enjoy school was a serious frustration. She had difficulty in writing, remembering, and understanding intellectual material with time limits. As a child, Erika possessed a very important psychological capacity, in that, she was able to emotionally separate herself from her mother's pathology. She did not feel she needed to remove herself from her father. She clearly felt her father's loving presence and concern for her. They shared a joint interest in art and intellectual pursuits. As a child, she remembers saying to herself when her mother would have an emotional fit or become emotionally detached, "What is wrong with her?" This was a moment when she was able to separate herself from her mother's pathology. It indicates she was not emotionally or symbiotically dependent on her disturbed mother. She also was not overpowered or allowed herself to be controlled by her mother. It's likely Erika had individuated from her mother from an early period of childhood. What is more, she maintained the separation, using her assertive and independent personality to be emotionally independent of her mother.

References

Bollas, C. (1983). Expressive uses of the countertransference-notes to the patient from oneself. *Contemporary Psychoanalysis.* 19(1).

Ferenczi, S. (1933). The Confusion of Tongues between adults and children: The language of tenderness and passion. In Balint, M. (Ed.) *Final Contributions to the Problems and Methods of Psychoanalysis* (E. Moscher, Trans.). New York: Bruner/Mazel, 1980, pp. 156–167.

Ferenczi, S. (1988). *The Clinical Diary of Sándor Ferenczi* (J. Dupont, Ed., M. Balint and N.Z. Jackson, Trans.). Cambridge, MA: Harvard University Press.

Freud, A. (1933). Report of the twelfth international psycho-analytic congress. *Bulletin of the International Psycho-Analytic Association.* 14: 138–140.

Freud, A. (1936). *Ego and the Mechanisms of Defense.* New York: International Universities Press.

Freud, S. (1954). *The Origins of Psychoanalysis: Letters to Wilhelm Fliess, Drafts and Notes, 1887–1902* (M. Bonaparte, A. Freud and E. Kris, Eds., Mosbacker and J. Strachey, Trans.). New York: Basic Books.

Herman, J.L. (1981). *Father-Daughter Incest.* Cambridge MA and London: Harvard University Press.

Jacobson, E. (1964). *The Self and the Object World*. New York: International University Press.

Jacobson, J.G. (1994). Signal affects and our psychoanalytic confusion of tongues. *Journal American Psychoanalytical Association*. 42(1): 15–42.

Mahler, M., Pine, F. and Bergman, A. (1973). *The Psychological Birth of the Human Infant*. New York: Basic Books.

Masson, J.M. (1984). *The Assault on Truth*. New York: Farrar, Straus, and Giroux.

Modell, A. (1990). *Other Times, Other Realities: Towards a Theory of Psychoanalytic Treatment*. Cambridge, MA: Harvard University Press.

Ogden, T.H. (1979). On projective identification. *International Journal of Psychoanalysis*. 60: 357–373.

Rachman, A.W. (1989). Confusion of tongues: The Ferenczian metaphor for childhood seduction and emotional trauma. *Journal of the American Academy of Psychoanalysis*. 17(2): 182–205.

Rachman, A.W. (1994). The Confusion of Tongues theory: Ferenczi's legacy to psychoanalysis. In Haynal, A. and Falzeder, E. (Eds.) *100 Years of Psychoanalysis*. London: Karnac Books, pp. 235–255.

Rachman, A.W. (1997). The suppression and censorship of Ferenczi's Confusion of Tongues paper. *Psychoanalytic Inquiry (Psychoanalysis' Favorite Son: The Legacy of Sándor Ferenczi)*. 17(4): 459–485.

Rachman, A.W. (2018). Ferenczi's confusion of tongues: A regressive idea conceived by a madman or one of the most important papers in the history of psychoanalysis. *Proposal. International Sándor Ferenczi Conference*. Florence, May 2–6.

Rachman, A.W. (2022). *Psychoanalysis and Society's Neglect of Sexual Abuse of Children, Youth, and Adults: Reassessing Freud's Original Theory of Sexual Abuse and Trauma*. London: Routledge Press.

Rachman, A.W. and Klett, S. (2015). *Analysis of the Incest Trauma: Retrieval, Recovery, Renewal*. London: Karnac Books.

Searles, H. (1979). The patient as a therapist to his analyst. In *Countertransference and Related Subjects*. New York: International Universities Press.

Shengold, L. (1989). *Soul Murder: The Effects of Childhood Abuse and Deprivations*. New York: Ballantine Books.

Chapter 8

Confusion of Tongues Contribution to the Evolution of Theory and Method in Psychoanalysis

Evolution of Psychoanalytic Theory

Ferenczi's introduction of the first alternative to the Freudian psychology of the Oedipal complex theory has been characterized as a paradigm shift in theory for psychoanalysis (see Chapter 7). Freud was threatened by Ferenczi's introducing an alternative perspective to the Oedipal complex (Gay, 1984). Ironically, Freud made an Oedipal interpretation about Ferenczi offering the Confusion of Tongues theory. He said Ferenczi was a symbolic son in rivalry with the symbolic father, playing out the Oedipal drama. Furthermore, the development of the Confusion of Tongues theory was interpreted not as a creative contribution to expand the evolution of psychoanalytic theory to include trauma, but seen as an attempt to kill off the rival father and overthrow him and become the head of the symbolic family, the community of psychoanalysis. As had been chronicled in other publications, Freud's idea of Ferenczi being an Oedipal rival became a preoccupation for Freud as witness the Totschweigen campaign he, along with Jones, launched to suppress Ferenczi's ideas and methods (Rachman, 1999, 2018a, 2022). Once Ferenczi began to develop his ideas and clinical methodology about understanding and treating trauma, Freud became antagonistic towards him. At some level of Freud's unconscious, Ferenczi's thinking and clinical functioning aroused rivalry, anger, and a desire to retaliate. Freud, as far as we can discover, never had a friendly conversation with Ferenczi about his dissident views, especially, the Confusion of Tongues idea and its implication for psychoanalytic theory and technique. He was willing to accept as the truth the rumors, accusations, rivalries, and antagonisms within the analytic community about Ferenczi: he accepted Clara Thompson's statement that she could kiss Ferenczi any time she wanted; he believed Ernest Jones's accusations that Ferenczi's

DOI: 10.4324/9781003265030-8

clinical behavior was a function of his personal psychopathology; he believed Joan Riverè's idea not to publish the Confusion of Tongues paper because Ferenczi was expressing negative thoughts about psychoanalysis that would do harm to the movement.

Freud had difficulty being an empathic father to his symbolic son, Ferenczi. He did not understand the necessity for a son to separate and individuate from the father to develop his own personal identity (Erikson, 1950). Ferenczi's Confusion of Tongues concept can be considered as a statement of an emancipation proclamation from Freud. First, it must be understood that Ferenczi did not develop this theory to rival, separate from, or elevate himself to be the new head of the psychoanalytic community (Rachman, 1997). His intention was to provide an evolutionary step for psychoanalysis to expand its boundaries for the study and treatment of trauma (Rachman, 2018a). The unfortunate and tragic circumstance was that Ferenczi began to separate from Freud because he felt devastated by his criticisms. Freud was angry at Ferenczi for developing his own ideas about psychoanalytic theory and technique. They never officially broke off their friendship, but they were not in loving contact during about the last years of Ferenczi's life. Their inability to reconciliate created a rift in psychoanalysis, Freud's psychology became the one and only perspective for the traditionalists. Ferenczi's or others like Adler, Jung, and Rank's additions to analytic thinking and functioning became the perspective of the unacceptable dissidents. If you want to be accepted in the traditional analytic community, you must accept the Oedipal complex theory as the cornerstone of your perspective.

The Confusion of Tongues idea was a paradigm shift in theory for psychoanalysis in several important ways. Ferenczi never rejected the Oedipal complex theory for understanding and treating neurotic disorders. His new theoretical paradigm was intended to help psychoanalysis understand that it could no longer remain a binary perspective, but it was necessary for the theory to evolve in order to treat traumas and borderline disorders. The treatment implications will be discussed more fully in the next section.

A significant shift in perspective was established in Ferenczi's understanding and treatment of trauma and borderline disorder that the role of the mother's interaction with the child was of utmost significance in the development of personality and psychopathology. The shift from focusing on the role of the father to the role of the mother in understanding human behavior and development of psychopathology was a significant idea as it changed the perspective of the male authority as the central figure in the development of human interaction. If one considers the Oedipal complex theory, the father and son play the central role in the interaction of neurotic disorder. The emotional tenure of the interaction is negative, an authority defending against the aggression of a subordinate, who is trying to overthrow him. The emotional undercurrent is anxiety, frustration, anger and danger. To underscore the interaction and emotional experience of the Oedipal complex, there is no hint of kindness, affection, compassion, or empathy. The philosophy of the analysis of the Oedipal complex reflects this theory. Clinical interaction highlights intellectual interaction where the authority of the analyst's interpretation dominates the interaction. The analysand awaits the wisdom of the analyst. When he deconstructed the primary influence of unconscious factors to include conscious or actual trauma experience, Ferenczi included both the mother and father as traumatogenic agents. Including the mother as a central agent in personality development was a pioneering moment in theory, which laid the foundation for Michael Balint, Ferenczi's foremost student, and D.W. Winnicott. These pioneers of the object relations perspective expanded on and further articulated the implications of the Confusion of Tongues idea for the evolution of psychoanalysis.

Ferenczi's understanding of the role of the mother opened up consideration of a different emotional role a mother played in a family in the interaction with the child. In the Confusion of Tongues perspective, the mother is conceived as the loving figure to the child. Whether it be a boy or girl, the mother is the closest figure to the child, providing attachment, empathy, attention, and love. The interaction with the mother becomes the architecture of the child's relationship with self, family, and others. As Ferenczi developed his interaction with trauma survivors, like Elizabeth Severn, the analyst role was as an affectionate parent/mother who is empathically connected to the analysand (Rachman, 2018a).

Balint, who was Ferenczi's successor to the presidency of the Hungarian Psychoanalytic Society and became one of the pioneers of the object relations perspective elaborated on Ferenczi's Confusion of Tongues paradigm. He described the search for primary object love as fundamental to understanding human development:

> I consider . . . primitive or archaic, object love . . . to be the fons et origo [source and origin]of human libido development. The original

and everlasting aim of all object relations is the primitive wish: <u>I must be loved without any obligation of return from me.</u>

(Balint, 1965, p. 233)

Balint believed that the primary wish of a child is for the intuitive, totally empathic, all-loving, maternal object. Balint maintained that the infant is born with a need to relate to its environment and an object (an individual). Development proceeds along the line of object relations, moving from archaic to mature object love. As the British object relations perspective developed, the major theoreticians, such as D.W. Winnicott, fully developed the mother's role during the transition of developmental stages in the life of the child. His object relations perspective described an instinctual need for the attachment and love of the mother. Love is considered the main motivating force in human behavior which also includes development of relationships (Winnicott, 1965, 1971). The balance between love and affection for another and the interest in and love for self is formed through thorough emotional bonds between self and another individual object.

Ferenczi's Concept of Tender Mothering

Isaiah's words as recorded in the Old Testament reflect Ferenczi's idea of the clinical interaction between analyst and analysand: "As one whom his mother comforts, so I will comfort you; and you shall be comforted in Jerusalem" (Isaiah, 66:13 – Stern, 1998).

Ferenczi used this Bible reference to develop a new clinical philosophy which was in marked contrast to Freud's philosophy of the analyst as a surgeon or clinical anthropologist. Freud's idea was the analyst as clinician who dissects the unconscious and digs into childhood amnesia in order to reconstruct the origins of the neurotic conflicts. Ferenczi, on the other hand, referred to a <u>tender-mother philosophy:</u>

It is important for the analysis that the analyst should be able to meet as far as possible without almost inexhaustible patience, understanding, goodwill, and kindness . . . The patient will then feel the contrast between our behavior and that which he experienced in the real family and knowing himself safe from the repetition of such situations.

(Ferenczi, 1931, p. 137)

A second quotation directly echoes the Old Testament statement from Isaiah:

> The analyst's behavior is this rather like that of an affectionate mother, who will not go to bed at night until she has talked over with the child all his current troubles, large and small, fear, bad intentions, and the scruples of conscience, and has set them at rest.
>
> (Ferenczi, 1931, p. 137)

Ferenczi's clinical philosophy, which Freud referred to as his tender-mother transference (Jones, 1957), was considered a significant deviation from tradition, so much so that Jones and Freud believed Ferenczi's philosophy of clinical interaction was a function of a personal need for love by the analyst, not the analysand's developmental need for love (Rachman, 1997, 2018b, 2022). Freud and Jones misinterpreted Ferenczi's noninterpretive clinical behavior of active interaction as arising from his personal need for the love and attention he missed from his family experience of maternal deprivation (Rachman, 1997). They did not understand his so-called maternal tenderness transference was developed from working with trauma survivors, such as Elizabeth Severn. She helped Ferenczi understand that childhood trauma caused developmental arrest, which can be alleviated by a new relational experience (Rachman, 2018a). Freud was clearly critical of Ferenczi's new formulation as he expressed his dissatisfaction to Max Eitingon (one of the members of the Society of Rings, which protected Freud from criticism within and without the analytic community) (Grosskurth, 1991).

It cannot be over emphasized that the Confusion of Tongues changed the perspective of clinical psychoanalysis from the focus on the father and the Oedipal rivalry to the attention to the role of the maternal experience with the attention to trauma and arrested development. Rather than discerning the existence of tension, frustration, and conflict, the focus switched to the psychological experiences in familial relationships which generated unfulfilled developmental needs. What is more, the clinical interaction moved to the analyst providing a compassionate, affectionate, and loving attitude which allows for empathic and responsive activity towards unfulfilled needs. In a personal conversation (AWR) had with Paul Roazen, the historian of psychoanalysis, reported that there were those who passed along the rumor that Sándor Ferenczi and D.W. Winnicott were considered homosexuals because they emphasized the maternal attitude in clinical interaction. It is interesting to note that Ferenczi's attention to the role of maternal affection, empathy, and unfulfilled need was interpreted as being the provenience of homosexuality. From the perspective of a relational orientation having the capacity to understand the role of the mother in human development and being able for a clinician to be tender, affectionate and empathic is essential and standard thinking and functioning (Rachman, 2018a).

Democratic Attitude and Two-Person Psychology

When Ferenczi reported he had submitted to Elizabeth Severn's idea that he should allow her to help him with analyzing his countertransference reaction to her, the idea of a democratic and two-person experience in the analytic encounter was introduced. This was a paradigm shift for clinical psychoanalysis because it invited the analysand to become a partner in creating and executing the analysis. Clinical interaction was deconstructed from the attitude that the analyst has the sole authority in the analytic encounter to an experience where the analysand is invited to share the authority of the interaction. The analysand became a co-contributor to the content and activity of the analysis. Shared responsibility for the clinical interaction can unfold in two basic ways: the analysand can request that he/she wants to contribute to the exploration of the emotional interaction and gives voice to this desire and the analyst empathically responds to the request; the analyst invites the analysand to contribute their ideas about the emotional issues and activity of their analysis.

Expanded Boundaries of the Active Role of the Analyst and Analysand

Ferenczi's role as a contributor to the pioneering period of psychoanalysis was as the analyst who helped move the boundaries of clinical theory and interaction towards the evolution of psychoanalysis. As has been discussed, Freud embraced the focus of his once most favorite student, Sándor Ferenczi, from 1908–1928, the first twenty years of their professional and personal relationship (Rachman, 1997). But once Ferenczi became involved in the analysis of Elizabeth Severn, which was the most challenging clinical experience of his career, Freud began to separate from him. This was a remarkable turnaround for both Freud and Ferenczi. At the height of Freud's affirmation of Ferenczi's clinical experiments in psychoanalysis, he told the Budapest Psychoanalytic Congress in 1918 that the future of psychoanalytic technique belongs in the hands of Ferenczi's idea of the role of activity of the analyst in the analytic encounter (Rachman, 1997). Why then did Freud abandon Ferenczi during his evolutionary theory and clinical behavior during the Severn analysis? Previously, reference has been made to Freud's irrational concern that Ferenczi was adding sexual acting out with analysands as a part of his trauma analysis methodology (Rachman, 2018a). Considering Ferenczi's introduction of the democratic and two-person experience as part of the Confusion of Tongues perspective, we need to add the idea that Freud was not only opposed to inviting an analysand to be partner in the analytic relationship but believed, along with Jones, that the basic authority of the analytic encounter should not be changed. Freud and his orthodox followers strongly believed that the analyst is the sole authority in the therapeutic relationship. Creating an analytic encounter where you consider the analysand your equal was considered an idea that was a function of a disturbed personality. Freud believed Ferenczi had an unresolved need to be loved, which he acted out, allowing analysands, like Elizabeth Severn, who "emotionally seduced" him, to provide her with all her emotional needs for love she missed in her traumatic childhood. It could be said that analysts include their own emotional needs in their expression of creative activity when attempting to meet the challenge of new and difficult analysands. It is possible that Ferenczi's need to be loved may have played a part in his empathic response to his trauma survivor analysands. But we must acknowledge the evolutionary pioneering contribution his clinical genius has made to psychoanalysis. Freud clearly recognized Ferenczi's clinical genius and innovations when, as mentioned, he declared in pioneering times that the evolution of clinical methodology would develop along the lines of Ferenczi's idea of noninterpretive activity of the analyst (Rachman, 1997).

The Confusion of Tongues perspective clearly expanded the boundaries of clinical empathy in psychoanalysis. Ferenczi's analysis of Severn can be seen as one of the stimuli for formulating this perspective. In order to successfully help Severn work through the harm of her horrific traumas of childhood, Ferenczi needed to call upon his natural capacity for empathy, in addition to his development of clinical empathy in order to therapeutically respond to Severn's desire to have her analyst respond to her need for a nonerotic/traumatic interaction from a parental figure. The analyst needed to respond to her developmental deficits. Severn's needs and demands were extensive because of her severe childhood traumas. Borderline personality disorder analysands with such unresolved developmental needs, present the greatest challenge for an analyst's capacity to translate emphatic understanding into meaningful analytic activity. Ferenczi has been criticized for his use of noninterpretive clinical measures with analysands, such as Severn. What needs to be understood is that special measures are sometimes necessary to meet the therapeutic challenges of severe trauma disorder. Ferenczi was able to expand the boundaries of his own special capacity for clinical empathy and translated it into an analytic experience which helped work through the damage of severe trauma (Rachman, 2018a). Analysts who are traditionally trained usually do not have the clinical training or emotional attitude to respond in a noninterpretive manner.

The formal introduction of noninterpretive clinical behavior emerges from the paradigm shift to the Confusion of Tongues paradigm from the Oedipal complex paradigm. Introducing the diagnosis, theory, and technique of trauma disorders necessitated developing creative clinical measures to analyze actual abuse, neglect, and deprivation. Ferenczi expanded the boundaries of clinical behavior because trauma survivors suffer from development arrest acquired from actual disturbed relational experience. What is more, trauma survivors ask for actual relational experiences which help alleviate childhood trauma deficits. Interpretations as the primary clinical intervention of the Oedipal complex issue has been criticized by analysands. Miss F. Heinz Kohut's famous analysand rejected his persistent Oedipal interpretations. It was only when Kohut terminated his need to use interpretation that Miss F. changed. He began to listen to her criticism of his interpretations; that was when the real analysis began. He finally stopped interpreting and realized he needed to intervene with a noninterpretive measure. When he responded with clinical empathy, Miss F. stopped her criticisms of him, and the analysis began to move in the direction of dealing with her developmental arrest (Kohut, 1971). It was unfortunate that Kohut did not remember Ferenczi's paper "Elasticity of psychoanalytic technique" (Ferenczi, 1928), in which he introduced clinical empathy into psychoanalysis (Rachman, 1989). Apparently, Kohut had read all of Ferenczi's papers before he had begun his own writings on self psychology, but did not acknowledge in presentations or publications that Ferenczi's ideas influenced him (Rachman, 1997). When he wrote about his difficult moments with Miss F., he acted as if he never was acquainted with clinical empathy or Ferenczi's pioneering contribution of it.

Besides clinical empathy, Ferenczi added a series of noninterpretive measures which centered around the clinical paradigm shift of changing the attitude, role, and behavior of the therapeutic dyad in the analytic dialogue and encounter. Three new noninterpretive measures were developed to contribute to the analysis of trauma disorders. They are among the most controversial clinical interactions, but these measures need to be taken seriously. They contribute to deconstructing traditional clinical interpretive behavior to reach unconscious material. This measures activity and the sharing of subjectivities to analyze trauma and developmental arrest. As Ferenczi deconstructed the nature of power, control, and status of the analysis, he opened up his activity to share his own subjectivity with an analysand. This occurred, not as Freud and Jones suggested, as a result of his need to be loved, and acquiesce to the analysand's request for fulfillment. Rather, his was a unique capacity to understand trauma and experience an analysand's need for empathic understanding and to develop the response that would address this need. Ferenczi would go beyond tradition and trust the analysand was asking for a necessary response and trust his response would aid the analytic process. The analyst sharing his/her power, control, and status in the relationship was developed by the analyst sharing his subjective experience in a judicious way with the analysand (Rachman, 1998). The analyst disclosing his/her subjective experience is intended to create a safe, empathic, need satisfaction interaction. This clinical philosophy deconstructs the idea of focusing on intellectual understanding of an analysand's neurotic conflicts. Analyst self-disclosure encourages a human experience in the analysis, an experience between two human beings, analyst and analysand, who are cooperating in helping the analysand confront, understand, and work through emotional problems.

Countertransference analysis is an essential expression of a deconstructed traditional approach to the analytic encounter. When Freud first discovered the countertransference reaction (Freud, 1910), he definitely did not see it as an essential ingredient in the analytic encounter. In fact, he wrote to Jung that countertransference should be a secret within the psychoanalytic community (Rachman, 1997). It is clear from Freud's reaction that there was something frightening about exposing the analyst's subjective experience. Freud did not want to expose his thinking and feeling to colleagues, and certainly not to analysands. It was essential for him to maintain his authority as the founder and head of psychoanalysis. He believed self-disclosure perforated his authority. Ferenczi did not share Freud's concern that self-disclosure was a danger to the analyst's authority. In his career, Ferenczi never sought political office nor entered into power plays with colleagues or analysands.

Mutual analysis, as developed by Ferenczi and Severn, stretched the clinical boundaries of the paradigm shift for clinical functioning. As mentioned in the previous section on analyst self-disclosure, Severn demanded that Ferenczi analyze his countertransference to her. What is more, she offered to help him with his countertransference analysis. They devised a methodology which involved analysand and analyst taking turns being analyzed and analyzing. Severn, of course, was involved in being an analysand before they changed their interaction. Ferenczi was successful being Severn's analyst, but he was also successful being her analysand. She used her therapeutic skills to help Ferenczi therapeutically regress to the time of his childhood sexual trauma. He confronted, worked through, and recovered from his childhood sexual trauma. He was able to integrate his experience and knowledge of trauma into his theory, as witness, the development of the Confusion of Tongues paradigm.

Freud and the traditional analytic community were severely critical of this noninterpretive measure because it was felt it relinquished the authority of the analyst. They did not understand one could share authority and not lose the essence of a therapeutic encounter. It is controversial to this day to introduce the method of mutual analysis Ferenczi and Severn employed. It is still considered controversial to encourage a mutual analysis between an analysand and analyst. Generally speaking, analysands may not be emotionally comfortable or interested in the responsibility of analyzing their analyst. If an analysand gave voice to this responsibility, the analyst would need to feel he/she was intellectually and emotionally capable of this therapeutic task. What is more, the analyst would need to trust his/her subjectivity to the analysand. Most analysts are not trained to be emotionally comfortable or vulnerable to an analysand. Allowing such vulnerability in an analytic encounter runs the risk, depending on the psychopathology and personality of the analysand, to engage the analysand to become more interested in analyzing the analyst than themselves.

There are instances when a mutual analytic encounter can be considered a meaningful technique: in a supervisory relationship, where such mutuality of sharing subjectivities were necessary to advance the supervisor's understanding and learning; mutuality could be used in a role-playing experience in training to help analytic candidates become more emotionally connected to their subjectivity.

Using the methodology of mutual analysis between two analysts who have been analytically trained and have years of post-graduate clinical experience can be useful as a therapeutic method. One of the authors (AWR.) has had such an experience. A mutual analysis between two trained analysts with about thirty years post-graduate clinical experience was developed. One member of this therapeutic dyad had been in analysis with three different psychoanalysts both during his training and afterwards. Although he said he enjoyed an excellent therapeutic relationship and respected the three former analysts, there was an emotional issue he was never able to work through. In his mutual analysis, he desired to work through this unresolved issue. He outlined his negative emotional issue with a family member that haunted him since childhood. In the mutual analysis he was responded to with empathy, compassion, and meaningful interpretation. After a period of several months, during which the issue was discussed for a one-hour weekly session, he felt he had worked through the emotional issue. When the mutual analytic partners analyzed the emotional breakthrough, the mutual analysand thought that the mutual analyst's clinical interaction was more helpful than his previous three analytic experiences because the issue of his relationship to an authority was dramatically changed. He realized that in the three previous analytic experiences, he had a negative transference reaction to the three previous male analysts. There was an underlying negative reaction to them because he felt subordinate to them, and they did not understand this negative transference. The analyst did not do anything to lessen the negative transference. In the mutual analytic experience, he felt his analytic partner's clinical attitude and interaction diminished the authority position by the use of clinical empathy and the sharing of his subjective experiences in similar emotional experiences. The mutual/analysand's previous negative transference did not emerge in the mutual analysis (Rachman, 2003a, 2003b). Apparently, this mutual analysis experience verified that Ferenczi's Confusion of Tongues clinical paradigm shift from a physician/ authority to an analyst/partner creates a democratic and helpful clinical experience (Rachman, 1997). Ferenczi's attention was clearly focused on being a healer. His learning about being a psychoanalytic healer, not only came from the theories and methodology of his colleagues in the analytic community, but from listening to and responding to his analysands.

The height of a countertransference analysis came to fruition in Ferenczi's analysis of his negative reaction to Severn. With her urging and help, he explored his childhood traumas with his mother and nurse, which left him with feelings of deprivation, abuse, and intense negative feelings towards women. He developed the insight that his childhood negative feelings towards women was a transference reaction to Severn, which he translated into a meaningful interpretation offered to his analysand. It changed the therapeutic impasse that had developed, and their analytic experience moved forward. Ferenczi developed countertransference analysis as an essential dimension of his trauma analysis (Rachman, 2018a).

References

Balint, M. (1965). Early development states of the ego: Primary object-love. In *Primary Love and Psychoanalytic Technique*. London: Tavistock.

Erikson, E.H. (1950). *Childhood and Society*. New York: W. W. Norton & Company.

Ferenczi, S. (1928). The elasticity of psychoanalytic technique. In Balint, M. (Ed.) *Final Contributions to the Problems and Methods of Psychoanalysis. Vol. III*. New York: Bruner/Mazel, 1980, pp. 87–102.

Ferenczi, S. (1931). Child analysis in the analysis of the adult. In Balint, M. (Ed.) *Final Contribution to the Problem and Methods of Psychoanalysis. Vol. III*. New York: Bruner/Mazel, 1980, pp. 126–142.

Freud, S. (1910). The future prospects of psychoanalytic therapy. *Standard Edition*. 11: 139–152.

Gay, P. (1984). *Freud: A Life for Our Time*. New York: W. W. Norton & Company.

Grosskurth, P. (1991). *The Secret Ring: Freud's Inner Circle and the Politics of Psychoanalysis*. New York: Addison-Wesley.

Jones, E. (1957). *The Life and Work of Sigmund Freud, Vol. III: The Last Phase 1919–1939*. New York: Basic Books.

Kohut, H. (1971). *The Analysis of the Self: A Systematic Approach to the Psychoanalytic Treatment of Narcissistic Personality Disorders*. Chicago, IL: University of Chicago Press.

Rachman, A.W. (1989). Ferenczi's contributions to the evolution of a self psychology framework in psychoanalysis. In Detrick, D.W. and Detrick, S.P. (Eds.) *Self Psychology: Comparison and Contrast*. Hillsdale, NJ: Analytic Press, pp. 81–100.

Rachman, A.W. (1997). *Sándor Ferenczi: The Psychotherapist of Tenderness and Passion*. Northvale, NJ: Jason Aronson.

Rachman, A.W. (1998). Ferenczi's "relaxation-principle" and the contemporary clinical practice of psychoanalysis. *American Journal of Psychoanalysis*. 58(1): 63–81.

Rachman, A.W. (1999). Death by silence (Totschweigen): The traditional method of silencing the dissident in psychoanalysis. In Prince, R.M. (Ed.) *The Death of Psychoanalysis: Murder, Suicide, or Rumor Greatly Exaggerated?* Northvale, NJ: Jason Aronson, pp. 154–164.

Rachman, A.W. (2003a). *Psychotherapy of Difficult Cases: Flexibility and Responsiveness in Clinical Practice*. Madison, CT: Psychosocial Press.

Rachman, A.W. (2003b). Freud's analysis of his daughter Anna: A Confusion of Tongues. In Roland, A., Ulanov, B. and Babre, C. (Eds.) *Creative Dissent: Psychoanalysis in Evolution*. Westport, CT: Praeger, pp. 58–71.

Rachman, A.W. (2018a). *Elizabeth Severn: The "Evil Genius" of Psychoanalysis*. London: Routledge.

Rachman, A.W. (2018b). Ferenczi's confusion of tongues: A regressive idea conceived by a madman or one of the most important papers in the history of psychoanalysis. *Proposal. International Sándor Ferenczi Conference*. Florence, May 2–6.

Rachman, A.W. (2022). *Psychoanalysis and Society's Neglect of Sexual Abuse of Children, Youth, and Adults: Reassessing Freud's Original Theory of Sexual Abuse and Trauma*. London: Routledge Press.

Stern, D.H. (1998). *Complete Jewish Bible: An English Version of the Tanakh (Old Testament) and B'Rit Hadashah (New Testament)*. Clarksville, MD: Jewish New Testament Publications, Inc.

Winnicott, D.W. (1965). *The Maturational Process and the Facilitating Environment*. New York: International Universities Press.

Winnicott, D.W. (1971). *Playing and Reality*. London: Tavistock Publication.

Chapter 9

Confusion of Tongues and the Language of Sexuality

Arnold Wm. Rachman and Paul Mattick

Sexuality as Analytic Construction

Ferenczi's ideas raise important questions about the very foundation of Freudian theory. The concept of a Confusion of Tongues was developed to understand such a situation as that in which a parent, for his or her own reasons, confuses a child's request for affection with a demand for sexual satisfaction. This conceptualization of such encounters suggests the need for a reevaluation of the psychoanalytic concept of infantile sexuality, which may itself represent the imposition of adult preoccupations on children's experience. It could even be argued that the most dramatic and widespread example of the Confusion of Tongues phenomenon is modern culture's bringing together of a wide variety of behavior by children and adults under the heading of "sexuality." Michael Foucault believed our society has spent a great deal of conversations about sex (Foucault, 1990). But this is not just a matter of talking more freely about a hitherto hidden phenomenon. Freud insisted that children are to be understood as explicitly sexual beings, in view of their oral, anal, and genital experiences. Freud wrote,

> There may perhaps, be an inclination to dispute the possibility of identifying a child's affection and esteem for those who looks after him with sexual love. I think, however, that a closer psychological examination may make it possible to establish this identity beyond any doubt" (Freud, 1975, p. 89). Why not, when he claims that the psychoanalytic method establishes that most of the so-called bladder disturbances of children younger than four: nocturnal enureis corresponds to a nocturnal emission.
>
> (Freud, 1975, p. 56)

DOI: 10.4324/9781003265030-9

Indeed he claimed that the whole surface of the body, and every internal organ, are potentially erogenous zones, that is, capable of sexual response. Thus an infant suckling at the mother's breast is not just feeding, but also enjoying the sensation, engaging in some sort of emotional contact, and exhibiting specifically sexual arousal. This is the beginning of infantile sexuality, in Freud's view: the infant discovers that the mouth is a source of pleasure. It is noteworthy that Freud makes no mention of the relational and affectionate component of the suckling experience; but then this is also missing from the picture he gives of adult sex also, described fundamentally as the satisfaction of individual libido needs. For Freud, sex is not a relational experience but a drive reduction experience within the individual. This is how he can insist that a sexual feeling is "independent of the object," transferable (in later life, in the perversions) to a material, animal, or oneself. It is only the terror of castration that restricts the object of desire to the world of socially acceptable relationships.

This conception of sexuality pictures the sexual abuse of children by adults as the interaction, however unfortunate, improper, or even damaging to the child, between two sexually desirous beings. The sexual excitability of children "seduced" by adults "show that an aptitude for [all kinds of sexual irregularities] is innately present in their disposition." Freud invokes an ancient comparison: "In this respect children behave in the same kind of way as an average uncultivated woman in whom the same polymorphously perverse disposition persists" (Freud, 1975, p. 57). It is hardly surprising that "the parents affection for their child may awaken his sexual instinct prematurely," since children "themselves behave from an early age as though their dependence on the people looking after them were in the nature of sexual love" (Freud, 1975, pp. 90–91).

Instead of saying that Freud discovered infantile sexuality, one can say that he imputed sexuality to an infant, thinking of it as similar to adult sexuality, although not necessarily located in the genitals. Classical psychoanalysis may be suffering from a Confusion of Tongues in its application of a vocabulary developed for the analysis of adults to the understanding of children and adolescents. What is more, they are misconstruing the expression of tenderness as an expression of sexuality. Such an emphasis on sexuality as the life force around which neurosis is formed could explain, at least in part, why Freud and the analytic community had such a negative reaction to Ferenczi's paper in Wiesbaden in 1932. Ferenczi's presentation raised very deep questions about the structure and conceptualization of psychoanalytic theory, striking at the prime dogma of the Freudian system. It raised a question about the assumption that you can use sexual vocabulary to talk about children as though they were adults.

The Oedipal conflict arises, in the Freudian system, as a result of the child's inner longing for sexual contact with a parent. Hence Anna Freud believed that giving up the Oedipal complex would mean giving up the cornerstone of psychoanalysis (Malcolm, 1984). Indeed, Ferenczi's idea was that the Oedipus complex did not accurately describe the experience of real trauma in instances where children were struggling with the after-effects of molestation by an adult. At several points in his clinical diary, Ferenczi suggested that the so-called sexuality of adults in relation to children had more to do with violence that with sexual expression (Ferenczi, 1988, pp. 79, 173ff)

Beyond the Confusion of Tongues between adults and children, Ferenczi's approach suggests a rethinking of the general category of sexuality. In Jane DeLynn's fictionalized tale of her sexual experiences, she described a visit to a dominatrix friend, who while spanking a female client, had a male kneeling outside her door like a dog. Comments DeLynn, "It was hard to sense the connection between these acts and sex, though I don't know what else you could call it," (DeLynn, 1990, p. 38). The implicit question here is a good one. It could be raised also of the child at the breast, as Freud saw it: why not classify this in physiological, affectional, and relational terms, rather than primarily libidinal ones? Why not take the S/M experience as an example of the exercise of power, control, and status, rather than of sexuality? The shiftability of such classifications is visible in the movement of the conception of rape over the last twenty-five years, from a primarily sexual to a primarily violent and abusive connotation.

To put the same point otherwise, what is the intellectual advantage of collecting these varieties of behavior, as Freud does, under the heading of sexuality? Freud's answer is that it allows us to classify behavior within a unitary framework. "It should be of a libido theory of neurotic and psychotic disorders to express all the observed phenomena and the inferred processes in terms of the economies of the libido" (Freud, 1975, p. 84). In particular, it allowed him to explain psychopathology as a matter of regression to infantile functioning. But perhaps such a unitary theory, while conceptually economical, does not do justice to the psychological, social, and historical complexities of human experience. Rather than take games of servitude and domination as formed by fundamental sexual energies, one could open an investigation of social- historical as well as psychological-historical into how it comes about that relational structures like sexuality and power can affect each other in these particular ways.

From this point of view, sexuality can be taken, for psychotherapeutic purposes, as a culturally-sanctioned classification of a variety of psychological experiences, interwoven with a host of emotional, interpersonal, and intellectual phenomena:

> Our experience of sexuality is all that there is to sexuality itself, and this experience was decisively and quite recently formed by a set of concepts of categories, among them "perversion," and related style of reasoning.
>
> (Davidson, 1992, p. 122)

This conceptualization differs from the view of sexuality as a drive; it starts from an attempt to understand the child's – or adult's – experience, rather than from positing a biologically rooted essence. As a classification, as a linguistic act, it can seek to impose a conceptual framework on experience; but it can also seem empathically to clarify and develop the subject's self-expression.

The role of language in the construction of sexual experience can be seen in an example of a Confusion of Tongues between a male college teacher and a female student. In the course of a discussion of her academic work, the student approached the teacher, putting her arms around him and making clear she had sexual desires for him. Taking this as a confusion on her part, and interpreting her action as a request for affection, he told her, "You don't have to have sex with me to get my attention." The effect of this was striking: she immediately relaxed her body, and the sexual embrace was converted into a child's embrace of a parent. After a moment of silence she confirmed his guess when he said, "Thank you for that." We interpret her acceptance of the teacher's redefinition of the interaction as suggesting that she had suffered from a confusion about her own desire, so that she experienced her desire for affection as sexuality. In Foucault's terms, this was an internalization of a socially dominant discourse of sexuality; more specifically it reflected a particular college subculture that accepted (and even encouraged) student-teacher sexual relationships, which provided a framework consonant with the results of her own intrapsychic struggles.

In understanding this situation the Confusion of Tongues vocabulary is very helpful. Redefining the experience as a desire for tenderness, transformed the encounter from a sexual to an affectionate one. That this redefinition was not arbitrary is shown by the student's response to it as allowing her to move in a direction she wished to take. She did not say, "No, I want sex from you, not attention." Apparently, a vocabulary for expressing the desire for parental tenderness was not available to her, other than in the form of sexuality. Once tenderness was offered, and named, the sexuality evaporated into thin air and never returned during months of continued meetings.

Ferenczi attempted to theorize such interactions in his analysis of the relations between analyst and analysand in the psychoanalytic situation. Just as he saw the intrusive parent as imposing passion (sexuality) on the longings of the child for tenderness (affection), so he saw that the analyst can impose his interpretation of sexuality on the longings of the analysand for tenderness (warmth, responsiveness, support, empathy). The form of this Confusion of Tongues, of course, is not that of seduction or emotional demandingness. The analyst acts in a detached, cold manner. Unwilling to form a mutual and emotionally sincere relationship, he or she is engaged in a matter of power and control. In psychoanalytic interaction as classically conceived, the doctor is in a position above the patient. A sick person is submitting to an expert who offers a diagnosis and a cure. Ferenczi did not deny that the analytic relationship was one of unequals, but he conceptualized the relationship as one of unequals who can influence each other towards change. By admitting when he has made a mistake, for instance, the analyst helps create a situation of trust, which helps the analysand to make use of the analyst's insights (Ferenczi, 1933).

By calling it a Confusion of Tongues, Ferenczi drew attention to the fact that language is a central medium of power in the psychoanalytic situation. The analyst is invested with the authority to interpret the analysand's experience in terms of his or her theoretical approach. John Forrester has emphasized "the fundamental rule of psychoanalysis: that the patient should say whatever comes into your head . . ." (Forrester, 1990, p. 35). What Forrester neglects to mention is the second rule of psychoanalysis, that the analyst reserves the right to tell the analysand the meaning of what has come into his or her head.

Interpretation is one of the main operations by which the analyst maintains power in the relationship. In particular, categorization of the analysand's responses as transference and resistance to interpretations can function as attempts to force the analysand to accept the analyst's way of thinking about the experience. If the former has a very different view of the experience, he or she runs the risk, in the classical situation, of having to submit to the authority of the latter, or else be seen as even more sick or disturbed. After all, if you fervently resist an interpretation intended to make you well, are you not clinging to your sickness? But if you submit to the interpretation despite it not matching your experience, you are having your reality redefined. So Ferenczi concluded, if the analysand is being critical of the analyst, wanting a more responsive interaction, the analyst who interprets this as a negative paternal transference reaction is creating a Confusion of Tongues experience for the analysand. In this way, the analyst recreates within the psychoanalytic situation the childhood trauma that brought the patient to treatment.

References

Davidson, A. (1992). Sex and the emergence of sexuality. In Stein, E. (Ed.) *Forms of Desire: Sexual Orientation and the Social Constructionist Controversy*. New York: Routledge.

DeLynn, J. (1990). *Don Juan in the Village*. New York: Pantheon.

Ferenczi, S. (1933). The Confusion of Tongues between adults and children: The language of tenderness and passion. In Balint, M. (Ed.) *Final Contributions to the Problems and Methods of Psychoanalysis* (E. Moscher, Trans.). New York: Bruner/Mazel, 1980, pp. 156–167.

Ferenczi, S. (1988). *The Clinical Diary of Sándor Ferenczi* (J. Dupont, Ed., M. Balint and N.Z. Jackson, Trans.). Cambridge, MA: Harvard University Press.

Forrester, J. (1990). *The Seduction of Psychoanalysis: Freud, Lacan and Derrida*. Cambridge: Cambridge University Press.

Foucault, M. (1990). *The History of Sexuality, Vol. I: An Introduction* (R. Herby, Trans.). New York: Vintage Press.

Freud, S. (1975). *Three Essays on the Topic of Sexuality* (J. Strachey, Ed. & Trans.). New York: Basic Books.

Malcolm, J. (1984). *In the Freud Archives*. New York: Alfred A. Knopf.

Chapter 10

A Contemporary View of Analyzing Childhood Sexual Trauma

Did Psychoanalysis Fail Survivors of Incest?

It is clear that an alternative view to the traditional psychoanalytic orientation is needed in order to treat the survivors of sexual trauma. Traditional psychoanalysis still greatly influences the way in which sexual trauma is viewed and treated. There are contemporary examples of these influences. A recent flyer announced a book being published by a child psychiatrist which compares the contemporary concerns about sex abuse with creating an atmosphere of tension and hysteria parallel to the Salem Witch trials in 1692. A supervisee told about his training experience at a therapy institute when he brought up a concern about a client's sexual abuse background in a classroom discussion. The faculty member, who was a trained analyst, assured him the best way to handle the situation was to encourage the repression of the trauma, rather than deal directly with it. In fact, she said, focusing on it just made it matters worse. My (AWR) own analytic training, which took place in a somewhat liberal analytic institute, never mentioned the seduction theory, Ferenczi, or the issue of sexual trauma (Rachman, 1997b).

If one uses the empathic method that Ferenczi pioneered that has been amplified by Balint, Kohut, Rogers, Searles, and Winnicott, among others, then clinical data provided by one's analysands can be a meaningful source of confirmation for the theory that childhood sexual trauma is an etiological factor in psychological disorder. Ferenczi, provided an emotional atmosphere where trust and safety are paramount. He was able to have adult analysands disclose their sexual molestation as children. Contemporary analysands have reported incidents of sexual seduction as widespread, but hidden in the highest levels of social strata. How many times, in the history of psychoanalysis, have analysands reported incidents of adult sexual molestation of children, either to themselves or others,

DOI: 10.4324/9781003265030-10

and how often have they been believed? As Masson has said, how many such analyses were incomplete because the pre-Oedipal sexual seduction trauma was never analyzed (Masson, 1984).

It is now clear in 2022 that Ferenczi's theoretical and clinical ideas about sexual abuse and its connection to the understanding and treatment of difficult cases were prophetic. Incest, of which Ferenczi spoke as being the most prevalent form of sexual trauma in difficult cases, was once thought to be a rare phenomenon. In the last ten years, clinical and epidemiologic studies have demonstrated that incest is a more common occurrence than both the professional and lay communities were willing to believe (Finkelhor, 1984, 1986; McCann & Pearlman, 1990; Quintero-Hernández, 2017). Prior to a recent study, it was thought that a 5 percent incidence of incest was the normative figure (Finklehor et al., 1990). But a current and thorough epidemiological study of adult women showed that 19 percent had an incest history (Russel, 1988).

Sexual Trauma Theory

An integration of the Confusion of Tongues theory and the development of trauma analysis can be used to develop a contemporary viewpoint for the treatment of sexual trauma.

1. Sexual seduction of a child by a parent (parental surrogate) does occur in all social strata in all Westernized industrialized societies (as well as in Asia, Africa, etc.); among all professions, including the healing professions (including doctors, teachers, priests, psychoanalysts); it is not limited by gender (mothers regularly seduce their sons and daughters; fathers not only regularly seduce their daughters, but also their sons); no religious group is exempt from incest, even ones that are the most fundamentalist, family oriented, and conservative in their interpersonal and religious practices. Incest has occurred in Muslim, Jewish, Born-again Christian, Universalist Unitarian, Mormon, and Atheist families (Rachman, 2022). There is no period in history when incest did not occur. What is different among contemporary life is that more individuals are willing to reveal their incest experiences, both in thoughtful as well as sensational ways.

2. As has been suggested, psychoanalysis and the general field of psychotherapy has neglected the issue of real sexual trauma (Rachman, 2022), for over the last 100 years. Psychoanalysis' neglect of incest

trauma had, during this period, negatively influenced the field of psychotherapy. Psychoanalysis needs to reorient its theoretical and clinical functioning in order to join the mainstream of contemporary treatment of incest trauma. There are several fundamental changes in thinking and clinical functioning that are necessary for this evolution.

3. Incest is a real event which causes trauma which can last a lifetime. If a real event is the cause of the trauma, then the treatment focus must be adjusted to this reality. Exploration, uncovering, and acknowledgment of a sexual seduction then becomes part of the analytic process. In the case of real trauma, Oedipal interpretations of the analysand's childhood for the adult, whether they be developmentally phase specific or exaggerated by trauma, do not relate to the emotional reality of trauma. Incest survivors want and need the analyst emphatically focused on the possibility of a real sexual trauma and acknowledge the hurt, rejection, betrayal, anger, and abuse that are part of the subjective experience of incest.

4. The empathic method is the fundamental means to create understanding, acceptance, trust, safety, and mutuality. <u>Empathy</u> is not an intervention to produce a desired effect or a response when a crisis arises; it <u>is a way of being for the analyst</u>. This form of empathy is not a routine, repetitive response, but a genuine desire by the analyst to understand the subjective experience of the analysand. If the analyst has difficulty discerning the subjective state of the other, he/she judiciously reveals the struggle to understand, thereby co-creating the analytic process. Analyst self disclosure is an invitation for the analysand to offer his/her idea in co-creating the analytic process.

5. A Confusion of Tongues explanation is a fundamental framework to understand the psychodynamics of childhood sexual seduction and the subsequent development of psychopathology. Childhood sexual experience is considered traumatic because: it is a betrayal of trust in the parent/child relationship; is an assault on the self of the child; disrupts the natural process of ego development; and overwhelms the child's capacity for metabolizing intense stimulation. In describing the manner in which the individual copes with the trauma, emphasis is placed on the self-actualizing capacity of the incest survivor. No stigma is attached to having been the victim of incest, nor is any attempt made to uncover the child's temptation of the adult. Sexual molestation of a child or adolescent by an adult is seen as the intrusion of the adult's

narcissistic needs onto the individual. Sexually seductive behavior between children or an adolescent and child is seen as behavior born of trauma.

6. Trauma analysis (Rachman, 2018) is based upon relational issues, for example, the disturbances in the object relations in the family of origin as well as significant relationship with authority figures/parental surrogates and peers. In the analytic situation, the relationship between analyst and analysand is part of the reparative process. As such, the relationship is open to examination by both parties in order to co-create the kind of flexibility and responsiveness that minimizes retraumatization, while providing reparative therapeutic experiences which heal the effects of the sexual trauma. The analyst takes an active role in the expression of empathic understanding, flexibility and responsiveness, reparative therapeutic experiences, and analyzing the core emotional issues. Particular awareness is directed towards the issue of retraumatization in the psychoanalytic situation. The analytic situation is a source of retraumatization when the analyst behaves with "clinical hypocrisy" (Ferenczi, 1933). Such hypocrisy develops when the analyst creates a one-person examination of the relationship, and the analyst's contribution to the treatment process is denied, omitted, or considered inappropriate (one must remember that the analytic tradition in almost all orientations does not favor analyst disclosure). If retraumatization does occur, the analyst moves quickly to reduce the trauma by taking responsibility for the disturbance, responds in a way to soothe the wound, and when the relationship crisis has subsided, an analysis of the trauma and its relevance to the original seduction experience is conducted.

7. "Analysis of the analyst" is essential to the analysis of the incest trauma. There are frequent incidents of interpersonal and emotional difficulty in the analysis of a survivor of childhood trauma. Such individuals can be hypersensitive in clinical interaction, experiencing unintentional, minor empathic breaks as abusive. When such impasses arise in the analytic situation, the analyst should not evoke a resistance interpretation. Rather, the focus is on a two-person analysis, where the countertransference analysis is an essential dimension in the analytic process (Ferenczi, 1933, Rachman, 1997a). In this relational approach, the analyst begins the analysis of the relationship crisis with a self-analysis. He/she begins an introspective process

where an attempt is made to uncover the analyst's contribution to the emotional difficulty. In fact, depending upon the severity of the individual's traumatic background and present emotional sensitivity, the analyst focuses on both self-analysis and the analysis of the analysand. Providing a therapeutic experience where the parental authority is willing, even eager, to analyze him/herself. This attitude contributes to the reparative therapeutic experience (Rachman, 1998) through the "tender mother transference" (Ferenczi, 1931), which is an essential part of the recovery process from childhood trauma.

8. A special form of retraumatization occurs when there is a real sexual seduction between analyst and analysand. It is ironic that Ferenczi's reputation was stained by the accusations made by Freud and Jones that he was sexually indiscreet with analysands. The "Elma Affair" was the vehicle for this false accusation (Rachman, 1993, 1997a). In actuality the Confusion of Tongues theory of sexual trauma specifically indicates that sexual contact between analyst and analysand is destructive for the analysand and the analysis. But since Freud rejected the ideas and techniques in Ferenczi's Confusion of Tongues paradigm, he did not understand that Ferenczi was specifically prohibiting sexual contact between analyst and analysand. It seems so self-evident that Ferenczi's Confusion of Tongues theory was actually a modern version of Freud's original rule of abstinence (Freud, 1915 [1914]). Freud introduced the rule of abstinence in order to help neophyte analysts cope with the difficulty of an erotic transference. He admonished young male analysts not to respond to the erotic longings of their female analysands, abstaining from fulfilling their neurotic wishes for love. Freud called it "transference love," realizing that such expressions of love and affection can have their genetic roots in childhood parental experiences. This does not mean the transference experience is not real, but it does mean a caution is sounded that the feeling not only comes from a childhood experience. The direct satisfaction of erotic feelings in the psychoanalytic situation would be detrimental to the individual and the therapeutic process. Freud cautioned not to satisfy a childhood neurotic need because it does not allow for personal growth. Direct satisfaction of the need by the analyst also encourages a form of romance and eventually an erotic component which produces an impasse. Erotic transferences are the most difficult to analyze because the analysand is encouraged to expect a real response

from a real person and not a therapeutic intervention from a clinician. Ferenczi was not only well aware of Freud's ideas about transference love, but fully accepted them. In fact, it was the rule of abstinence that began his formal clinical experiments with the analytic method (Rachman, 1997a). The Confusion of Tongues theory was a further development of this idea, evolving into the concept of "retraumatization" (Ferenczi, 1933). An analyst who has sexual interaction with an analysand, whether it is emotional seduction, verbal expression of sexuality or direct physical contact is demonstrating the most dangerous form of retraumatization, that is, the analysis itself becomes a seduction trauma, and the analyst becomes the seducer. In turn, the seduction in the psychoanalytic situation triggers the Confusion of Tongues trauma in the analysand. The analysand becomes the victim of the analyst who has caused an "etatrogenic trauma." The relationship between analyst and analysand is intended to be a curative of the Confusion of Tongues trauma. When the analyst contributes erotic passion to the interaction, he/she recreates childhood sexual trauma and changes from a therapeutic agent to a sexual predator.

9. The analyst has to assume a new role in the psychoanalytic situation in order to prevent or minimize retraumatization. It is clear that intensive clinical work with "difficult cases" uncovers trauma etiology, a finding that Freud first uncovered (Freud, 1954). What made Ferenczi's clinical thinking so significant, is that he used the data of clinical experience to examine the functioning of the psychoanalyst, realizing that retraumatization can be a function of the interpersonal encounter between analyst and analysand. The most fundamental characteristic of this examination of the therapeutic relationship is the following aspect of the analyst's behavior:

    (a)   To evoke an empathic attitude to understand the analysand's subjective experience as embedded in the interpersonal crisis in the psychoanalytic situation, the following needs to be understood:

    (b)   A willingness to admit mistakes or errors in his/her functioning. The analyst is co-creating with the analysand a democratic, two-person psychological experience.

    (c)   A no-fault attitude towards the analysand is established. There is no desire to blame analysands for their emotional difficulties, no matter how they may have caused a crisis in the ongoing therapeutic relationship. A nonjudgmental personal and therapeutic attitude predominates.

(d) The fundamental analogy for the analyst's role is "the tender mother." By tenderness is meant the expression of accepting, kind, warm, compassionate, loving feelings towards the analysand for the purpose of repairing the fundamental trauma. Being loving never means erotic contact. Being a tender parent was described by Ferenczi (1931) as

> It is important for the analysis that the analyst should be able to meet the patient as far as possible with almost inexhaustible patience, understanding, goodwill, and kindness . . . The patient will then feel the contrast between our behavior and that which he experienced in his real family and knowing himself safe repetition of such situations (p. 132).
>
> The analyst's behavior is rather like that of <u>an affectionate mother</u>, who will not go to bed at night until she has talked over with the child all his current troubles, large and small, fears, bad intentions, and scruples of conscience, and has set them at rest (p. 137).

10. An awareness is developed towards the occurrence of an abusive parental transference (Rachman, 1993). As has been emphasized, the sexual trauma survivor is emotionally and interpersonally hypersensitive to any experience in the relationship that triggers feelings of abuse, betrayal, manipulation, control, violence, or sexuality. As we know, there is no long-term, intensive relationship where empathic failures do not occur (Balint, 1968, Ferenczi, 1933, Kohut, 1984, Searles, 1979, Winnicott, 1965). All analysts must confront this, whether they are neophytes or training analysts. Experiencing the damage of real trauma from an analysand's childhood abuse can move analysts to tender feelings with which Ferenczi felt and identified.

11. An ethos of clinical experimentation in embraced, where active and noninterpretive measures are integrated into the analytic process to both soothe the wounds of the traumatized analysand when uncovering the areas of the basic fault (Balint, 1968), as well as to provide the working through of trauma through both the analysis of the genetic material, the therapeutic relationship, and reparative therapeutic measures.

Any meaningful adjunctive modality is employed which can aid the analysis (e.g., group therapy, family sessions, couple therapy, intense individual sessions, referral to 12 step, self-help groups, etc.). What is more, the analyst is particularly attuned to the requests by the analysand for therapeutic measures that he/she believes would be especially useful in dealing with the effects of childhood trauma. Sexual trauma survivors are particularly interested in suggesting esoteric therapeutic measures, which expresses a two-fold emotional process. On the one hand, the survivor has lost faith in the norms and traditions of society which have not protected him/her from incest. On the other hand, early childhood trauma can create a receptivity to any means which holds the promise of cure in a hostile and unresponsive world. Perhaps survivors turn to nontraditional, even other worldly measures because there is a psychic wisdom and openness about what may be curative when one is sensitized to trauma in early life.

12. A "benign regression" (Balint, 1968) is allowed to unfold where the individual can reach the archaic self in the safety of the psychoanalytic situation. The therapeutic milieu functions as a "container" (Winnicott, 1971) for the negative parental introjects, in order to metabolize the toxicity of the transference. With these considerations, the clinical work with survivors of incest trauma can, in an ironic way, return us to the most exciting period in psychoanalytic history, when both Freud and Ferenczi both struggled with these significant issues in human behavior.

References

Balint, M. (1968). The disagreement between Freud and Ferenczi and its repercussions. In *The Basic Fault: Therapeutic Aspects of Regression*. London: Tavistock Publications, pp. 149–156.

Ferenczi, S. (1931). Child analysis in the analysis of the adult. In Balint, M. (Ed.) *Final Contribution to the Problem and Methods of Psychoanalysis. Vol. III.* New York: Bruner/Mazel, 1980, pp. 126–142.

Ferenczi, S. (1933). The Confusion of Tongues between adults and children: The language of tenderness and passion. In Balint, M. (Ed.) *Final Contributions to the Problems and Methods of Psychoanalysis* (E. Moscher, Trans.). New York: Bruner/Mazel, 1980, pp. 156–167.

Finkelhor, D. (1984). *Child Sexual Abuse: New Theory and Research*. New York: The Free Press.

Finkelhor, D. (1986). *A Sourcebook of Child Sexual Abuse*. Thousand Oaks, CA: SAGE.

Finkelhor, D., Hotaling, G., Lewis, I.A. and Smith, L. (1990). Sexual abuse in a national survey of adult men and women: Prevalence, characteristics and risk factors: *Child Abuse and Neglect*. 14: 19–28.

Freud, S. (1915). Instincts and their vicissitudes. *Standard Edition*. 14: 109–140.

Freud, S. (1954). *The Origins of Psychoanalysis: Letters to Wilhelm Fliess, Drafts and Notes, 1887–1902* (M. Bonaparte, A. Freud and E. Kris, Eds., Mosbacker and J. Strachey, Trans.). New York: Basic Books.

Kohut, H. (1984). *How Does Analysis Cure?* (A. Goldberg and P.E. Stepansky, Eds). Chicago, IL: University of Chicago Press.

Masson, J.M. (1984). *The Assault on Truth*. New York: Farrar, Straus, and Giroux.

McCann, L. and Pearlman, L.A. (1990). Vicarious traumatization: A framework for understanding the psychological effects of working with victims. *Journal of Traumatic Stress*. 3(1).

Quintero-Hernández, Y.A. (2017). Social, cultural, and family practices as determinants of narratives and the self of 11 women with histories of child sexual abuse. *Open Journal of Social Sciences*. 5(5): 121–133.

Rachman, A.W. (1993). *The Abusive Parental Transference in Group Analysis of the Incest Trauma* (Presentation). San Diego, CA: American Groups Psychotherapy Association.

Rachman, A.W. (1997a). *Sándor Ferenczi: The Psychotherapist of Tenderness and Passion*. Northvale, NJ: Jason Aronson.

Rachman, A.W. (1997b). Sándor Ferenczi's contributions to the evolution of a self psychology framework in psychoanalysis. In *Progress in Self Psychology, Vol. 14*. New York: Analytic Press.

Rachman, A.W. (1998). Ferenczi's "relaxation-principle" and the contemporary clinical practice of psychoanalysis. *American Journal of Psychoanalysis*. 58(1): 63–81.

Rachman, A.W. (2018). *Elizabeth Severn: The "Evil Genius" of Psychoanalysis*. London: Routledge.

Rachman, A.W. (2022). *Psychoanalysis and Society's Neglect of Sexual Abuse of Children, Youth, and Adults: Reassessing Freud's Original Theory of Sexual Abuse and Trauma*. London: Routledge Press.

Russel, P. (1988). *Trauma, Repetition and Affect Regulation: The Work of Paul Russell*. New York: The Other Press.

Searles, H. (1979). The patient as a therapist to his analyst. In *Countertransference and Related Subjects*. New York: International Universities Press.

Severn, E. (1916). "Dictated in a subjective or trance state." *Friday Morning, January 14*. In Rachman, A.W. (Ed.) *Elizabeth Severn, The "Evil Genius" of Psychoanalysis*. London: Routledge, 2018, pp. 246–248.

Winnicott, D.W. (1965). *The Maturational Process and the Facilitating Environment*. New York: International Universities Press.

Winnicott, D.W. (1971). *Playing and Reality*. London: Tavistock Publication.

Chapter 11

The Confusion of Tongues between Freud and Dora

Dora's Psychopathology and Analysis
The Analysis of Dora

Having abandoned his famous seduction hypothesis in 1897, Freud was motivated to publish the case of Dora in order to substantiate his new theoretical tour de force, the Oedipal complex theory of neurosis. The case was published in 1905a, the actual therapy having been conducted for eleven weeks in 1900. Freud was motivated to present his first case study because he wanted to demonstrate that his new Oedipal theory was the cornerstone of psychoanalysis, providing an understanding of neurosis and its treatment. Even though Freud wanted to be scientific in presenting the case material, there is material presented or omitted which makes the case clearly beyond the Oedipal theory. It is naive to believe that Freud, a physician, male authority, and parental figure would openly explore the sexual feelings and experience of an adolescent girl, at the beginning of the 20th century, in Vienna, without producing significant issues for both Dora and Freud. The issue is sexual matters, such as sexual arousal, sexual countertransference, sexual trauma, and sexual abuse can inform an undercurrent of this case study. This undercurrent can be considered to be a classic example of a Confusion of Tongues trauma between Freud and Dora.

Freud's famous case study of Dora was of Ida Bauer (1882–1945). This is the first of Freud's iconic case histories, taking its place as one of the classic reports in the literature of psychoanalysis (Lowenberg, 1985; Marcus, 1986). The other cases were Little Hans, Dora, The Rat Man, Schreber, and the Wolf Man (Decker, 1998). Freud's case study of Dora was considered as highlighting the issue of transference:

> The story of Freud's patient Dora . . . not only illumines the concept of transference but also shows how Freud missed the all-important

DOI: 10.4324/9781003265030-11

transference that occurred during Dora's treatment an omission that may have had significant consequences in her life.

(Decker, 1998, p. 2)

In October of 1900, Dora, Ida Bauer was seen by Freud, referred by her father, Phillip Bauer, a 47 year-old prosperous textile manufacture. The Bauer family can be described as having been typical upper-middle class. The father was the dominating figure. Ida was emotionally close to her father. Freud believed the mother suffered from "housewife psychosis," that is, she was confined largely to the household, obsessed with order and cleanliness in the home. Dora's brother had a distant emotional attachment to his father. On the other hand, he tended to side in all financial disputes with his mother. Dora defended her father (Billig, 2012, p. 520). Dora's symptoms, which worried her father and made him consult Freud about his daughter were dyspnoea, that is, difficulty breathing, hysterical choking, depression, avoidance of social contact, leaving a suicide note, fainting spell, and aphonia, loss of voice. Freud described Dora as being completely hysterical by the age of 14 years old. In her later years, Dora suffered complete loss of voice as well as vaginal discharge.

The case study also clearly revealed the presence of a sexual abuse trauma suffered by the teen-aged Dora perpetrated by Herr K., a middle-aged male family friend. Yet, this issue of actual sexuality is neglected in Freud's analysis in preference to his idea of the unconscious psychodynamic of the Oedipal drama being played out in Dora's negative reaction to Herr K.'s sexual advances to her. Freud believed her negative reaction was a transference reaction from her father to Herr K. The description of Herr K.'s actions indicates he set out to seduce Dora from an early age and that he persisted in the endeavor, presenting her with flowers and valuable gifts as she grew older. There were two important events in the Herr K. and Dora relationship that were significant in her adolescence. When she was 14, Herr K. arranged to be alone with her in his office and made a sexual advance to her:

[he] suddenly clasped the girl to him and pressed a kiss upon her lips . . . [Dora reacted with a] violent feeling of disgust.

[Then she ran away] (Freud, 1905b, p. 28)

A second experience of seduction took place when Dora was sixteen years old. She and Herr K. were taking a walk by a lake in the Alps. Dora told Freud:

[Herr K.] had the audacity to make her a proposal [a proposal of love]. No sooner had she grasped Herr K.'s intention than without letting him finish what he had to say, she gave him a slap in the face and hurried away.

(Freud, 1905b, pp. 25, 46)

In this instance, Dora first told her father she wanted to leave the lake immediately and then told her mother about the seduction attempt. The mother conveyed the incident to the father:

Freud believed Dora's report of her seduction experience with Herr K.:

the conclusion of Dora's story must correspond to the facts in every respect.

(Freud, 1905b, p. 46)

This affirmation of her seduction by Freud was commendable. But because he was so motivated to establish his Oedipal theory, he was intellectual and emotionally blind to the implication of the sexual trauma suffered by Dora. He neglected to analyze the sexual seductions of Herr K. towards Dora because he believed his seduction theory of neurosis was incorrect. In actuality, Freud's original formulation on the origin of psychological disorder was meaningful. As we can see from contemporary psychoanalytic theory and clinical practice, the seduction hypothesis and Ferenczi's Confusion of Tongues expansion of it were clearly relevant to understanding and treating childhood sexual trauma seduction (Rachman & Klett, 2015).

Dora's So-Called Resistance to Freud's Interpretations

On October 14, 1900, Freud wrote to Fliess that he has a new patient and the analysis, he believed, began with success fully exploring her Oedipal complex. There was, however, a host of issues that needed to be understood, confronted, analyzed and worked through. This zealous scientist emotionally overtook the psychoanalyst as healer. Freud viewed the analysis from a one-person perspective, mainly his own. He was, unfortunately, intellectually and emotionally blind to the second person in the analytic encounter, his patient, Dora. She was in analysis not because she wanted to be analyzed. Dora was in analysis because her father brought her to Freud because he thought she was ill. In truth, she was what Ferenczi called a difficult analysand: she didn't recall her childhood; she was not forthcoming with psychic material; she rejected interpretations; she used denials, silence, and resistance as responses to Freud's intervention. On December 31, 1900, eleven weeks after she began, in an act of liberation, she terminated her analysis:

> Dora had listened to me without any of her usual contradictions. She seemed to be moved; she said good-bye to me, very warmly, with the heartiest wishes for the New Year, and – came no more.
>
> (Freud, 1905b, pp. 108–109)

Dora's father assured Freud she would return. She did return for one visit but did not resume the analysis. Freud believed Dora's termination was an act of angry acting out:

> breaking off so unexpectedly, just when my hopes of a successful termination were at their highest, and her bringing these hopes to nothing – this was an unmistakable act of vengeance on her part.
>
> (Freud, 1905b, p. 109)

His interpretation of Dora's vengeance is consistent with his diagnosis of Dora as neurotic. Her premature termination verified for him that she was resistant and a difficult analysand. In Freud's view, Dora could not metabolize the truth of his correct interpretations. Freud was absolutely convinced that her psychopathology had its origin in her unresolved Oedipal conflict with her father. Dora came to analysis with several emotional issues: she was unhappy with her relationship with her mother and her father; she was depressed; she felt alone with her disturbed feelings. Basically, she had no one to support her thoughts or feelings that she was traumatized. There was an enormous discrepancy between this teenage girl's view of her emotional life and the adults in her life. A dramatic and significant example of this emotional discrepancy was Freud's completely different view of the sexual trauma Dora faced with Herr K. One of these dramatic sexual traumatic experiences was described by Freud as a hysterical event:

> Herr K. contrived to get Dora alone . . ., and the without warn-
> ing . . . clasped the girl to him and pressed a kiss upon her lips.
> This was surely just the situation to call up a distinct feeling of
> sexual excitement in a girl of fourteen who had never before been
> approached. But Dora had at that moment had a violent feeling
> of disgust, tore herself from the man, and hurried past him to the
> staircase and from there to the street door.
>
> (Freud, 1905b, p. 28)

Dora kept the event a secret until she revealed it to Freud in her analysis. Dora suffered from intense emotional disturbance from Herr K.'s
attempt at sexual seduction. But Freud interpreted Dora's negative reaction to Herr K.'s sexual advance as a sign of her repressed Oedipal conflict. Freud did not note that when a middle-age male forces a sexual
experience on a teenage girl, it produced a negative emotional response.
But the emotional response is not a desire for sex as a result of an Oedipal conflict. Freud believed Dora should have been receptive to Herr
K.'s predatory sexual behavior. Her negative reaction, he thought was a
neurotic conflict. A contemporary view would believe it was a reaction
to a traumatic experience due to a relational disturbance. Marcus (1986)
believed this episode was the precipitating agent for the severe stage of
Dora's illness." (p. 419)

Sexual abuse of a 14-year-old girl is an event of serious emotional disturbance, which can lead to a trauma disorder, especially when it continues
to occur, as it did in Dora's case. Freud did not view Herr K.'s behavior as
sexual abuse, which it was then and would be considered so now. Freud
believed Dora was a severe neurotic when she entered analysis:

> In this scene . . . the behavior of the child of fourteen, was already
> and completely hysterical. I should without question consider a person
> hysterical in whom an occasion for sexual excitement elicited feelings
> that were predominantly or exclusively unpleasurable.
>
> (Freud, 1905b, p. 28)

Freud's interpretation of Herr K.'s sexual abuse of Dora assumed that she
was sexually stimulated by him, rather than traumatized by his physical
and emotional intrusion. Rather than her need to escape his aggression
against her, he said she repressed her sexual feelings, which overwhelmed

her. Building a theoretical system based on the unconscious blinded Freud to being aware of real experience, such as sexual abuse, being determinants of the psychodynamics of human behavior. Freud believed that if Dora wasn't a severe neurotic, she would have responded positively to Herr K.'s sexual advance as a normal woman: "should have responded to the embrace with specific genital heat and moisture" (Marcus, 1986, p. 421).

As Marcus (1986) astutely concluded that Freud's description of the case of Dora was written

> with a model in mind, but it turned out that <u>the model either didn't fit or was the wrong one.</u>
>
> (p. 422)

It is perfectly obvious that Freud had his Oedipal complex model in mind in presenting the case of Dora, feeling it illustrated the clinical verification of the theory. Rather than verify the efficacy of the Oedipal model, the case of Dora illustrates the use of power, control, and status by an analyst in attempting to convince an analysand of the analyst's frame of reference. Freud's model did not fit Dora's psychological problems, which was a trauma disorder, not an Oedipal disorder. Freud was so motivated and enthusiastic to fill the void between the seduction hypothesis and the Oedipus complex, that he injected the Oedipal theory into the understanding of the case. What is missing was an empathic attunement to Dora's traumatic sexual abuse experience. Dora's analysis needed empathic understanding of her trauma and help working through the actual trauma as it affected her psychological functioning (Rachman & Mattick, 2012). She did not need to be convinced that she was neurotically unable to sexually respond to the advances of a middle-aged male, three times her age. Dora needed affirmation that she was sexually abused as a teenager by an adult male predator (Rachman, 2018, 2022). Freud had freely admitted to being a man possessed with intellectual thought, which drove his clinical interaction with an analysand:

> a man like me cannot live without a hobby horse, a consuming passion – in Schiller's words a tyrant. I have found my tyrant, <u>and in his service I know no limits</u>. My tyrant is psychology; it as always been

my distant, beckoning goal and now, since I have hit on the neurosis, it has come so much the nearer.

(Freud, 1954)

In the case of Dora, Freud also demonstrated he possessed:

The demon of interpretation had taken hold him and it in this power that proceeds over the case of Dora.

(Marcus, 1986, p. 432)

In the literature amassed on the discussion of the case of Dora, we need to acknowledge the scholarly and astute article by Steven Marcus (1986), which is a comprehensive, informative, and valuable resource. However, we differ significantly from the remarkably positive assessment of Freud's theoretical and clinical accomplishments in this case. Marcus believed the case of Dora to be a turning point in his theoretical development of an understanding of neurosis in continuing the Studies of Hysteria by Breuer and Freud, and Freud's Interpretation of Dreams. Marcus (1986) also believed this case represents the theory in Three Essays on the Theory of Sexuality. How can the case of Dora be such an important theoretical contribution to analysis when it is generally considered a clinical failure. It can also be considered an uninformed example of treating an adolescent analysand and a trauma survivor. Shouldn't a case study demonstrate that the analysand's reaction to the analyst interpretations demonstrate that the theoretical argument is correct? In this case, Dora's reaction to Freud demonstrate a confused, dissatisfied, unhappy individual, not someone who accepted Freud's interpretation and gained emotional insight into her so-called highly neurotic emotional life.

As has been presented in this book, Ferenczi's Confusion of Tongues concept is considered a better fit, a more parsimonious, appropriate theoretical model for the case of Dora. A psychoanalytic model for understanding sexuality, trauma, clinical analysis, empathy, and the analyst behavior is needed. We can become enlightened by comparing Freud's case of Dora to Ferenczi's case of Rosa K., which was published during the same period Dora was in analysis with Freud (Ferenczi, 1902). Ferenczi's clinical behavior with Rosa K. is in marked contrast to Freud's with Dora. Rosa K. preferred to be called Robert as she was a transgender woman. The political and public attitude towards homosexuality and transgender individuals was draconian at the turn of the 20th century, which included imprisonment and public abuse. Ferenczi's clinical method of treatment was pioneering in that he showed a compassionate, empathic attitude towards Rosa K. His understanding was that her sexual orientation created abusive treatment towards her. He did not share the political, public, or psychiatric attitude of the time that only heterosexuality was normal and should be the only orientation to be affirmed. Ferenczi wrote a letter for Rosa K, which she could show to the police when stopped in the street for being dressed as a man. As she was a woman dressed as a man, the Ferenczi letter informed the authorities she was under treatment and should not be incarcerated. Ferenczi's clinical attitude was built upon empathic understanding. There was no blaming the analysand for their emotional issues, no forcing interpretations which the analysand needed to accept; no talk of resistance if the analyst and analysand had differences of opinion. Ferenczi attuned to the subjective experience of the analysand rather than prove his was correct in his theoretical perspective (Rachman, 1997).

Dora's Suicide Note

This teenage girl entered analysis in an emotionally difficult state: she was dissatisfied with herself; she became unfriendly with her father, with whom she had grown close; she was on bad terms with her mother. Her emotional disturbance reached a crescendo in writing a suicide note saying she could no longer endure her life. What was the participant factor in writing a suicide note? Dora could not speak directly to her mother and father about her sexual abuse trauma with Herr K. because she didn't feel they were emotionally available to hear and confront the issue. She was depressed, feeling alone, suffering from trauma. Dora needed to give voice to her traumatic experience, but could not. Freud did not address the harmfulness of sexual abuse when he devoted himself to the Oedipal complex. The seriousness of Dora's suicidal ideation was not taken into consideration in the clinical interaction of the analysis because interpretation took precedence over empathy. We need to understand the psychodynamics of suicide, as Freud outlined it, to present a reassessment of what was missing in Dora's treatment. The psychodynamic, which was part in Freud's thinking about suicide when he saw Dora, involved killing of the unconscious introject, which is the parent. The anger the individual harbors for a parent is acted out against the self. A child feeling vulnerable and powerless blames themselves for the emotional disturbance. In Dora's case she was angry at her father for not confirming his friend Herr K. was sexually abusive towards her. What is more, because of his detachment he did not do anything to stop her assailant. As a result, Dora harbored intense anger towards her father for neglecting the trauma and the harm the assault caused her. Dora was also angry at her mother because the mother was not available to emotionally respond to her daughter's trauma nor give the emotional support that her daughter desperately needed. Dora felt alone in her silent misery.

It is instructive to understand Dora's subjective experience of feeling suicidal if we search from a two-person relational perspective where empathy supplants interpretation. We can ask an analysand to share with us his/her self-disclosure of the phenomenology of their suicidal thoughts and feelings. Here is the statement of an adult male who described his feelings when he attempted suicide when he was 14 years old.

> Entertaining suicide means you feel totally alone in the world. There is no one who cares about you, you have no one to turn towards. You feel helpless, nothing good can happen to you. You do not feel you have the strength to go on. You feel alone with no one to understand or help you.
>
> The only way out of this darkness is someone reaching out to you. You need for someone to understand that you are suffering, accept your trauma, believe what you are saying is hurting you. Do not tell us what we are feeling, listen to what we are saying to you – believe us – reach out to us.

Neither Dora's mother, father, or analyst Freud was attuned to her in the way described by the analysand quoted. When Dora returned to Freud 15 months after her termination, he did begin to reflect on his contribution to the difficulties in the analysis:

> I do not know what kind of help she wanted from me, but I promised to forgive her for having deprived me of the satisfaction of affording her a far more radical cure for her troubles. (Freud, 1905b, p. 122)
>
> Its [analysis] great deficit which led to its being broken off prematurely . . . [was] I did not succeed in mastering the transference in good time.

(Freud, 1905b, p. 118)

The analysis ended without Freud addressing Dora's traumatic sexual abuse with Herr K.

Whose Reality Is It Anyway?

The question remains – whose reality is it, the analyst or the analysand? Marcus (1986) believed Freud's analysis of Dora was iconic; it was the analyst's understanding of the emotional issues that were of importance. In the Freudian perspective, the analyst bring meaning to the emotional struggle because he/she can interpret the

> several unconscious mental processes simultaneously.
> (Freud, 1905b, p. 47)

It was Freud's belief that he had to confront Dora with his interpretations. At no time did he approach Dora for her understanding of what had happened to her. Freud reproaches Dora, clearly believing she was an obstacle to her treatment when he said:

> she was never quite able to accept this version of reality, of what "really happened."
> (Marcus, 1986, p. 423)

Actually, Freud could not accept and understand what really happened to Dora. On the basis of an analysis of two dreams, as well as their interaction in the sessions, Freud sees Dora brimming with sexual desire for Herr K., her own father, and Freud himself. Despite her clear denials of sexual interest or feeling for any of these people, Freud insists that she unconsciously wanted an erotic relationship with Herr K. This yearning evoked an earlier Oedipal wish for her father that she had transferred this erotic longing to Freud. If you don't understand what was just said, imagine what Dora's experience was when Freud attempted to convince her of this. One must add that the confabulation was not an indication of Freud's hostility but his ardent desire to prove his newly etched Oedipal theory of neurosis. To Dora's credit she resisted Freud's interpretations, although she did consider them. After two months of sessions, she decided to terminate the analysis because she felt she was not understood, did not receive empathy, nor was she fully helped with her emotional issues through interpretation.

The most telling passage from Freud, in which he attempted to muse about his contribution to the difficulties in the therapeutic relationship with Dora, turns out to be the most telling and significant statement of the Confusion of Tongues dilemma that Dora faced with Freud:

> Might I perhaps have kept the girl under my treatment if I myself had acted a part . . . if I had exaggerated the importance to me of her staying on, and had shown a warm personal interest in her a course which, even after allowing for my position as her physician, would have been tantamount to providing her with a substitute for the affection she longed for? I do not know.
>
> (Freud, 1905a, p. 131)

Dora, in telling her side of the story to Freud, obviously talked about her inadequate relationship with her mother and father. Freud believed Dora longed for a warm personal interest and affection. So Dora was successful in expressing to Freud her subjective experience of affection and tenderness. Freud was attuned to her need, but he chose not to share his empathy with Dora, thinking she needed to better understand her Oedipal conflicts. The Confusion of Tongues theory provides a much needed understanding of a trauma disorder which Freud could have used to understand Dora.

Freud's Confusion of Tongues

Freud insists on taking Dora's wish for adult affection – with all that is implies for an adolescent, as an expression of sexual desire. He takes her refusal to accept his Oedipal analysis as an indication of her anger at his providing her valuable insights. Interestingly, one can take Freud's effort to impose his theory on Dora as an unanalyzed sexualization of the relationship. Whatever Dora wanted to talk about, Freud turned the interaction towards the Oedipal wish for sexual expression with a parent. She wanted to talk about affection, deprivation, abuse, he called it sexual desire. He sees her behavior as symbolically sexual. Freud is trying to control her, make her submit to him. He openly suggested she has thoughts about kissing him as an interpretation to a dream fragment. She plays with her purse in the session, which he interprets as masturbation. But even aside from this, his encounter with Dora can be seen as a reenactment of traumas at the source of Dora's troubles, such as lack of adult (parental) affection and denial of her perceptions, as well as insistence on the appropriate-ness of a sexual relationship with an older man she doesn't want. Freud insisted on telling her what she wants, even though she does not respond. What would have been curative of the Confusion of Tongues experience for Dora? There are many meaningful clinical interactions which show her some aspect of the affection she longed for by a parental figure: to show her tenderness; to encourage her to voice her thoughts and feelings and accept them as her subjective experience; to be an empathic figure, with no desire to convince her of the analyst's interpretations; to empathize with the feelings of betrayal, abuse, mistrust, intrusion, confusion, and anger that occurs when an adult tries to sexually seduce you against your will, and no adult accepts your reality of the situation or that it happened; to try to empathize with the experience of being driven to despair as a result of the seduction and the conspiracy of silence between adults; to help Dora understand that she needed to develop somatic symptoms and suicidal thoughts in order to be heard.

Dora's Confusion of Tongues

Dora is literally confused about what she wants to say because no one, including Freud, wants to hear her. The Confusion of Tongues was an evocative term to use in the context of a form of treatment described as a "talking cure." Ferenczi's paper, after all, was an extended comparison of the psychoanalytic situation with childhood sexual trauma. The difference between the two is that in the psychoanalytic situation, it is speech itself which carries the burden of the work. So Ferenczi's comparison draws our attention to the analogy between Herr K.'s physical assault on Dora, as when he grasps and kisses her, and Freud's verbal insistence on Dora's sexual longing for Herr K., her father, and Freud. Despite his consistent denial, Freud continued to confuse her with his interpretations. It was ingenious on Ferenczi's part to consider the analogy between the adult/child relationship and the analyst/analysand relationship because speech is a form of structured behavior that underlies both experiences. The capac-ity "to find one's voice" in such an interaction is clearly determined by the relational quality of the interpersonal experience. As it should be the goal of a parent to help their child speak of their confusions, it should be the analyst's mandate to help an analysand speak of their confusion, discon-tent, relationship disturbance, both from childhood and in contemporary existence. Freud had not yet discovered the countertransference reaction at the time of Dora's analysis. When he did report on this five years later, he made it clear how significant countertransference analysis is to a meaningful analysis:

> We have become aware of the "counter-transference," which arises in him [the psychoanalyst] as a result of the patient's influence on his unconscious feelings, and we are almost inclined to insist that he shall recognize this counter-transference in himself and overcome it . . . <u>no psychoanalyst goes further than his own internal resistances permit.</u>
>
> (Freud, 1910, pp. 141–142)

Unfortunately, Freud never took his own advice in the quotation presented, as he concentrated on being the physician authority in the analytic encounter. What Ferenczi was presenting in his Confusion of Tongues concept was that a two-person analytic experience is needed to help sexual trauma survivors to confront, work through, and recover from sexual abuse.

References

Billig, M. (2012). Freud and Dora: Repressing an oppressed identity. *British Journal of Social Psychology*. 3: 518–535.

Decker, H.S. (1998). Freud's "Dora" Case: The crucible of the psychoanalytic concepts of transference. In Roth, M.S. (Ed.) *Freud: Concept and Culture*. New York: Knopf.

Ferenczi, S. (1902). Homosexualitas Feminina (Female sexuality). *Gyögyazat*. 11: 167–168. (Translated by Gabor Kalman).

Freud, S. (1905a). Three essays on the theory of sexuality. *Standard Edition*. 7: 125–243 (London, England: Hogarth Press, 1955).

Freud, S. (1905b). *Standard Edition*. 7: 1–122 (London: Hogarth Press).

Freud, S. (1910). The future prospects of psychoanalytic therapy. *Standard Edition*. 11: 139–152.

Freud, S. (1954). *The Origins of Psychoanalysis: Letters to Wilhelm Fliess, Drafts and Notes, 1887–1902* (M. Bonaparte, A. Freud and E. Kris, Eds., Mosbacker and J. Strachey, Trans.). New York: Basic Books.

Lowenberg, P. (1985). *Decoding the Past: The Psychohistorical Approach*. Berkeley, CA: University of California Press.

Marcus, S. (1986). Freud and Dora: Story, history, case-history. In Bernhumer, C. and Kahane, C. (Eds.) *In Dora's Case*. London: Virago.

Rachman, A.W. (1997). *Sándor Ferenczi: The Psychotherapist of Tenderness and Passion*. Northvale, NJ: Jason Aronson.

Rachman, A.W. (2018). *Elizabeth Severn: The "Evil Genius" of Psychoanalysis.* London: Routledge.

Rachman, A.W. (2022). *Psychoanalysis and Society's Neglect of Sexual Abuse of Children, Youth, and Adults: Reassessing Freud's Original Theory of Sexual Abuse and Trauma.* London: Routledge Press.

Rachman, A.W. and Klett, S. (2015). *Analysis of the Incest Trauma: Retrieval, Recovery, Renewal.* London: Karnac Books.

Rachman, A.W. and Mattick, P. (2012). The confusion of tongues in the psycho-analytic relationship. *Psychoanalytic Social Work.* 19(1–2): 167–190.

Chapter 12

The Analysis Between Sándor Ferenczi and Elizabeth Severn

Origin of the Confusion of Tongues Paradigm and Trauma Analysis

The therapeutic relationship between Sándor Ferenczi and Elizabeth Severn has been severely criticized and dismissed as a wild analysis (Rachman, 2012). The Totschweigen campaign was successful in removing the significance of the Confusion of Tongues paper as well as the study of the psychoanalysis between Ferenczi and Severn (Rachman, 2018). In neglecting this analysis, the analytic community has not understood that this pioneering analysis of trauma helped develop the Confusion of Tongues paradigm and trauma analysis (Ferenczi, 1988; Rachman, 2018). We need to understand the pioneering relationship that emerged in their analytic relationship. Their relationship was complex and multidimensional, which helped develop paradigm shifts in theory and technique for psychoanalysis. The analysis can viewed as a mutual analytic experience, which reached its zenith in the last year of their analysis (Ferenczi, 1988; Rachman, 2018). There were several dimensions to this relationship; analysand, student, mutual analytic partner, friend. It was clear that Severn came to Budapest as a last chance analysand of Ferenczi. Severn sought out Ferenczi for what can be called a last chance analysis. She had tried analysis on several occasions with four different analysts, but they were not successful (Rachman, 2018). Otto Rank sent her to Ferenczi; realizing his version of a trauma analysis was not sufficient. Severn was clearly dissatisfied with Rank's birth trauma analysis (Eissler, 1952). In particular, Severn was critical of Rank because she experienced him as being absorbed in teaching her a course about birth trauma therapy, rather than engaging her in an analysis of her emotional disturbances. In her previous analyses prior to seeing Rank, she was dissatisfied with the personality of the analyst and the relationship that was established. Another analyst was not able to analyze her trauma and the other had personal issues. When she

DOI: 10.4324/9781003265030-12

went to Rank, she wanted and needed a psychoanalysis because she was severely depressed, entertained suicide, and felt she was on the edge of her emotional existence (Rachman, 2018). After Rank, she was intent on being with an analyst who would target her depression, suicidal ideation, and severe emotional disturbance. She went to Budapest to see Ferenczi as her last chance to salvage her life. As depressed as she was, Severn was an individual who never lost her desire and motivation to explore and change her life and work through her emotional difficulties.

Severn and Ferenczi also developed a teacher and student relationship. Ferenczi, by the time Severn sought him out, was one of the outstanding figures in the pioneering era of psychoanalysis and was considered the analyst of difficult cases (Rachman, 1997). Severn had been a student of psychology and psychotherapy before she met Ferenczi and became a self-taught successful psychotherapist. She brought her intellectual and clinical interests with her when in analysis with Ferenczi. He considered Severn to be in a training analysis with him. In the pioneering days, a psychiatrist, psychologist, or a professional with an intellectual interest in psychoanalysis and becoming a psychoanalyst, used their analysis as a training experience. Training institutes were just being established, and standards for training were not firmly established. With the approval of a senior member of psychoanalysis, they accepted exceptional individuals as trainees. By the time Severn terminated with Ferenczi, and the years afterwards, she considered herself a psychoanalyst, as did Ferenczi.

Ferenczi and Severn enjoyed a dimension of a therapeutic relationship rarely established. Ferenczi considered Severn a colleague and referred to her as such in a photograph he gave her of him (Rachman, 2018). Severn also considered him a colleague and partner as she discussed their interaction (Severn, 1933). By being colleagues and partners, they played out aspects of their complex relationship by exchanging ideas about their therapeutic interaction. They discussed during their analytic sessions and personal visits their philosophy and ideas about what was salutary about the psychoanalytic encounter. Severn openly revealed to Ferenczi her feelings and thoughts about what she needed to feel safe, cared about, understood, and analyzed. Two remarkable people were brought together by severe emotional illness to become both the healer and the healed. Their collegial relationship and analytic partnership reached its zenith in their development of mutual analysis. This clinical methodology, which was controversial, then and now, emerged from their willingness, openness, and motivation to solve analytic problems in a difficult therapeutic relationship. As has been discussed in a previous publication (Rachman, 2018), mutual analysis was created by Severn in order to help Ferenczi analyze his countertransference reaction to her, which had produced a therapeutic impasse. Severn, possessing personal assertiveness, and possibly some form of unconscious capacity to communicate with Ferenczi (Rachman, 2019a) needed to work through his negative feelings about her so that her analysis could be successful. Severn had the audacity to tell Ferenczi she could help him with his countertransference analysis. Remarkably, Ferenczi did not initiate an interaction which suggested Severn had lost her mind, was in the midst of a severe therapeutic regression, or was in massive resistance. Rather, he struggled greatly to understand, accept, and integrate Severn's invitation for mutual analysis. He described his year-long struggle with all the doubt, confusion, and skepticism that a thoughtful psychoanalyst would have in allowing an analysand to analyze him. Most analysts have considered Ferenczi's decision to join Severn in a mutual analysis of his countertransference reaction as a disaster and a giant analytic mistake (Rachman, 2018). An alternative response can view Ferenczi's controversial response as a pioneering clinical experiment in empathic understanding and clinical creativity. Ferenczi was willing to transcend his traditional Freudian training and allow his work with trauma survivors and trauma analysis to change his thinking and functioning. He realized that Severn's interpretation of his countertransference reaction needed to be understood and analyzed. Remarkably, he had the emotional courage to allow an analysand to inform him of his clinical functioning and allowed her to help him to move from an empathic failure to an emphatic breakthrough. Ferenczi's capacity to empathize with Severn's criticism of their relationship rather than analyze her criticism of him, was a landmark breakthrough in the origins of relational psychoanalysis. The mutual analysis of countertransference produced the following positive changes:

1.   The therapeutic impasse was reduced and Ferenczi and Severn were able to return the negative interaction to the analysis of trauma.
2.   Severn reduced her feeling that Ferenczi had negative feelings towards her. He began to take responsibility for his countertransference feelings that were negative because he experienced her as masculine, assertive, and domineering.

3. Severn began to feel that Ferenczi had developed empathy rather than contempt for her. Consequently, she felt understood and emotionally safe with Ferenczi. Then she was able to return to accepting and responding positively to Ferenczi's analytic interventions.
4. Severn and Ferenczi resumed their trauma analysis, which, of course, was the main purpose of their relationship.
5. Their therapeutic breakthrough allowed the analysis to proceed towards a meaningful success. Severn was able to work through her childhood traumas during the analysis. After she left Budapest, she led a successful career as a psychoanalyst and had meaningful relationships with her daughter, friends, and colleagues.
6. Ferenczi also benefited from the mutual analysis in a very dramatic and unexpected way. Severn was influential in helping Ferenczi retrieve his own sexual seduction in childhood. Ferenczi was able to retrieve a childhood sexual experience with a nursemaid. With that retrieval of a trauma, as well as a significant dream, Severn helped Ferenczi retrieve his own childhood sexual trauma and analyze and develop insight into his countertransference reaction towards Severn.

This analysis also produced insight into Ferenczi's negative feelings about women traced back to his relationship with his mother (Rachman, 2018). Ferenczi's retrieval and analysis of his personal childhood sexual trauma contributed to successfully analyzing Severn's trauma disorder. Their analysis became the pioneering case for the diagnosis and treatment of trauma disorder, the analysis of the analyst, mutual analysis, and expanding the analysis boundaries of empathy.

It would not be an exaggeration to describe the Severn/Ferenczi relationship as being one of analyst and analysand who were also friends. There was an unspoken understanding that analyst/analysand maintains an emotional and interpersonal distance during the psychoanalysis. The Freudian philosophy of analytic clinical interaction focused on establishing a neutral working therapeutic experience. Becoming interpersonally and emotionally intertwined did occur; consider the warm, affectionate, and personal relationship between Freud and Ferenczi (Rachman, 1997). Severn's psychological and developmental needs combined with her assertive and outgoing personality moved her to desire a more human than neutral therapeutic relationship. Her traumatic background, as far as we can ascertain from Ferenczi's report (Ferenczi, 1988) and the research recently developed from the Elizabeth Severn Papers (Rachman, 2018), indicated Severn's trauma were induced by her father. Ferenczi believed that a trauma disorder needed to be understood in non-Oedipal terms. Trauma did not only emerge from an unconscious conflict, but rather from actual psychosocial interaction between an abusive parent and an innocent child. An abusive interaction overwhelms the developing and fragile sense of the child, producing serious psychopathology. This is the Confusion of Tongues paradigm that Ferenczi and Severn developed from their understanding of Severn's severe psychopathology and the need for Ferenczi's empathic understanding and activity towards Severn. As has been mentioned, Severn was looking for something different in her last chance psychoanalysis with Ferenczi that she needed and did not have in her previous analyses. What was clearly missing was an analytic experience that was embedded in a human experience. Ferenczi and Severn were intellectually, emotionally, and interpersonally compatible. They naturally became friends. Severn's outgoing and assertive personality, her emotional vulnerability, a desire to express her inner struggles, and a wish for an emotionally safe and nonabusive relationship with a father figure matched Ferenczi's warm, outgoing personality, identity as a healer, creative and experimental attitude as a clinician, democratic and friendly interpersonal interaction, and dedication to working with difficult cases.

The personal and professional compatibility between Ferenczi and Severn was related to their developing the Confusion of Tongues theory and trauma analysis. Severn's analysis helped establish this landmark accomplishment in the following ways:

1. Non-Oedipal trauma disorders were an important category of psychological disturbance that can be treated by psychoanalysis. Severn had been living with trauma all her life and it was never diagnosed or treated properly. Even Rank, who considered himself a trauma specialist, was more interested in treating Severn with an intellectual trauma method than integrating trauma therapy with an analytic philosophy as Ferenczi was able to accomplish.
2. Ferenczi used his positive personality characteristics therapeutically with Severn because he realized her traumatic childhood demanded a human experience with an analyst. She suffered from a traumatic childhood from a severely abusive father, who was likely a psychopath (Ferenczi, 1988; Rachman, 2018). His experience with difficult cases

(Rachman, 1997) helped him develop an active analytic role in the analytic encounter as he realized that certain analysands need an analyst who practiced empathy and activity in dealing with trauma. Such analysands could not associate in the prescribed way and respond to the Oedipal interpretations of the analyst. Ferenczi became the analyst of difficult cases because he was the most successful of the pioneering analysts with so-called difficult cases. Analysands with severe neurosis, character disorders, and borderline and trauma disorders responded to Ferenczi as an analyst because he responded with concern, compassion, empathy, and activity to their emotional difficulties, in addition to interpretation (Rachman, 1998).

3. The analysis with Severn expanded the boundaries of the active and empathic analytic approach because she demanded Ferenczi's attention to her unfulfilled developmental and interpersonal needs. She also contributed to her analysis. Severn had developed her own clinical methodology to reach her inner subjective emotional state before she was in analysis with Ferenczi. Her subjective or trance state method (Severn, 1916) allowed her to retrieve her childhood feelings, which she used to develop insight into her emotional disorder. Ferenczi and Severn used her method to retrieve her traumas. This became an important part of trauma analysis (Ferenczi, 1988; Rachman, 2018). The Ferenczi/Severn analysis can be seen as the pioneering trauma analysis which tested and expanded the boundaries of empathic understanding and activity.

4. The analysis between Severn and Ferenczi, based upon the Confusion of Tongues paradigm introduced a two-person, relational perspective for psychoanalysis (Rachman, 2019b, 2022). The analytic relationship is deconstructed from a one-person experience where the analyst is the sole authority and interpretive voice in the relationship into the creation of a democratic, two-person human experience when an empathic relationship informs the therapeutic activity of the analysis. The analysand is encouraged to contribute to the understanding and clinical interaction of the analysis. In a two-person experience, the analyst develops an open, cooperative, and emotionally responsive relationship with the analysand, who responds with their own ideas, criticisms, and contributions to the analytic encounter. The two-person relationship experience deconstructs the issues of power, control, and status in an analytic relationship. The analyst is no longer in charge

of the relationship where an analysand is compelled to adhere to the analyst's definition of the process and content of the analytic encounter. An analyst who accepts this perspective also feels free to conduct the interaction in a way that satisfies the developmental needs of the analysand. The analysand is also free to contribute in a way to help construct the analysis to meet their needs.

5. The Ferenczi/Severn analysis can also be considered an experimental clinical demonstration of the introduction of the use of noninterpretation measures in a trauma analysis (Ferenczi, 1988; Rachman, 2018). It became totally understandable that trauma is treatable by measures which were not interpretations developed to produce insight, since the products of actual trauma were not the result of Oedipal conflicts. Trauma produces psychopathology, which originates in relational experiences. Trauma analysis focuses on trauma disorders which were caused by the maltreatment between an authority and a subordinate, for example, a parent and child; a teacher and a student; a cleric and religious observer; an employer and employee. Severn's previous analyses were conducted with an Oedipal conflict theory as the perspective. Ferenczi's approach was to create an emotional bond with her which helped to retrieve her childhood trauma. It created an analysis which worked on and through the emotional disturbances of her abusive father. To reiterate, in the previous analyses, Severn's childhood traumas were neglected. Through Severn's joint efforts with Ferenczi, they were able to introduce both the idea of trauma disorder and its treatment.

References

Eissler, K. (1952). *Interview with Dr. Elizabeth Severn. December 20, 1952. Container 121. Sigmund Freud Papers*. Washington, DC: Manuscript Division, Library of Congress.

Ferenczi, S. (1988). *The Clinical Diary of Sándor Ferenczi* (J. Dupont, Ed., M. Balint and N.Z. Jackson, Trans.). Cambridge, MA: Harvard University Press.

Rachman, A.W. (1997). *Sándor Ferenczi: The Psychotherapist of Tenderness and Passion*. Northvale, NJ: Jason Aronson.

Rachman, A.W. (1998). Ferenczi's "relaxation-principle" and the contemporary clinical practice of psychoanalysis. *American Journal of Psychoanalysis*. 58(1): 63–81.

Rachman, A.W. (2012). Confusion of tongues between Sándor Ferenczi and Elizabeth Severn. *Presentation. International Sándor Ferenczi Congress – "Faces of Trauma."* Budapest, June 3.

Rachman, A.W. (2018). *Elizabeth Severn: The "Evil Genius" of Psychoanalysis.* London: Routledge.

Rachman, A.W. (2019a). The psychoanalysis between Sándor Ferenczi and Elizabeth Severn: Mutuality, unconscious communication and the development of countertransference analysis. *Psychoanalytic Inquiry.* 39(3–4): 1–6.

Rachman, A.W. (2019b). The Confusion of Tongues: Sándor and the Budapest School of Psychoanalysis: A revolutionary paradigm shift in psychoanalysis. *Presentation, Irish Psychoanalytic Society.* Dun Laoghaire, May 10.

Rachman, A.W. (2022). *Psychoanalysis and Society's Neglect of Sexual Abuse of Children, Youth, and Adults: Reassessing Freud's Original Theory of Sexual Abuse and Trauma.* London: Routledge Press.

Severn, E. (1916). "Dictated in a subjective or trance state." *Friday Morning,* January 14. In Rachman, A.W. (Ed.) *Elizabeth Severn, The "Evil Genius" of Psychoanalysis.* London: Routledge, 2018, pp. 246–248.

Severn, E. (1933). *The Discovery of the Self: A Study in Physiological Cure.* London: Rider and Co.

Chapter 13

The "Two-Person Psychology"

The Necessity to Extend the
Freudian Theory to the Reality
of the Interpersonal Traumatic
Development

Clara Mucci

I would like to start this chapter quoting Judith Herman's pioneering work on child abuse and incest:

> Female children are regularly subjected to sexual assaults by adult males who are part of their intimate social world. The aggressors are not outcasts and strangers; they are neighbors, family friends, uncles, cousins, stepfathers and fathers. To be sexually exploited by a known and trusted adult is a central and formative experience in the lives of countless women.
>
> (Herman, 1981, p. 7)

As extreme and appalling as this statement might sound, it is confirmed by clinical practice and by statistics, as Arnold Wm. Rachman has already documented in this book. In my own country (Italy) the National Institute of Statistics (ISTAT) attests that 31.5 percent of women between the age of 16–70 have undergone some form of physical abuse; 20.2 percent physical violence; 21 percent sexual violence. Very often the perpetrators are in the family: partners, relatives, and friends. Often, more than we might want to think, abuse is linked to incest, with the special blurring of boundaries and particular consequences on identity and self-esteem that incest implies for the victims. Particularly high are in Italy the numbers of women killed by family members: even though Italy looks like rather secure in terms of crimes and homicides in general in comparison to other countries, there is an extremely high number of women killed within the family, mostly by a partner or an ex-partner: a woman is killed every other day in a home (111 in 2019, 88.3 percent by a family member or someone they knew). There has been even the need to create in the last few years a new word in

DOI: 10.4324/9781003265030-13

the Italian language to describe this phenomenon: "feminicide" = killing
of females. It should be noted that the very word "femmina," (female in
Italian) carries the same root of "fe-minus" in Latin, meaning that women
would be less worthy of faith or in a word, less accountable (than men).[1]
This origin goes back to Medieval times when women, with their impuri-
ties, most linked to their bodies and sexual reproductive capacities, were
considered closer to the devil than to God (compared to male subjects).
The persecution of so-called witches in many countries in Medieval and
Renaissance times testifies to this social, historical and psychological
prejudice (Mucci, 2001). In Italy, during the pandemic months in 2020,
the number of women calling to ask for help from social services has
increased up to 79.5 percent in comparison to 2019. Homes can become
dangerous prisons for women. And moreover, as shown in many countries
in the world right now, see for instance the latest news about Afghani-
stan after the departure of US forces, when freedom is at risk in a nation,
women are the first to be restricted or even incriminated and killed. Notoriously, Freud had started his theoretical and clinical pioneering work giving voice to women who suffered from hysteria, whom he thought had
been seduced (we would nowadays say molested) by uncles, fathers, and
other males or caregivers in the family. The word "incest" was never mentioned, but for years he very honestly had to acknowledge, often in notes
written years or decades afterwards, that this was very often the case. The
perpetrator was in the house and was known to the victim and, actually,
often very dear to her, a figure of attachment. Equally known is Freud's
repudiation of his own theory of seduction, in 1897, in favor of the conflictual origin of psychopathology. He claimed in that moment that at the
root of hysterics' mental disorder and psychological suffering was, indeed,
not a real event, but an internal conflict between ego, id, and super-ego,
the three partitions of the human mind (according to his later description).
He maintained at that point that hysterical women in particular were conflictual about their sexual desires, and this was also a sign that their psychological development, rooted in what he termed Oedipal complex, was
not healthy or had suffered a psychological arrest. He therefore rooted in
repression, a defense mechanism, the very cause of the disturbance: these
women, conflicted about their desires and sexual fantasies towards their
fathers or family members, had forgotten or repressed, removed from their
conscious awareness, their desires and sexual fantasies, and this had led to

pathology: "Hysterics suffer from reminiscences," he states in *Studies on Hysteria* (Freud & Breuer, 1895, p. 7), and the very act or experience of retrieving those painful memories and giving words to the event or series of disturbing events was the cure. In this way, from his first belief in a real event, a real interpersonal trauma of abuse, Freud went back to a fantasy or conflictual origin for the symptoms. This took place right after the death of his father in 1897 when we found in his letters to Fliess his renunciation to believe their "neurotica" (September 21, 1897: "I no longer believe in my neurotica" [theory of the neurosis]; Mucci, 1998). From this moment onward, not only for Freud but for the psychoanalytic establishment following him, a phantasmatic and conflictual origin to psychopathology, not a real traumatic event, was considered the man etiopathogenetic cause. It followed that repression (a further developmental defense), not dissociation, a primitive defense which we now understand as connected to an earlier or severe traumatic development, became the foundational psychodynamic for Freud and his followers. I have described the link between Freud's renunciation of the trauma theory and his privileging, as a consequence of this disavowal, repression over dissociation, in my previous work (Mucci, 2008, 2014, 2017, 2021).

When I teach at various training institutes or in university courses discussing these theoretical as well as historical events pertaining to the origin of the psychoanalytic preference for choosing a phantasmic origin of trauma instead of a real event, and therefore, describing the serious divide created in the practice and the theory of trauma between Freud and Ferenczi, students and candidates both in the US and in Europe are always very surprised that real traumatizations have been so easily discounted and that psychoanalysis after Freud has preferred to follow the road of repression and denial of the real seduction rather than believing that interpersonal trauma does have the worst consequences for the human mind, causing internal fractures and distortion that, for example, natural trauma caused by a hurricane or a typhoon will never create. In fact, the repudiation of the reality of traumatic theory, namely the fact that a real abuse has happened, and it does not originate from a mental fantasy, is still haunting, in my opinion, the conscience of several institutions and individuals who follow the road that Freud has traced for them, without listening and inquiring further. I can testify to several occasions, in supervising cases, in which I am told how a previous supervisor, usually belonging to a more traditional psychoanalytic institute, having to face the choice of believing in a serious abuse in the family or even incest or doubting this truth, prefers to question it and unmistakably asks: "are we sure it is not a fantasy?" as though they had to protect both the theory and themselves from exposure to a possible, unbearable truth. That it is indeed the real trauma, not the fantasy of it, that has created suffering and the psychopathology. It is as though entertaining the idea that the event was reality and not fantasy opened paths that they cannot beat, either because the mainstream theory does not hold that or because countertransferential emotions that would be issued in the case of a real event would be overwhelming for them, or both. Very often, even nowadays, one century and a half after Freud's denial of the reality of sexual trauma as the major cause for psychopathology, the victims of abuse or incest, often women, are less worthy of faith or really less worthy of being believed than the perpetrator himself (most often a male). The words or testimony of rape, abuse, or violence of a woman are often tainted by prejudice. And even if the reality is attested, the prejudice runs like: what did *she* do to cause that? And was she not really the initiator, therefore provoking the response of the male counterpart? And finally, I've heard even senior and very renowned male psychoanalysts say this: "Didn't they feel pleasure after all?" as though they might have been even lucky. In this way, abused women (or even children) become not the victim of abuse but almost the initiators, the "provocateurs" of it. And sometimes it does not matter how young the child is, it is or was "her innocent beauty," her vivaciousness, her desire for closeness that are to blame, as though there were no difference, after all, in the responsibility between an adult and a child.

For Freud, what was not easily acceptable was that the behavior of respectable families was in question. As Herman underlines:

> If his patients' reports were true, incest was not a rare abuse, confined to the poor and the mentally defected, but was endemic to the patriarchal family. Freud refused to identify fathers publicly as sexual aggressors. Though in his private correspondence he cited "seduction by the father" as the "essential point", in hysteria, he was never able to bring himself to make this statement in public. Scrupulously honest and courageous in other respects, Freud falsified his incest cases. In "The Aetiology of Hysteria", Freud implausibly identified governesses, nurses, maids, and children of both sexes as the offenders. In

Studies on Hysteria, he managed to name an uncle as the seducer in two cases. Many years later, Freud acknowledged that the "uncles" who had molested Rosalia and Katharina were in fact their fathers.

(Herman, 1981, p. 9)

Silence (about the relevancy and frequency of sexual abuse and incest) in most cases covered the issue for a long time and even when it was dispelled, the secret became as foundational as the reality it was covering. To speak of trauma, especially within the family, and denounce fathers of their misdeeds would make the author less worthy of faith, and in danger of frightening the patriarchal rule. And I would like to stress, if still necessary, that patriarchy does not mean only the rule of fathers on wives and children, but of males in power over males with less power or who are younger, as between fathers and sons, and as in the case of authoritative figures in general. I therefore agree with Rachman's move in linking incest and Confusion of Tongues trauma theory to all the situations in which an authoritative figure exerts their power on the less powerful:

one can extend this clinical paradigm to include the functioning of any authority figure with a subordinate, or more clearly stated, any relationship where there is an imbalance of status, power, and control.

(Rachman & Mattick, 2012, p. 48 of this volume)

This means that it is not simply a matter of gender and sexual position but namely first and foremost of power and domination, running throughout all gender positions and sexual practices.[2]

Notoriously, a different attention was tributed to trauma and abuse in general especially after the 1980s, after research on the symptoms reported by Vietnam veterans and the aftereffects of trauma and violence onto women suffering of depression and other disorders lead the major Diagnostic and Statistical Manual of Mental Disorders (DSM-III, 1980), to recognize the new diagnosis of PTSD (post-traumatic stress disorder). In DSM-V (APA, 2017), a reference to dissociation to the previous diagnosis was added. Still no distinction has been made between trauma created by abuse, the only trauma leading to dissociation in fact (see Liotti, 2005; Mucci, 2018), and trauma due to a natural catastrophe, which cannot induce a structural fragmentation as dissociation. The long-term devastating effects of interpersonal violence and abusive relationships has been recognized so far only by the Psychodynamic Diagnostic

Manual, Second Edition (PDM-2, Lingiardi & McWilliams, 2017) and by the International Classification of Diseases, 11th edition (ICD-11). But at least since 1980 the interest in the consequences of trauma has created a renewed desire to study and reevaluate the effects and the dynamics of interpersonal trauma and violence, from the point of view of several interdisciplinary connections, and for clinicians and theoreticians with a cognitive behavioral or psychodynamic and psychoanalytic background. It is in lieu of the different views on the consequences of trauma for mind and body, even within the psychoanalytic tradition that to reevaluate psychoanalytic theory and Freudian trauma theory is a must. I could not agree more with Rachman when he stresses that

> Child sexual abuse is an important psychodynamic in the development of psychopathology. In particular, child sexual abuse leads to a trauma disorder. This was the introduction of a new category of psychological disorder, which was in contrast to Freudian view of neurosis whose origin was in the Oedipus Complex.
>
> (see Chapter 1, p. 12, this volume)

And therefore:

> It is necessary to expand the psychoanalysis to the presence of trauma disorders, keeping in mind that "Ferenczi was not moving away from psychoanalysis, as Freud believed, but asking to expand the boundaries of psychoanalysis to include diagnoses and treatment of trauma disorders" (see Chapter 5, p. 40) and that "psychoanalysis needs to reorient its theoretical and clinical functioning in order to join the mainstream of contemporary treatment of the incest trauma."
>
> (see Chapter 10, p. 106)

The psychodynamic of sexual abuse takes a different route towards the development of identity compared to the Oedipal process, as has been magisterially analyzed with its psychological painful dynamics and clinically by Rachman (Chapter 7, this volume, pp. 56–79).[3] This traumatic development has been disregarded by minor or major psychoanalytic theoreticians or has been silenced by mainstream psychoanalysis when Ferenczi himself tried to point out to this etiological reality so clear in his patients. He tried strenuously as early as the '20s and '30s to raise his voice against his master and analyst and to fight the silence that has covered the truth of the real etiopathogenesis of psychological and mental disorders, but notoriously he encountered ostracism and rejection. It is interesting that the rejection that he suffered within the psychoanalytic establishment took the form of a feminization and a pathologizing of the author: against the (myth of the) all male paternal Freud, the image of a feminized and mentally ill Ferenczi was proposed. He was considered the "mother" of psychoanalysis, and he was considered psychotic (Jones, 1957). This feminization also goes back to a cultural bias in which women are the sentimental, weak, and unreliable or crazy subjects, while men are the rational, strong, and reliable or even moral and healthy ones.

To stress the importance for the optimal development of a good interpersonal relationship between parent and child in particular or with any attachment figure in general is necessary for a new developmental psychoanalysis. It calls forth, in my opinion, a rewriting of the theory and, therefore, a different attitude in clinical practice. The relational and interpersonal nature of human (and I suppose any living being's) development and the evolution of the human personality and identity as a dyadic enterprise, constantly co-constructed and foundational in the first two years of life cannot be denied anymore and has, in fact, received more and more attention from many sources: through the rehabilitation of Bowlby's theories of attachment; through the findings of infant research and of developmental studies of psychology; through a rediscovery of Ferenczi's theory of trauma and consequent indications for therapy, and more recently and finally, thanks to the development of neuro-psychoanalysis and relational affective neuroscience, including the field of interpersonal neurobiology as developed eminently by Allan Schore, Dan Siegel, and Louis Cozolino, to whose field I have contributed with my last volume (Mucci, 2018). Since the first caregiver is usually a mother or female figure (because of a mixture of natural and cultural motivations), not to recognize that human life bears a clear debt to women is a clear attack on their implicit power, as the attempt by male doctors to control the birth process, starting as early as Medieval and Renaissance times with the ambivalent or threatening position held by midwives in many cultures. Nonetheless, the relevance of women to birth and caregiving practices should not make women the culprit of dysfunctional developments because if there is insecurity of attachment or trauma in a child, it means that there has been trauma in the caregivers as well: the reason for this being that it is a long-term integrational process that needs to be taken into consideration and possibly healed in order to avoid the transmission of trauma in the future generations (see

Mucci, 2022). Attachment is, in fact, the first means of transposition of trauma intergenerationally and is considered at the same time the actual force (biological as well as psychological) of human development, issuing and allowing all neurobiological and physiological processes, as epigenetic studies of families of rodents on children have shown (Hofer, 1984; Meaney, 2001; Cassidy, 1994; Van Ijzendoorn et al., 2011). We need to stress that humans in contrast to other animals are endowed with the possibility of developing a symbolic capacity and therefore the potential to develop a representation of those biological transactions linked to a human caregiver that are going to influence their behavior even in lack of the real person to whom they are attached. It is the biological care and the presence of a caring other that relationally engages in the process of caretaking intensely, constantly, and with sensitivity for at least two years that, in humans, allows the frontal areas and higher order faculties to mature and be established. For this reason, as is amply demonstrated and also as clinical practice shows, this symbolic higher development in humans is not a given, but a capacity that requires the proper caregiving and cure of an adult in order to be developed, not necessarily a biological parent; it is this integrative symbolic capacity that is hampered and reduced in severe psychopathology, which derives from adverse experiences in growing up, with the development of insecure or even disorganized attachment with the caretaker; therefore this disorganization is of traumatic origin.[4]

So there is a need for a shift or extension of psychoanalytic theory as a two-person psychology for two reasons: 1. human development is the result of a dyadic development (Tronick, 2007; Schore, 1994; Beebe & Lachman, 1994); 2. we are in need also of differentiating not only a healthy or neurotic development, where the Oedipal construct might be applied, but also a kind of traumatic or dysfunctional development, where the usual track or Oedipal development cannot be tracked, as in borderline and narcissistic personality developments. Therefore, in order to understand the complete continuum of development from healthier to more pathological, we need to differentiate different routes, all including the necessity of interpersonal exchanges without which no life is possible; but we need to distinguish between a healthier development (which according to traditional Freudian theory implies the development and overcoming of the Oedipal complex) and another route for the psychosexual stages of development, which therefore have to be reconsidered when there has been interpersonal trauma and abuse. It is as though the necessity to cover the reality of potential traumatic development or sexual abuse and real trauma, in favor of a fantastic elaboration of it, has affected the potential extension of psychoanalytic theory, as Rachman underlines.

It is also interesting, in this regard, to notice how Bowlby himself had been notoriously cast out from the psychoanalytic British establishment in the major years of his practice because he had the courage or honesty to affirm or to go back to the real conditions of upbringing, which when marked by a loss or severe deprivation could cause depression and severe psychopathology in the child (Bowlby, 1969). Again, the dyadic origin of possible pathology and the stress on the real event or the series of events at the origin of those difficult dysfunctional developments were not received favorably. The prejudice here affected the entire theory of attachment: it would seem that to deal with real, even historical traumatic circumstances would lead beyond the realm of deep psychoanalysis or outside of the traditional psychoanalytic concern, rooted in the dynamic unconscious and away from the Freudian terrain situating pathology in intrapsychic fantasy and conflicts. Again, one of the problems in the acceptance of Bowlby's theories for mainstream psychoanalysis was his concern for the real conditions of childhood and the stress on the fact that development is not only intrapsychic and innate (as his supervisor Melanie Klein would maintain) but an interpersonal, epigenetic, relational process, and this process sees as their protagonists, when all is said and done, a child and their mothers or caregivers. Going back to others is always a bit problematic, it would seem, for a psychoanalysis that is rooted in the Oedipal complex of the privilege of a male lineage, so that the version of the Oedipal complex for women, it is maintained, is a reversal of the prevalent one, the male version (as is any binary structure). After all, Freud maintained, women want mainly to give a child to their father, overcoming in this way the penis envy (Freud, 1905a). It can be credited to Freud's honesty the fact that often he has to say, nonetheless, on various occasions, that on women's desire (what do women want) he knew very little, and finally, it is the knowledge that poets have of women that he referred us (Freud, 1933, p. 135 "Femininity"), as though male poets inhabited an in-between terrain between female and male knowledge, as inhabitants of mysterious borders.

Reality seems to be something that psychoanalysts have problems with, starting from the real conditions of upbringing (as in Bowlby's attachment) going on with Ferenczi's theory of relational trauma and abuse. For a rewriting of psychoanalytic developmental theory, going back to Bowlby, through Winnicott (who wrote that there is no child without a mother) and Ferenczi especially means to go back to a two-person psychology of development that sees mothers as co-constructors of the process, instead of repressing, silencing, or controlling the relevance of women's contribution to the very existence and development of humanity in ourselves. The fact that a caregiver can be of any sex does not obliterate the reality that in most existing cultures, the first months are dominated, for better or worse, by women. Our own development, optimal or less optimal, rests in the first and most precious years of growth on this dual, reciprocal encounter, and it is governed by biological, genetically preorganized by finally epigenetic processes ruled by conscious and unconscious dynamics starting in utero and in the very expectations the parents have on the child, prenatally. When we speak of unconscious here we do not necessarily refer to the dynamic unconscious as discovered and defined by Freud, but as what is nonconscious (i.e., implicit relational knowledge) and, nonetheless, through relationally imprinted models of self and others encoded very early on the amygdala (the emotional center of the limbic system linked to somatic memories and sensorial imprintings and the basis of implicit memories), does influence future development. In this regard, Allan Schore has presented a view of the unconscious as an implicit, amygdala-based, not-conscious process that leads our choices and behavior without our full awareness (something probably closer to Freudian preconscious, see Schore, 1994, 2001, 2003a, 2003b, 2012, 2019a, 2019b). Following Bowlby we can speak of "internal working models," which I would revise, thanks to the extension of present neuroscientific contributions, as "implicit" working models. With the term "implicit" we also refer to implicit memory, where the bodily, somatic, and primary memories, devoid of words, are kept, a kind of procedural memory based in the amygdala. This area of the limbic system organizes mostly emotions in connection with higher areas which is already formed and working since birth. The declarative and episodic memory is based in the hippocampus, also located within the same limbic system, but which starts functioning after two and a half years since birth. This latter brain development explains why the first two years of life are covered by amnesia of an inability to record our memories since they were not encoded in symbolic processes like words, therefore not narratable.

Particularly influential in this expanding theory and the practice of psychoanalysis through a two-person psychology, Schore has brilliantly explained in his painstaking interdisciplinary research carried through four decades how the mother or the first caregiver works as the first regulator of all biological and psychological interpersonal systems. The first caretaker provides optimal or less than optimal care, influencing epigenetically the evolutionary and developmental path, so that interpersonal neuropsychology and neuropsychoanalysis allows to trace how the process of attunement between the two, or on the contrary of disattunement or even actual abuse, functions to dramatically influence the development of the brain and the psychic systems of the newborn, resulting in secure, insecure, or disorganized attachment. Consequently, the neurobiological consequences connected to stress and excess glucocorticoids among which cortisol, which is the major stress hormone, can have very severe consequences in the delicate process of development.

In this attempt to better understand the functioning of the interpersonal exchanges and possible traumatic development between the two components of the dyad, I have introduced (see next chapter) a model of what I define "trauma of human agency" with three levels of severity (Mucci, 2013, 2018, 2022; Mucci & Scalabrini, 2021), in which "early relational trauma" as studied by Schore is constituted mainly by the disattunement in the regulatory process, resulting in a deficit in the development of the child and affects dysregulation, even in the case that abuse and maltreatment are not present. Abuse, maltreatment, severe deprivation, and incest constitute, in my opinion, a different, higher level of trauma, possibly cumulative, with special dynamics. This psychodynamic is the introduction of the victim-persecutor dyad in the psyche of the child, which I derive in part from Ferenczi's theory of the identification with the aggressor. Then I identify, within the trauma of human agency, a third level, in which we have massive traumatizations as in war and genocide as in the Holocaust. I present this model in detail in the next chapter. My aim in this model is also to distinguish the effects of trauma of human agency from other traumata of natural origins, such as earthquakes or hurricanes or typhoons, in which the relational trust that is the foundation of life and empathy is not touched, therefore natural catastrophes do not create dissociation in the child, proving how human relationships are at the foundation of good development, creation of humanity, and empathy and health. This distinction is very important for future psychopathology because, as Italian psychologist

Giovanni Liotti has argued (Liotti, 2004), only interpersonal trauma causes dissociation (or disorganization of attachment which creates the vulnerability towards dissociation), which should now be considered as the structural foundation of severe fragmentation of the human mind and the basis of the most severe psychopathology, in contrast to what Freudian theory still maintains, privileging repression as the major cause of psychopathology. Severe psychopathology, in fact, should be understood to be based on dissociation, causing borderline and more severe disorders, not on repression (a further developmental defense that we now understand as the basis only of neurotic pathologies, not of borderline or psychotic disorders). This also means that at the basis of severe pathology there is real interpersonal trauma, not intrapsychic conflicts of fantasies (see also Mucci, 2013, 2018, 2021).

The particularly negative consequences of trauma of human agency underline the fact that positive interaction with a caring other is at the basis of a healthy and harmonious psychological development, showing how we are primed to develop relationally. No psychological growth and optimal development are possible without the intervention of a sensitive constant and caring other, as early research by Rene Spitz studying children left in orphanages showed (Spitz, 1945). The human intention of doing harm has particularly negative consequences on the human psyche, even in the case that it was not a family figure causing the harm, since each human figure is potentially an attachment figure, while an accident or natural catastrophe is devoid of ill intentions (and does not damage relational trust and hope). This also stresses how it is the meaning of the traumatization, even though it might remain unconscious or not fully conscious, that affects the response of the human mind to trauma for a very long time, if not healed, interpersonally, collectively, and/or in therapy. Repositioning the etiology of mental psychopathology in a dual relationship means to lead psychoanalysis to a new theoretical and clinical development and to process a different route for metapsychology, necessarily relational, dual and then triadic: in order for the symbolic and social connections to be created in the psyche, the human mind needs the intervention of a symbolic "third" entering and intervening in the first dyadic relationship, as explained, among others, by Benjamin (2013, 2018), by Schore (1994) and myself (Mucci, 2013, 2018). It also means to go beyond the intrapsychic and the innate to give evidence to the importance of experience for development and the epigenetic and environmental processes, all deriving by the social and interpersonal dynamics. What is implied in this new turn is not any-more or not simply a psychoanalytic use of the dynamic unconscious, as intrapsychic and mostly innate, in the description of Freud, but, on the contrary, to describe, define, and work with the concept of a "two-person unconscious" as Lyons-Ruth proposed (Lyons-Ruth, 1999), within the Boston Change Process Social Group: to work with a two-person uncon-scious in psychoanalysis means to

> sketch outlines of a theory of psychoanalytic and developmental change based in unconscious of implicit enactive representation and patient-therapist transactions rather than in the content of symbolized meanings of interpretation. This focus on the two-person process is intended to establish a theoretical framework through which long-standing clinical insights on the interplay of affect, conflict, defenses and resistance can be further extended into a two-person realm and given a scientifically credible developmental base.
>
> (Lyons-Ruth, 1999, p. 580)

This new version of a "dual unconscious," relationally co-constructed and created by real human encounters and bodily deep communication (for Schore they would be described as right brain processes) can also include an "unrepressed unconscious," as explained by Schore himself and by Ital-ian neuroscientist and psychoanalyst Mauro Mancia (2006). In Schore's description, this earlier version of the unconscious (compared to Freud's dynamic unconscious) is an implicit nucleus of the self (Schore, 2012), originally created responding to the genetic inherited possibilities but actu-ally developed through their regulatory movements between the first car-egiver's right brain and a child's right brain in the first year or first year and a half of life, the critical period of attachment, before the intervention of a second caregiver that helps implement the growth and development of the left hemisphere which usually becomes dominant. Both hemispheres work in conjunction, but with different tasks, and both are necessary for the full emotional, cognitive, empathic, and social development of a human being. The right brain (and the limbic system within it in particular) can be con-sidered the bodily basis, interpersonally created, of this unrepressed uncon-scious. Since early trauma and insecure or disorganized forms of attachment are encoded in implicit memory and stored in the amygdala mostly, these memories are somatic memories and not hippocampus-based memories. We remind the reader that the hippocampus develops after the first two years and a half and is the bodily basis (the brain is body, meaning cells, neurons, axons, neurobiological processes) for episodic, declarative memory, while the amygdala is the basis of somatic and procedural memory so that trauma happened in the first two years of life can only be stored and remembered somatically in the amygdala, without words and narratives attached to it. Moreover, we should point out that future severe traumatizations (after the first two years of life) cannot be stored through the connection with the hippocampus because traumatic stress creates an excess of glucocorticoids (cortisol and other hormones) that impede the usual storage of events to be remembered within the hippocampus, therefore they remain dissociated or cast out from episodic and narratable memory (controlled by hippocampus) and can only be remembered through the body, as Rachman (this volume), reminds us, ready to be kindled by somatic triggers such as odors, lights, and other apparently unexplainable triggers. This is the complex traumatic process that Van der Kolk describes as "the body keeps the score" (Van der Kolk, 2014). The entire debate about the possibility of retrieving memories of abuse (at least the cognitive components of the debate, disclaiming the possibility that memories of abuse are not actually fully remembered but can nonetheless be retrieved in their own truth afterwards) does not take into full consideration the new neuroscientific findings. Memories of abuse, given either the extreme stressful circumstances in which the abuse has taken place or sometimes because of the early age of the victim, cannot be stored in the hippocampal memory but only in the amygdala, creating somatic memory without the possibility of being narrated as episodic events so that only the safety of a very empathic and committed therapy can possibly retrieve them. But it needs to be a two-person relational psychotherapy with a deeply empathically committed other, what I call "embodied" – meaning also empathic because empathy needs connection to the other's body – "witnessing" (Mucci, 2018). I take the testimonial process from Ferenczi himself (Ferenczi, 1988), as I need to clarify, and from Dori Laub's clinical observations and definition of therapy for the traumatized (Laub, 2005a, 2005b) but I explain it in neurobiological and neuroscientific terms. To follow Rachman (1997, 2003, 2018, 2022) on this point as well, and as Ferenczi would say, what has been damaged in a relationship needs to be repaired in a relationship (more on this point in Chapter 15). In contrast with Freud's views, "abreaction is not enough" (Ferenczi, 1988, p. 108). We need a true relational experience to be imprinted even implicitly in the working models and in the unconscious (with the meaning of what is not fully conscious but nonetheless affects our behavior and personality). We still think, as Freud had maintained, that both the healthy and pathological development or functioning share the same dynamics or defenses. It is mostly a matter of degree. We now understand in clear detail how the best caregiving leads to affect regulation: with integration of all the systems with internalization of well-functioning dynamics; with optimal self-esteem, self-care, best development of affective emotional and cognitive potential with a balanced personality capable of functioning in relationships, in work and love, while disattunement or even abuse create dysfunctional developments up to the point of dissociation and destructiveness.

As Rachman (this volume) reminds us, it is enough that one of the dyad does not respond to the need of the other to create the possibility of trauma (p. 13). Developing a two-person psychoanalysis, as Rachman and Schore among others insist on, is a necessary deconstruction of Freud's authoritarian version of psychology and subjectivity rooted in a center that is mostly male and intrapsychic and includes a concept of drives that were fundamentally of genetic origin (not historical origin but genetic in the sense of innate). It is possible for relational theory to provide an analytic perspective without the one-person Oedipal complex structure (Rachman & Mattick, 2012; Rachman et al., 2023). Carrying on decades of interdisciplinary research in neuro-psychoanalysis and affective neuroscience and interpersonal neurobiology, Schore has described this movement as the right brain to right brain continual communication that is vital to the first year and a half for the human mind to develop. Most traumatic memories remain in the right hemisphere. After this first period, in which the right brain is dominant, the left brain develops and usually becomes dominant, allowing for further affective, cognitive, social, and symbolic interaction and capacities, as in language and social competences. No brain and therefore no subject develops to its full potential without the intervention of a caring other. The intervention of multiple caregivers (not necessarily of different sex and gender, of course) is essential to the best development, stabilizing the internalization of affect regulation (first learned in connection to the other, then internalized by the self) to the development of further cognitive and symbolic processes. Affect regulation and bodily processes are at the basis of the complex systems that will develop into identity and personality; the same foundational importance that Freud gave originally to the bodily process needs to be understood nowadays as a complex interpersonal procedure, calling for a rewriting of the theory as a larger dyadic and the triadic system, not an innate and intrapsychic development. Here is Freud's understanding:

> The Ego is ultimately derived from bodily sensations, chiefly from those springing from the surface of the body. It may thus be regarded as a mental projection of the surface of the body, besides representing superficies of the mental apparatus.
>
> (Freud, 1923, pp. 364–365; footnote added in the English Edition of 1927)

Notoriously, Freud made the drive a bodily based energetic concept: the physical representative of the stimuli originating from within the organism and reaching the mind (Freud, 1915, p. 122). But even the body and the internalized image of one's body within the mind is a deposit of the images sedimented in one's psyche in early implicit interactions, marked by care, fostering optimal self-esteem and good interpersonal capacity and adaptation to life and further exchanges, or marked by traumatic relationships whose difficult developments I will describe in the next chapter.

This move towards a two-person psychoanalysis is also necessary because of the consistent danger of considering the psychoanalytic process as influenced by a dominant subject, the analyst, who happens to know what is best for the other, to help relieve the suffering of the other, the patient, from an authoritative position. Freud's difficulties in accepting the idea of a countertransference is nowadays amply surpassed by the actual study of how the healing process in deep psychotherapy follows a continual flux of interactive communications, implicit-corporeal unconscious and explicit verbal conscious, between the two subjects and the two minds in relation so that countertransference and enactive movements are a fundamental tool in the therapeutic process of the joint work (Schore, 2012, 2019a). Enactments and a constant flow of carefully orchestrated dual regulation are considered nowadays the major tools of psychoanalytic treatment. Besides, it is not only a meeting of minds (as eminently and cogently explained by Lewis Aron (1996) in his pioneering work on a new relational turn in psychoanalysis) but of two bodies, in so far as the right brain to right brain process (if the right brain is the basis of the relational implicit unconscious as clarified by Schore) is a bodily based process. This for me creates the basis for a therapeutic model of relational therapy that I have defined as "embodied witnessing," which I will describe in full length in Chapter 15.

Notes

1 Notoriously, in Freudian theory, the Oedipal route was considered a bit more flexible in women, so that developmentally for a certain kind of psychoanalysis women remained less worthy of faith, linking the male gender to a more strict or better developed morality.
2 Years ago, when I was still a professor of English Literature and Shakespeare Drama, I explained how even a play that looks like the most traditionally patriarchal example in the literary Western canon of male domination over female subjection, Shakespeare's *The Taming of the Shrew* (1623), follows in fact the major rule of domination of the most powerful onto the less powerful, regardless of sex: the fact that Katherine is a woman, or female, in fact, just confirms the rule of power over binarism so that the first of the sequence (man) is the most powerful and prevails over the less powerful in the binarism (woman), not because of an essence or a biological quality of sex or gender, but simply because politics and culture have privileged the rules of fathers and males over mothers and women in all of the major cultures. If it were a matter of gender and sex only, then why are there in homosexual couples still power positions relegating to a female dominated position the one more nurturing and more emotional of the couple while the dominant one, perceived as more masculine, is usually less emotional, less nurturing, more rational, and so on? Power is a force of domination regardless of sex and gender, but it certainly structures positions of gender. I hint at this also in the final pages of *Borderline Bodies* (Mucci, 2018), to show how in clinical work we have to be aware of structures of dominance and subjection, regardless of gender positions, or actually we have to consider gender positions as imbued with power positions.
3 I will go into more detail about the dynamics analyzed by Rachman in the next chapter.
4 For a description of cases with these severe developmental difficulties, due to insecurity or disorganization of attachment, resulting from interpersonal trauma and early relational trauma, see the cases I presented from multidimensional diagnosis to completed treatment in *Borderline Bodies* (Mucci, 2018), organized in a crescendo of severity, from less severe (hysteric-hystrionic) to more severe narcissist disorders in a continuum of severity passing through borderline per se and going towards the severe psychosomatic and psychotic spectrum.

References

APA (American Psychiatric Association). (2017). *Diagnostic and Statistical Manual of Mental Disorders* (5th ed., DSM-5). Washington, DC. American Psychiatric Association.

Aron, L. (1996). *A Meeting of the Minds: Mutuality in Psychoanalysis*. Hillsdale, NJ: Analytic Press.

Beebe, B. and Lachmann, F.M. (1994). Representation and internalization in infancy: Three principles of salience. *Psychoanalytic Psychology*. 11(2): 127–165.

Benjamin, J. (2013). *The Bonds of Love: Psychoanalysis, Feminism, & the Problem of Domination*. New York: Pantheon Books.

Benjamin, J. (2018). *Beyond Doer and Done to: Recognition Theory, Intersubjectivity and the Third*. New York, NY: Routledge.

Bowlby, J. (1969). *Attachment and Loss: Attachment* (Vol. 1). New York: Basic Books (Cambridge, MA and London: Harvard University Press, 1988).

Cassidy, J. (1994). Emotion regulation: Influences of attachment relationships. *Monographs of the Society for Research in Child Development*. 59(2–3): 228–249.

Ferenczi, S. (1988). *The Clinical Diary of Sándor Ferenczi* (J. Dupont, Ed., M. Balint and N.Z. Jackson, Trans.). Cambridge, MA: Harvard University Press.

Freud, A. (1923). Beating fantasies and daydreams. In *The Writings of Anna Freud* (Vol. I). New York: International Universities Press, pp. 135–157.

Freud, A. (1933). Report of the twelfth international psycho-analytic congress. *Bulletin of the International Psycho-Analytic Association*. 14: 138–140.

Freud, S. (1905a). Three essays on the theory of sexuality. *Standard Edition*. 7: 125–243 (London, England: Hogarth Press, 1955).

Freud, S. (1915). Instincts and their vicissitudes. *Standard Edition*. 14: 109–140.

Freud, S. and Breuer, J. (1895). Studies on hysteria. *Standard Edition*. 2(32): 1–335 (London, England: Hogarth Press).

Herman, J.L. (1981). *Father-Daughter Incest*. Cambridge MA and London: Harvard University Press.

Hofer, M.A. (1984). Relationships as regulators: A psychobiologic perspective on bereavement. *Psychosomatic Medicine*. 46(3): 183–197.

ICD-11 (2021). *International Classification of Diseases* (11th ed.). Geneva: World Health Organization.

Jones, E. (1957). *The Life and Work of Sigmund Freud, Vol. III: The Last Phase 1919–1939*. New York: Basic Books.

Laub, D. (2005a). Traumatic shutdown of narrative and symbolization: A death instinct derivative? *Contemporary Psychoanalysis*. 41: 307–326.

Laub, D. (2005b). From speechlessness to narrative: The cases of Holocaust historians and of psychiatrically hospitalized survivors. *Literature and Medicine*. 24: 253–265.

Lingiardi, V. and McWilliams, N. (Eds.) (2017). *Psychodynamic Diagnostic Manual: PDM-2*. New York: The Guilford Press.

Liotti, G. (2004). Trauma, dissociation, and disorganized attachment: Three strands of a single braid. *Psychotherapy: Theory, Research, Practice, Training*. 41(4): 472.

Liotti, G. (2005). Trauma e dissociazione alla luce della teoria dell'attaccamento. *Infanzia e adolescenza*. 4(3): 130–144.

Lyons-Ruth, K. (1999). The two-person unconscious: Intersubjective dialogue, enactive relational representation, and the emergence of the new forms of relational organization. In Aron, L. and Harris, A. (Eds.) *Relational Psychoanalysis: Innovation and Expansion* (Vol. 2). Hillsdale, NJ: Analytic Press, pp. 311–349.

Mancia, M. (2006). Implicit memory and early unrepressed unconscious: Their role in the therapeutic process (how the neurosciences can contribute to psychoanalysis). *International Journal of Psychoanalysis.* 87(pt 1): 83–103.

Meaney, M.J. (2001). Maternal care, gene expression, and the transmission of the individual differences in stress reactivity across generations. *Annual Review of Neuroscience.* 24(1): 1161–1192.

Mucci, C. (1998). *Tempeste. Narrazioni di esilio in Shakespeare e Karen Blixen. Campus, Pescara.* Napoli: Ristampa Liguori.

Mucci, C. (2001). *Il teatro delle streghe: il femminile come costruzione culturale al tempo di Shakespeare.* Naples: Liguori.

Mucci, C. (2008). *Il dolore estremo. Il trauma da Freud alla Shoah.* Roma: Borla.

Mucci, C. (2013). *Beyond Individual and Collective Trauma: Intergenerational Transmission, Psychoanalytic Treatment, and the Dynamics of Forgiveness.* London: Karnac Books.

Mucci, C. (2014). Trauma, healing and the reconstruction of truth. *American Journal of Psychoanalysis.* 74(1): 31–47.

Mucci, C. (2017). Ferenczi's revolutionary therapeutic approach. *American Journal of Psychoanalysis.* 77(3): 239–254.

Mucci, C. (2018). *Borderline Bodies: Affect Regulation Therapy for Personality Disorders (Norton Series on Interpersonal Neurobiology).* New York: W. W Norton & Company.

Mucci, C. (2021). Dissociation vs repression: A new neuropsychoanalytic model for psychopathology. *The American Journal of Psychoanalysis.* 81(1): 82–111.

Mucci, C. (2022). *Resilience and Survival. Understanding and Healing Intergenerational Trauma.* London: Confer Books.

Mucci, C. and Scalabrini, A. (2021). Traumatic effects beyond diagnosis: The impact of dissociation on the mind-body-brain system. *Psychoanalytic Psychology.* 38(4): 279–289.

Rachman, A.W. (1997). *Sándor Ferenczi: The Psychotherapist of Tenderness and Passion.* Northvale, NJ: Jason Aronson.

Rachman, A.W. (2003). *Psychotherapy of Difficult Cases: Flexibility and Responsiveness in Clinical Practice.* Madison, CT: Psychosocial Press.

Rachman, A.W. (2018). Ferenczi's confusion of tongues: A regressive idea conceived by a madman or one of the most important papers in the history of psychoanalysis. *Proposal. International Sándor Ferenczi Conference.* Florence, May 2–6.

Rachman, A.W. and Kooden, H. (2021). *Different Journeys Towards Becoming a Psychoanalyst and Psychotherapist: Personal Passions, Unusual Journeys.* London: Routledge.

Rachman, A.W. and Mattick, P. (2012). The confusion of tongues in the psychoanalytic relationship. *Psychoanalytic Social Work*. 19(1–2): 167–190.

Rachman, A.W., Mattick, P. and Mucci, C. (2023). The death of the oedipus complex (in preparation).

Schore, A.N. (1994). *Affect Regulation and the Origin of the Self: The Neurobiology of Emotional Development*. Mahwah, NJ: Erlbaum.

Schore, A.N. (2001). The effects of early relational trauma on right brain development, affect regulation and infant mental health. *Infant Mental Health Journal*. 22(1–2): 201–269.

Schore, A.N. (2003a). *Affect Regulation and the Repair of the Self*. New York: W. W. Norton & Company.

Schore, A.N. (2003b). *Affect Dysregulation and Disorders of the Self*. New York: W. W. Norton & Company.

Schore, A.N. (2012). *The Science of the Art of Psychotherapy (Norton Series on Interpersonal Neurobiology)*. New York: W. W. Norton & Company.

Schore, A.N. (2019a). *The Development of the Unconscious Mind (Norton Series on Interpersonal Neurobiology)*. New York: W. W. Norton & Company.

Schore, A.N. (2019b). *Right Brain Psychotherapy (Norton Series on Interpersonal Neurobiology)*. New York: W. W. Norton & Company.

Spitz, R. (1945). Hospitalism: An inquiry into the genesis of psychiatric conditions in early childhood. *Psychoanalytic Study of the Child*. 1: 53–74.

Tronick, E. (2007). *The Neurobehavioral and Social-emotional Development of Infants and Children*. New York: W. W. Norton & Company.

Van der Kolk, B. (2014). *The Body Keeps the Score: Mind, Brain and Body in the Transformation of Trauma*. London: Penguin.

Van Ijzendoorn, M.H., Bakermans-Kranenburg, M.J. and Ebstein, R.P. (2011). Methylation matters in child development: Toward developmental behavioral epigenetics. *Child Development Perspectives*. 5(4): 305–310.

Chapter 14

Three Levels of Trauma of Human Agency and the Problems of the Diagnostic and Statistical Manual (DSM) Categories for Post Traumatic Stress Disorder – PTSD

Clara Mucci

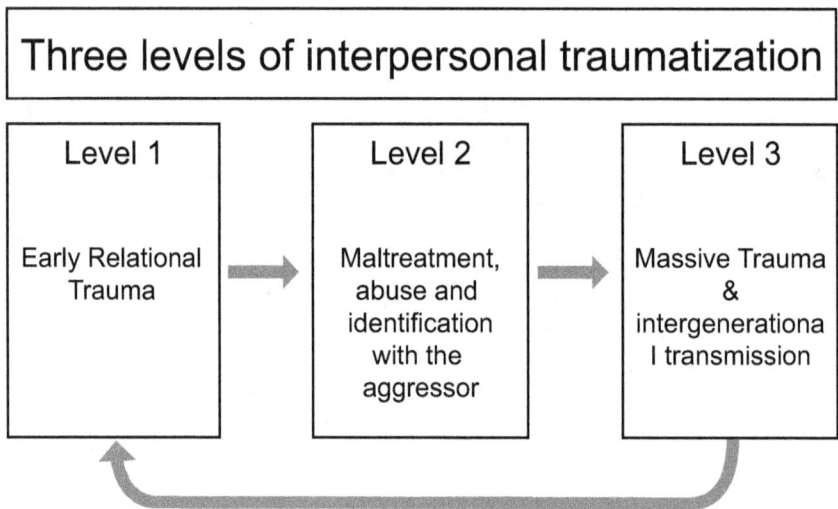

Figure 14.1 Three Levels of Interpersonal Traumatization

In contrast to the commonly accepted definition of traumatic consequences as described by the category of PTSD in DSM-5 (APA, 2017), I have distinguished three levels of trauma of human agency, and I have stressed, following Liotti's research, that only trauma of human agency creates dissociation, while natural catastrophes do not. Dissociation induced by interpersonal trauma is the basis for severe psychopathology (Mucci, 2013, 2018, 2022; Mucci & Scalabrini, 2021), in contrast with Freud's theory of repression as the basis for psychopathology. There are differences between the various levels of trauma of human agency, from the first level, less

DOI: 10.4324/9781003265030-14

severe, namely early relational trauma (Schore, 1994), with disattunement between the needs of the child and the capacity of the caregiver to provide constant and sensitive care, to the second level, with abuse, severe deprivation, and incest to the most severe, massive social trauma, such as in war, political torture, and genocide, which I define as the third level of trauma. *Nonetheless all these levels share the same major feature, "human agency" as opposed to "natural casualty."* Only human agency and the intention to harm or enact violence (sometimes even without full conscious awareness) against another individual create the most severe traumatic consequences for the human psyche, resulting in a dissociative structure or a split in personality. Ferenczi wrote as early as 1933 about this in the *Clinical Diary*, and as we still maintain today in the etiological understanding of personality disorders (Mucci, 2018, 2022).

The first level of trauma of human agency, i.e. early relational trauma, does not include active maltreatment and abuse, but can nonetheless create stress and deficit in the regulatory processes of the child as in the thorough description of traumatic development presented by Schore in his interdisciplinary research (1994–present). Schore speaks of "early relational trauma" as a disattunement between caregiver and child which results in affect dysregulation of all the physiological systems, and even dissociation, creating deficit in the development. Besides disattunement and disruption of the communication between caregiver and child, I think *we need to differentiate a "second level of trauma of human agency," with interpersonal violence, emotional and physical abuse, incest, or severe neglect especially when caused by a family member or an attachment figure* because it has more severe consequences psychologically. In fact, besides creating affect dysregulation (as in the first level of trauma), this second level, besides the affect dysregulation of the systems impeding optimal growth, creates an internal dyad of internalized aggressiveness and guilt, as described by Ferenczi in both the *Clinical Diary* and the "Confusion of Tongues" paper. In these writings Ferenczi clearly described how trauma from being outside and external becomes internal, resulting in the internalization of guilt and aggressiveness which in reality belong to the perpetrator but are internalized and mostly revolved against the self as a survival mechanism. It is internalized as an aggressiveness which can be directed against the other, perpetrating a cycle of violence in families and societies, but mostly against the self (as in all psychopathologies, especially of the borderline level of organization and most often in women). In this regard, I see a gender difference about internalization of guilt and aggressiveness: women tend to internalize violence and guilt, while men tend to externalize them. These differences I suppose occur for cultural reasons, since violence and aggressiveness are usually more accepted in cultural prescriptions of a masculine role. I have applied this internalized dyad of interpersonal traumatic origin to the structure and dynamics of personality disorders as I have seen them at work or enacted literally especially in borderline women (Mucci, 2018). The women I have depicted in *Borderline Bodies* (Mucci, 2018) demonstrate guilt and aggressiveness against one's own bodies with self-cutting, self-loathing, suicidal attempts, eating disorders, and alcohol and drug addictions. Sometimes, they might become aggressive towards their children (felt as part of their own selves).

With the term "borderline" here I refer to the organization that Otto Kernberg (1975) has described, with identity diffusion, severe defenses (such as denial, splitting, dissociation, projective identification, severe idealization and devaluation, omnipotent control and grandiosity) and maintenance of reality testing. It is an organization that describes a pre-Oedipal structure with destructiveness in love, work, relationships and does include several types of personality disorders at this level of severity (hysteric-hystrionic, borderline proper as in DSM, as well as narcissistic, paranoid and schizoid personality disorders). But in contrast with Kernberg's view of an innate aggressiveness, following the tradition of Klein and Freud, *I see this internalization of violence and the destructiveness of this psychopathology as a direct consequence of having undergone violence and severe neglect, therefore, it is not an innate process, but aggressiveness is an epigenetic and environmentally created consequence, as a result of interpersonal trauma.* Describing this internalization of the victim-persecutor dyad of traumatic origin (in the II level of interpersonal trauma), I analyze the affective and emotional components and psychodynamics in detail in the treatment of clinical cases of personality disorders (Mucci, 2018), following not only Ferenczi's revolutionary concept of the identification with the aggressor but also utilizing and revising his indications for a therapy that sees the analyst as a "benevolent and helpful observer" and a "witness" (Ferenczi, 1988, p. 24) to traumatic interpersonal situation. I finally propose a therapeutic model of intervention that I can synthesize as "embodied witnessing," described in details in my previous work (Mucci, 2018), and summarized in the chapter on therapy (see Chapter 15) for the traumatized. I, therefore,

integrate Ferenczi's principles of trauma theory with interpersonal neurobiology (Schore, 1994, 2019a, 2019b) with neuroscientific explanations of
how the human mind develops relationally, casting a different etiopatho-
genic light onto the origin of borderline disorders, and I describe what kind
of treatment can restore healing in the damaged self (see Chapter 15).

These traumatic developments with all of their complex and varied symp-
tomatology should be considered developments of long-term dysfunctional
relationships, what we refer to as Complex PTSD, so far still unrecognized
in DSM-5 and only accepted by PDM-2 (Lingiardi & McWilliams, 2017)
which acknowledges Complex PTSD in the second edition (C-PTSD)
in the subsection S41.3 (pp. 190–193) and by ICD-11. Complex PTSD
describes the long-term consequences and distortions on mind, body and
personality development of ongoing abuse and dysfunctional relationships,
usually within the family or with significant relationships and caregivers.
Borderline disorders and PTSD reactions might share some symptoms and
difficulties (for example anxiety, or sleep disorders and memory difficulties) but overall refer to very different structures, dynamics and outcome.
As already stressed, a hurricane or a typhoon will not cause Complex PTSD
and a personality disorder. In the last version, DSM-5 (APA, 2017) has
included dissociation as a symptom within PTSD, which adds to the confusion in so far as there is still no distinction between the different consequences of trauma according to the presence or lack of evil human intention
(which in my opinion is the cause of the real mental fracture). We therefore
agree with Liotti and Farina (2011), that a PTSD diagnosis is not adequate
to describe the consistent and long-term suffering and personality distortions that follow repeated and continual abuse by a caregiver. These kinds of
cumulative traumatizations are often the reason for adult psychopathology
(such as depression, anxiety disorders, addictions and eating disorders) and
are difficult to trace back immediately to childhood abuse, since memory
blocks are connected to disorganized attachments and dismissive attitudes.
These kinds of cumulative traumata result in psychopathologies and psychosomatic diseases. To synthetize, my reasons to introduce within the second level of trauma of human agency the "confusion of tongues trauma,"
has to do with the following considerations:

1) Only trauma of human agency (usually of the second level) creates the disposition for dissociation in the child, as explained by Liotti
(1995) and Schore (1994): dissociation seems to be the major structure of
response to severe human agency trauma (Mucci, 2018, 2020), splitting

the personality and leading also to severe destructiveness and maladaptation to reality and difficulties in self and other relationships. *Dissociation is a split or fragmentation of the human mind, creating a discontinuity in the states of the self, which bear the most destructive consequences for mental health.* Dissociation, not fully considered by Freud, implies an attack on the human psyche much deeper than the damage created by repression. Ferenczi spoke of this split of the mind of the child because of abuse and incest as "fragmentation" (Ferenczi, 1988, pp. 38–40), on which we will return. This is how Ferenczi's describes interpersonal trauma and subsequent dissociation and distortions in personality

> from the moment when bitter experience teaches us to lose faith in the benevolence of the environment, a permanent split in the personality occurs. The split-off part sets itself up as a guard against dangers . . . thus the splitting of the world, which previously gave the impression of homogeneity, into subjective and objective psychic systems; . . . Actual trauma is experienced by children in situations where no immediate remedy is provided and where adaptation, that is, a change in their own behavior, is forced on them – the first step toward establishing the differentiation between inner and outer world, subject and object. From then on, neither subjective nor objective experience alone will be perceived as an integrated emotional unit.
>
> (Ferenczi, 1988, p. 69)

2) what we are discussing with the concept of "Confusion of Tongues Theory of Trauma" as presented here by Arnold Wm. Rachman in the previous chapters and in his previous writings (1994, 1997a, 1997b, 2018b, 2022; Rachman & Klett, 2015), falls in my opinion within the second level of trauma of human agency and in the category of Complex PTSD, which defines the long-term affective difficulties, emotional disturbance, symptoms, destructiveness and cognitive distortions caused by long-term exposure to abuse, incest and severe neglect. This recognition is long overdue but has been rejected by the psychiatric board of APA on the basis that there is not enough research data, only clinical evidence.

  3) the dynamics of maltreatment, abuse and incest as discussed here, for their consequences on the human psyche, for the first time introduced by Ferenczi with his trauma theory and the concept of identification with the aggressor, describe an alternative developmental route which is in contrast

with Freud's definition of Oedipal complex. This means that Freudian theory needs to be expanded in order to consider other kinds of development such as pre-Oedipal ones, to include clinical cases of severe personality disorders, namely, traumatic developments. In fact, I see this kind of development as the etiopathogenesis of a borderline or narcissistic disorder, as opposed to the healthy or neurotic development in the description of Freud, rooted on the Oedipal process dynamics. Borderline disorders are "pre-Oedipal" disorders if we want to retain this kind of language and distinction.

In the present lack of acknowledgment of Complex PTSD by mainstream diagnostic categories I see the same attitude in both the medical and lay community that prevented Freud from retaining his own trauma theory. It is the sign of a persistent difficulty in accepting the reality that the worst consequences of trauma are due to abuse that happens most often within the family or with people of trust or attachment figure. This is a sign of the same unease that we found in the heated debate in the '90s in the retrieval of memory of abuse in therapy, in which cognitivist researchers and psychodynamic clinicians could not agree on the possibility of actual retrieval of memory of abuse even many years after the episodes. This prejudice or difficulty is certainly still existing nowadays since renowned experts in the fields feel the need to call infantile abuse and particularly incest "the hidden epidemic" (Lanius et al., 2010). For years Bessel Van der Kolk and Judith Herman among others have asked the board of APA for proper recognition of the long-term consequences of abuse and trauma from attachment trauma to traumatic developments and incest, to no avail. In a letter published by Van der Kolk in his recent book *The body keeps the score*, a passage of the letter received by the board has been published as an exergue at the beginning of Chapter 10 (Van der Kolk, 2014, p. 168): for the Board, there is clinical evidence for the long-term consequences of abuse in childhood but, at present, not enough research to prove it.

Contrary to this statement, the Adverse Childhood Experience research (ACE) (Felitti et al., 1998) is still ongoing and carried out so far on 18,000 patients with medical conditions and psychological illness. Even though it is an epidemiological research, it has indicated a high correlation between levels of childhood adverse conditions (including having had experienced physical, sexual or psychological abuse, in conjunction with other dysfunctional conditions in the family such as depression and mental disorders, antisocial conduct, aggressiveness and violence between family members and use of drugs), and mental and physical illness. Among the mental disorders correlating with abuse were depression, addictions including food and use of drugs, suicidal tendencies, eating disorders and personality disorders; among the physical ailments were cardiovascular and circulatory diseases, metabolic disease, immune system disease, and liver and kidney disease. *To receive harm instead of sensitive care especially in developmental phases and by attachment figures seems to cause the worse consequences, up to the possibility of provoking early death and accidents.* If we think of the psychological consequences, it is well known to whoever is in the field of psychological and mental disorders, without being necessarily psychoanalytically oriented, that to have received abuse and neglect in the early phases of life leaves permanent and pernicious traces in the mind and emotional life, something that will need years of therapy to be repaired and healed. In this way the human relation, which we claim to be the basis of *a two-person psychology, is not only the fundamental element for development, but also the one which might create the most damage and disruption in the other dependent being, depending on the other's care for their growth and health. Trauma of human agency impacts on our capacity to maintain the positive affects and emotional resources that sustain life (inside, intrapsychically, and outside, interpersonally, influencing our behavior and our processes of care, control, planning and decision-making), hampering the optimal functioning of all the systems, and reducing the capacity for resilience.* Resilience, at the other end of vulnerability and traumatic exposure, seems to be based on trust and hope and good self-esteem (Panskepp & Biven, 2012) allowing the creation and maintenance of a feeling of connectedness and integration or continuity in the self that finally promotes health and well-being individually, in the families, and in society (see Fonagy, Steele, Steele, Higgitt, Target, 1994; van Ijzendoorn, Palacios J. et al, 2011; Mucci, 2022).

Description of the Neurobiological Consequences of Level I of Trauma of Human Agency or Early Relational Trauma

In all levels of trauma of human agency there will be consequences at the neurobiological level, first of all hyperarousal, with high levels of stress and glucocorticoids. Such consequences are in excess, and the possible dissociative structure at the basis of further destructive behavior and psychopathology, since the stressful information and traumatic event cannot be

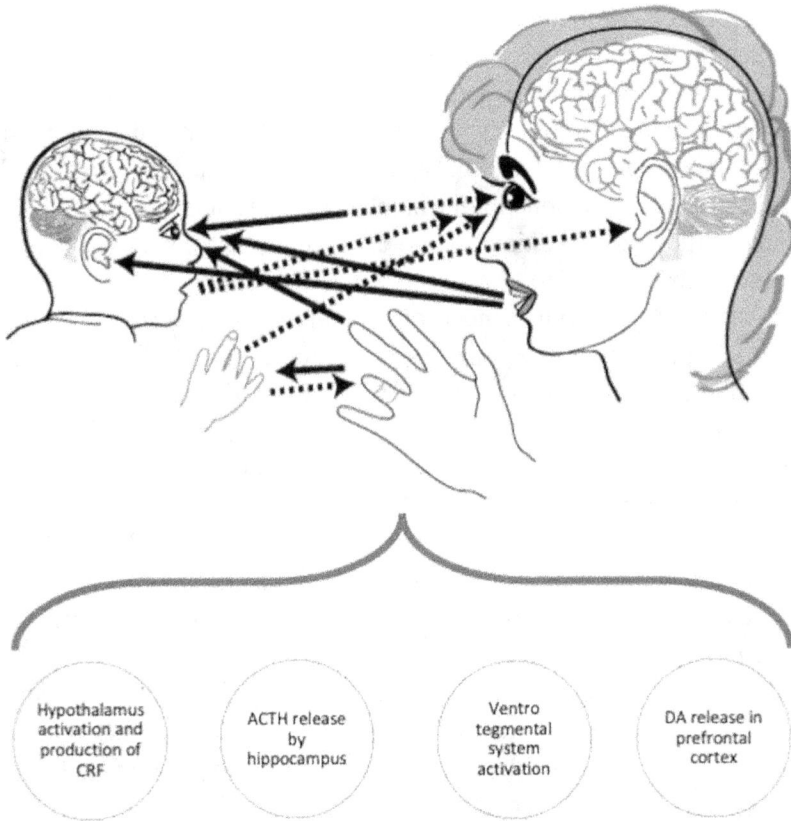

Figure 14.2 Trauma Resulting from Disattunement Between Caregiver and Child Adapted from Mucci, 2018, p. 22

properly encoded within the labeling prescribed by hippocampus episodic memory because of extreme stress and excess of glucorticoids and corti-sol (as already explained). This affect dysregulation negatively impacts all neurobiological and neuroscientific levels of development. As Schore describes cogently:

At the end of the first year right lateralised cortical-subcortical circuits imprint, in implicit procedural memory, an internal working model of attachment which encodes affect regulation that non-consciously guide the individual through interpersonal contexts.

(Schore, 2011, p. XII in Bromberg, 2011)

It is the progressive maturation of limbic circuits thanks to the attachment relation that connects (with a special input at the end of the first year), amygdala, cingulate cortex, insula and orbitofrontal areas (Schore, 1997, 2000, 2001). Through the connection with hypotalamus and brain stem, regulation controls instinctual and bodily drives, through a representational system that is unique for the human being (what in psychoanalysis goes under the object relation theory, a relationship connected through affect (see Kernberg, 1976).

Even though dissociation is most common in second level trauma, while the first level usually creates only dysregulation of affect, the first level could nonetheless cause dissociation in the child even in lack of maltreatment and abuse, because the caregiver might have dissociative areas that are communicated unconsciously from the right brain of the parent to the right brain of the child. In fact, when the caregiver has unresolved traumatizations (what in the Adult Attachment Interview is called U, Unresolved Trauma), or when there is a lack of violence and severe maltreatment of the child, the dissociated parts of the personality and of the behavior of the parent can be transferred to the limbic system of the child in the attachment bond, mostly through the right-limbic brain of the infant in connection to the right-limbic brain of the (still traumatized) mother, so that the attachment relationship itself becomes a vehicle for intergenerational transmission of trauma making dissociation in the child possible EVEN IN LACK OF ACTUAL MALTREATMENT AND ABUSE (one more reason to treat traumatizations in the caregivers as soon as possible, possibly before the child is born, in mothers at risk). We can speak therefore of an intersubjective and psychogenic mechanism of intergenerational traumatization and of the dissociative defenses towards overwhelming and disturbing negative affects in the child (Schore, 2010). Research shows that severe maternal dysfunctions (not paternal, unless the main caregiver is the father), such as mental disorder, unresolved mourning especially in the first two years of the child, addictions, traumatizations, correlate with dissociation in the child (Liotti et al., 1991). Confirming the necessity to extend psychoanalysis to different routes in development and possible psychopathology, we can say that the brain in fact is socially constructed (meaning, through human relationships), as Eisenberg writes (Eisenberg, 1995). Schore has extensively explained (Schore, 1994, 2019b) how the brain is wired for potential optimal social and empathic and intelligent and symbolic development. The way the human brain will develop depends on the appropriate and caring response of the environment, namely on the relationships of care experience in the upbringing. Those experiences can promote the best possible outcome in terms of ontological development and behavior, given the genomic input, or the final outcome can be negatively affected or even damaged. At birth, the brain is a very undifferentiated organ, and early experiences determine how neurons connect with each other, creating specific circuits that give origin to the various mental connections and processes. Brain structures develop differently according to the different stimuli they receive, influencing:

a. the growth of neurites (the nervous terminations of the cells), that extend in localized regions or distribute themselves in different areas;
b. the creation of new or wider synapses;
c. the formation, along the axons, of the myelin sheath, which speeds up the conduction of electric signals, making the connection quicker;
d. changes at the level of the post-synaptic membrane of the receiving cells;
e. determining cellular death phenomena, due to insufficient usage or degenerative processes (such as chronic stress).

What is interesting for our purposes is that trauma can be considered a fundamental example of how environmental (mainly relational) experiences can modify the structure of the brain and the cerebral functions beyond what was genetically determined for the individual (Tuttè, 2004; Van Ijzendoorn et al., 2011)*, and is, therefore, the best evidence for brain plasticity and epigenetics. From the point of view of neuroscience, relational traumatic experiences are stored in the imagistic procedural memory of the visuo-spatial right hemisphere, the locus of implicit and autobiographical memory* (Schiffer et al., 1995; Schore, 2010; Hugdahl, 1995; Markowitsch et al., 2000). The major container of somatic memories is in the amygdala in the limbic system, not related to episodic memory.

Disattunement and disruption of regulation in the primary dyad leading to affect dysregulation led to lack of autonomic control and impulse control, with impulsivity, lack of deferral of impulses, and even dissociative moments between mind and body. The lack of attunement, in fact, might cause vulnerability to dissociation in the communication (visual, tactile, prosodic, verbal, and nonverbal) between the amygdala (within the limbic system, as mentioned, eminent in the connection of emotions to higher order control areas) of the mother and the amygdala of the child. Moments of disruption might be present if the mother herself is traumatized so that during the dissociative moments of the mother, the child is left alone with dysregulated internal chaotic affects that cannot be elaborated and processed. This lack of impulse control and dissociation between body and mind might lead in the future to addictions, destructiveness, and aggressive behavior, while the emotional ups and downs create states of anxiety, depressive symptoms, and instability in relationships. On the contrary, when the care is sensitive and well-tuned, the development of the limbic areas (amygdala, thalamus, hypothalamus, hippocampus, among the others), leads to affective response and empathic connection with the other, nontraumatized caregiver, capable of insuring this constant regulation of the child with the capacity for prompt repair in the normal moments of dysregulation. It is this regulatory attunement, first external then internalized, that insures the proper development of cortical areas, especially the orbitofrontal and ventro-medial areas that guarantee, with their connection with the limbic system, the mature control of emotional input and determine the capacity for future self-regulation, ideation, and control of higher capacities, starting from the first hemisphere, the right one, going to the proper development of the left hemisphere, which starts a critical growth after the second year of life (Cozolino, 2002; Henry, 1993; Schore, 1994; Siegel, 1999; Sasso, 2011). The orbitofrontal areas undergo a fundamental growth between 10–12 months of the child (Diamond & Doar, 1989, p. 70; Schore, 1994). It is this connection between the amygdala and what is emotionally experienced and the control provided by the orbitofrontal areas that is lacking in personality disorders, especially of the borderline type as described in DSM.

Tronick et al. (1978) have strikingly demonstrated through the protocol of the "Still Face" how even very few moments of disruption in the visual and emotional communication mostly through gaze, visual exchanges, tone of voice, and vocalizations between the dyad can have the most dramatic effects. In the protocol, the two participants (a few months old child and her mother) are nonverbally communicating through gaze, smile, and all the minor vocal sounds normally exchanged between the two, in a very harmonious and alive kind of play and communication when the mother receives the command to interrupt the flow of communication. The mother's face goes still, that is, motionless and without any emotions and intention to communicate even for seconds, interrupting what

Trevarthen has called "proto-conversation." What happens in a matter of minutes is incredible. The child first tries to attract the mother's attention, then tries to protest with gestures and movements of face and body, then starts crying aloud, protesting disappointment for having been abruptly abandoned. We can imagine when the lack of correspondence is rare or when the disruption of the communication happens frequently, as in dissociated, traumatized, or depressed mothers and caregivers how difficult the relationship becomes and how the child is left alone in complex developmental processes (affective, cognitive, social) that require the active participation of the other, in order to be regulated at first by this adult and in order to internalize the ability to regulate these states in the future. This bodily based affect regulation learned in relation becomes the bodily base for higher order symbolic development, creation of internal good object and capacity for empathic connection and understanding of the other's needs. I have explained at length in previous writings how this bodily based regulation beginning with an other and then internalized becomes the basis for the internalization of the (symbolic) object, good or bad, according to the primary early experiences, also establishing implicit relational models between self and other in future relational experiences, including psychotherapy (see Mucci, 2018). A mother who is always depressed and interacts very poorly visually or vocally, leaves the child constantly in a state of lack and deprivation, even though she does not abuse the child. It is the starting place of the so-called dead mother complex as indicated by psychoanalyst André Green (1993), that can be understood also in terms of a relational developmental neuroscientific model in which emotional mirroring and psychic presence and exchange is lacking. It means, psychologically and psychodynamically, that the mother is not responding emotionally (because she might be depressed, ill, or dissociated), so that the child experiences this absence. This lack not only of mirroring but of a real interaction with a caring human being feels like a ghostly absence and is experienced as emptiness and a disquieting void instead of a sustaining participation, as we see in many borderline young subjects.

The affect dysregulation and emotional ups and down typical of the first level of trauma of human agency means that there is lack of regulation of the HPA (Hypothalamic-pituitary-adrenal) axis so that hormones, peptides, and neurotransmitters are not properly regulated. This influences the response to stress even in future situations (therefore influencing permanently the capacity for resilience) and contributing to anxiety and negative emotions in face of stress. But why is there trauma of first level or lack of attunement? In this case the caregiver, because of previous and present stress or trauma, use of drugs, depression, severe loss, and other serious difficulties cannot perform at their best the level of caring that the child requires for optimal development. In terms of psychopathological effects and symptoms, affect dysregulation in the developing being may result in incapacity to control fear, anxiety, and elaborating negative emotions in general and in dangerous behaviors, such as drug and alcohol abuse or addictions, eating disorders, especially obesity (where food is used as affect regulator of negative emotions), and dependent behaviors in relationship, with impulsivity and lack of control, which also implies amygdalar activation without control of higher areas of the brain, orbitofrontal and frontal areas, leading to impulsive destructive acts against self and others (Schore, 1994) and deficit in symbolic object formation. In addition (and this is true for all levels of trauma of human agency and for trauma due to natural catastrophes or accidents) the major stress hormone, cortisol, when too high or too low, affects the immune system influencing high levels of inflammation in the body and contributing to infections and disease. This was indicated by the Adverse Childhood Experience Research (ACE) and as clear already in the research carried through by René Spitz in American orphanages in the United States, where children were physically fed but emotionally abandoned. They were often prone to infections and would often die from them. In addition, adrenaline, noradrenaline, and dopamine, all fundamental neuro-transmitters, would be dysregulated, creating emotional ups and downs and affecting all the other neurobiological and neurophysiological systems, impeding stability of emotions and capacity for mentalization (Spitz, 1945). These further connections made possible in the brain thanks to the regulations of underlying systems allow for the further social and empathic levels of development, endowing the human subjects precisely with precious and unique symbolic higher order capacities, including language, aesthetics, and higher ethical and moral capacities, contributing to meaning and value and spirituality. It means that the very development of empathy and compassion, which seem to be decreasing nowadays together with emotional and social capacities for adaptation and respect in a society of narcissists are not a given by default but are created in long-term intergenerational dynamics, which might result in antisocial behavior and even violence. *This also means that aggressiveness and the death drive are not innate, but at least in great part a reaction to the abuse and violence and difficulties and deprivation experienced in relations.* In this way, even the Freudian view that aggressiveness is innate cannot hold; and aggressiveness *is better explained by the internalization of aggressiveness and violence experienced in the family and intergenerationally and often against oneself. This is also Ferenczi's view of how violence and aggressiveness are the deposit of experience and introjected as in the model of identification with the aggressor,* better explained in the second level of trauma of human agency.

Level II: Maltreatment, Abuse, Severe Deprivation, Incest

The second level of trauma of human agency, namely *maltreatment, severe neglect, abuse, and incest, demonstrate, in several studies, that children whose parents suffer from unresolved mourning, depression, substance abuse, problems connected to divorce* (Ainsworth & Eichberg, 1991; Carlson & Sroufe, 1995; Liotti in Ammaniti & Stern, 1992; Liotti in Solomon & George, 1999; Main & Hesse, 1990) *are more vulnerable to developing disorganized attachment, with a vulnerability to dissociation* (see Liotti, 1995) *and therefore future psychopathology.* Psychodynamically, we can imagine how severe the consequences of the maltreatment are when the parent is not only nonresponsive or often mentally or emotionally vacant because they are: in an abusive marriage or other traumatic circumstances; they are using drugs; are in deep mourning and grief; have difficulties of various kinds; consciously or actively beats the child, abusing them physically, psychologically, or even sexually; or treat the child with cruelty and punishes them in bizarre inhuman ways. In some adult attachment interviews I have heard of parents who kill the pet of their children as exemplary punishment for the child, while they are only teaching them cruelty. A mother who is in an abusive marriage is also often unable to adequately protect the child, contributing, unfortunately, to a vicarious traumatization, instead of being a witness to the abuse carried on by the partner. The importance of the presence of a third term, the other parent or caregiver who can be a testimony to the abuse going on, was stressed by Ferenczi, who often wrote about the fact that the abused child would lose all hope in the environment not only because of the actual abuse received, but also by the lack of support and comfort from the environment; often the other person is indeed emotionally non responsive, absent or in denial or dissociated because of trauma and abuse. As Ferenczi lucidly writes in the paper "Confusion of Tongues," it is a second person of trust that can reduce or redeem the traumatic experience in the child, and it is the lack of comfort from the environment that adds cumulative traumatization:

> Usually the relationship to a second person of trust, in the chosen example the mother, is not intimate enough either to provide help. Timid attempts of this kind [on the part of the child] are rejected by the mother as nonsense. The abused child turns into a mechanically obedient being or becomes defiant, but can no longer account for the reason for the defiance, even to himself; his sexual life remains undeveloped or takes on perverse forms; I will not mention at this time the neuroses or psychoses that could result from such a situation. The scientific importance of this observation is the assumption that the still not well-developed personality [of the child] responds to sudden unpleasure, not with defense, *but with identification and introjection of the menacing person or aggressor, or identification based on fear.*
>
> (Ferenczi, 1933, pp. 298–299, emphasis in the text)

The child turns first to the other parent for support, but often there is denial or dissociation in the other parent, who is often an abused mother. It is only afterwards that, in lack of emotional comfort, support, and witnessing, the child finally surrenders and identifies with the aggressor and their negative feelings, buying into their untruth. It is this fundamental distortion that annihilates the truth of what has happened and distorts reality and identity or splits the identity, permanently. Many studies indicate, in fact, a high correlation between disorganized children (children with insecure attachment with dissociative features) and mothers who in the AAI (Adult Attachment Interview) have transcripts classified as U (Unresolved Trauma), CC (cannot classify), or HH (hostile-helpless) (Hesse & Main, 2000; Hesse et al., 2003; Lyons-Ruth et al., 2003; Solomon & George, 1999). Clinical evidence testifies to the presence of abuse, trauma, and depression very often in the mother and abuse and incest with the father. It is clearly an intergenerational chain that leads to the abuse of a child. If the negative experience is not properly worked through and elaborated by the parent, the model of early relational trauma implies the tendency to perpetrate or be subjected to the same abuse, repeating a victim-persecutor pattern. Sometimes the parent might express their control and more or less violent coercion with their emotional withdrawal and lack of responsivity, as for instance, when the mother "does not hear" the child crying. Some clinicians (Fraiberg et al., 1975; Lyons-Ruth & Block, 1996) have found that mothers who were themselves victims of infantile abuse could react with emotional withdrawal or with a negative or intrusive behavior (mothers who had been victims of physical abuse are more likely to be controlling than mothers who had been victims of sexual abuse). It is because of the lack of support in the environment, according to Ferenczi, that the child, while the traumatic relationships goes on, responds with an identification with the aggressor, based on fear. In Ferenczi's description of the dynamics of abuse and deadening of the soul with the dynamic of identification of the aggressor as a result we read:

> 7 August 1932: Only a very small proportion of the incestuous seduction of children and abuse by persons in charge of them is ever found out, and even then it is mostly hushed up. . . . Moreover, the child is intimidated by the threat of the withdrawal of love, indeed of physical suffering. *Soon it begins to even doubt the reality of its own senses, or, as more frequently happens, it withdraws from the entire conflict-situation by taking refuse in daydreams and complying with the demands of waking life, from now on, only like an automaton. . . . The early-seduced child adapts itself to the difficult task with the aid of complete identification with the aggressor.*
>
> (Ferenczi, 1988, pp. 189–190, italics added)

Here I want to stress also how abused children become disconnected from the truth of their own feelings ("it begins even to doubt the reality of its own senses"), starting that dramatic fragmentation that is represented by the disconnection between mind and body, sometimes up to an "out of body experience" as explained by Rachman and Klett (2015). The child takes refuge in daydreaming, withdraws from reality disavowing their own feelings and the very truth of what happened, with depersonalization, derealization (two of the most common dissociative levels of traumatic origin, the others being absorption and a sense that the body does not belong to the subject, in a mind-body divide, which is the basis of dissociation).

Very interestingly and decades in advance of what we now understand as the typical freezing disconnection or parasympathetic response to attack and trauma as described by neuroscience (see Panskepp, 2012;

Schore, 2011), Ferenczi writes in *The Clinical Diary* in the entry called "Fragmentation":

> a child is the victim of overwhelming aggression, describing what he termed "giving up the ghost" ["Aufgeben des Geistes"], with the firm conviction that this self-abandonment (fainting) means death . . . . Therefore someone who has "given up the ghost" survives this "death" physically and with a part of his energy begins to live again; he even succeeds in reestablishing unity with the pre-traumatic personality, although this is usually accompanied by memory lapses and retroactive amnesia of varying duration. But this amnesic piece is actually a part of the person, who still is "dead", or exists permanently in the agony of anxiety. The task of the analysis is to remove this split.
>
> (Ferenczi, 1988, p. 39)

Ferenczi calls "fragmentation" what we now consider "dissociation." Dissociation as a term and concept for a defense originating by trauma was already in use by Pierre Janet at the time, but Freud did not consider it, possibly as a consequence of his own disavowal of his traumatic theory (Mucci, 2017). It is really interesting to see how many connections are in Schore's description of the neurobiological traumatic response of the child in this "freezing" response or parasympathetic response to trauma, as we will say in contemporary neurobiological language:

> The parasympathetic dominant state of conservation-withdrawal occurs in helpless and hopeless stressful situations in which the individual becomes inhibited and strives to avoid attention in order to become "unseen" (Schore, 1994, 2001). The dissociative metabolic shutdown state is a primary regulatory process, used throughout the life span, in which the stressed individual passively disengages in order to conserve energies, foster survival by the risky posture of "feigning death", and allow restitution of depleted resources by immobility. In this passive hypometabolic state heart rate, blood pressure, and respiration are decreased, while pain numbing and blunting endogenous opiates are elevated. It is this energy-conserving parasympathetic (vagal) mechanism that mediates the "profound detachment" of dissociation.
>
> (Schore, Foreword, in Bromberg, 2011, p. xvii)

The subsequent splitting of personality is another major and permanent resource of the individual for adaptational purposes; it is done at the cost of sacrificing the truth ("they have done that to me") and through the deadening of the body: not only the reality is distorted – the identification of the self becomes one with the persecutor, through the identification with the aggressor – but the renunciation applies also to physical bodily sensations with disconnection between mind, body, and brain: the subject is an automaton, a living dead; and the disconnection between truth, reality and mind-body-brain consciousness leads in the long run to alexithymia, a lack of physical sensations, emotions, and an impossibility to feel and to speak about them. It is not surprising, therefore, given the high occurrence of abuse and neglect in our times in an inter-generational cycle that we find an increasing number of personality disorders, addictions including alcohol, food, and internet, all connected to alexithymia as the incapacity to feel and name emotions, which also is at the basis of the growing number of somatic disorders or psychosomatics.

As Rachman has thoroughly and convincingly explained, psychologi-cally, incest and long-term abuse coming from a family member or an attachment figure disrupt the boundaries of safety and break of trust, with the betrayal of the assumptions that regulate the care and the protec-tion of the child, implying for the child that the other should be there for them and for their well-being and to promote their best development, not to exploit them and their body (Rachman & Klett, 2015). Several bor-derline women are often survivors of incest or of severe and continued abuse received by figures of (potential) trust, as demonstrated by research (Gabbard, 2000; Gunderson, 2008; Zanarini et al., 1997; Van der Kolk, 2014; Mucci, 2018). The link between mind, body, dissociation, and trauma has been thoroughly explored by several neuroscientific research studies. In fact, the right brain is also fundamental for maintaining a coherent sense of one's body (Tsakiris et al., 2008), for attention (Raz, 2004), and for pain processing (Symonds et al., 2006), and represents the ultimate defense for blocking emotional bodily-based processes (Schore, Foreword to Bromb-erg, 2011, p. xxix). This also explains why dissociation is a major fracture between mind and body, and it is mostly a disconnection in the right hemi-sphere, where the feeling and awareness of one's body (through the right insula, in the limbic system is dominant (Craig, 2004). Schore states that:

> neurobiologically dissociation reflects the inability of the right brain cortical-subcortical implicit self-system to recognize and process the

perception of external stimuli (exteroceptive information coming form the relational environment) and on a moment-to-moment basis integrate them with internal stimuli (interoceptive information from the body, somatic markers, the "felt experience"). This failure of integration of the higher right hemisphere with the lower right brain and disconnection of the central nervous system from the autonomic nervous system induces an instant collapse of both subjectivity and intersubjectivity. Stressful affect, especially those associated with emotional pain are thus not experienced in consciousness.

> (Bromberg "not-me" self-states) (Schore, Foreword, in Bromberg, 2011, p. xxiii)

Incest Trauma and what it Disrupts in the Child

Chapter Seven of this book describes in subtle and cogent details the dynamics of what Rachman defines "parental sexual seduction" or incest. The sensuality that can be present within the relationship between fathers and daughters (to name the major dynamics, since seduction between fathers and between mothers and sons or daughters is remarkably less common), Rachman underlines that parental/child sexuality must be kept

> at the level of fantasy. When the father, or other abusing adult or adolescent, under the pressure of his/her own narcissistic needs distorts the total motivation of the child, reducing it to a predominantly sexual one, the stage is set for pathological, incestuous, acting out with the child.
>
> (this volume, p. 55)

Confusing the normal and developmental need for attachment and tenderness, the parent, according to Rachman (ibid.)

> initiates a part-object relationship, and uses the child as a discharge-object rather than as a whole object in which the capacity for nonerotic affection predominates. . . . Molesting the child is really overpowering the child. It is actually aggressing against the child. Therefore there are at least two unrealities, e.g., distortion of reality in the experience.
>
> (Modell, 1990)

The child is forced to accept because tenderness is a vital source of life. As Rachman writes, the child is saying: "I will give you the sex you want because I need the affection or love you say you will give me" (p. 56 this book).

This is the essence of the distortion and subjection that the Confusion of Tongues trauma contains at all levels. Moreover, what I find extremely important to stress, "the sexual contact between parent and child disrupts the intrapsychic fantasy process" (this volume, p. 56). In another outstanding paper, Rachman has further analyzed this dynamic as follows:

> The child, in order to maintain self-cohesion, protect an affectionate tie to the parent, and continues the interpersonal contact necessary for survival, developing a serious of coping mechanisms. One could also label them "trauma surviving measures", that is, intrapsychic, interpersonal, and intellectual measures to reduce the intensity of the emotional crises that threaten to overwhelm the child. The need to deny the act of seduction loosens the child's hold on reality. Such a process of adaptation to trauma alters one's capacity to relate to one's inner world and the world of significant others. A clinical detachment and even dissociation mechanism can develop which encourages an amnesia for the feelings, thoughts, and behavior of the seduction experience: All that may remain is a somatic memory or a fragment of the experience, such as an odor, a body sensation, or an unusual thought. In the most severe cases, individuals are so dramatically split-off selves and are created to cope with the severe violence and abuse. Once repressed dissociated state becomes encapsulated, and the child becomes what Ferenczi (1953, p. 362) referred to as an "automata."
>
> (Rachman, 2005, p. 3)

In lack of an external validation by an adult, and of the support of the environment, the child goes on with thinking that the abuse was not real, discrediting their own bodily truth. Ferenczi described with extraordinary insight the process of discrediting one's own perception and connection between what the mind knows and what the body feels, and the beginning of the split between mind and body (the root of the first major dissociation), a split that only therapy through different and restorative emotional experience can repair.

Rachman, going further in his explanation, shows us of how trauma can belong and properly describe my definition of second level of trauma of human agency. It is extremely important to stress that the need to deny the act of seduction loosens the child's hold on reality. In other words, in order for abused children to accommodate within their own reality of incest, they need to distort, dissociate, or deny what has happened. Through cognitive distortion and blurring of boundaries, which predisposes them to further abusive relationships with distortions of borders, it is the very hold on reality that is loosened. Rachman does not openly speak of psychotic traits or dynamics for incest survivors, but I think this distortion can have psychotic consequences. In women suffering from borderline personality disorders, reality testing is retained, but in presence of particularly stressful moments or especially when a future intimate relationship recalls the incestual or incestuous trait of the past, reality testing is very weak or sometimes missing. An abuser can become an affectionate lover in the mind of an abused individual for very long, unfortunately, until the abuse becomes too obvious to be denied or too dangerous. Moreover, the trespassing of rules and order to the point of obliterating the truth and reality has very dangerous consequences for the social interaction, disrupting the very participation to the social world and the understanding and capacity to follow commonly respected rules. In my clinical practice I have seen this blurring of boundaries, and sometimes difficulties, to belong to social groups following the rules of institutions. More than an anti-social behavior, these women seem incapable of decoding, following, or simply acknowledging the rules of the group or social institution, as though the incest trauma disrupted the very belonging to a symbolic order in which the subject has transgressed the Oedipal boundary (being the victim of this transgression), a boundary which is the very foundation of rules in most social groups, constructing the order itself in most of societies. It is not antisocial behavior but a psychotic incapacity to distinguish self and other, me and you, and to discriminate symbolic representations of belonging to an order where identity and the self are located. It is as though incest disrupted the very possibility of distinguishing between self and other, between right and wrong, leaving sometimes the child in a confusion that impedes the growth and membership into any further order and community. We can imagine how a daughter victim of incest can maintain boundaries and help define, recognize, and construct the identity of a child of her own, male or female does not matter. It is also very interesting, I think, that what maintains the scaffolding and safety of identity is precisely this necessary preservation of the fantasy of incest from becoming a reality. To breach that fantasy and make it real corresponds to a breach into the safety of reality and the piercing through of an horrific and appalling reality, as in the Holocaust or as in massive extermination, where, as Grubrich-Simitis correctly acknowledged, "the camps made real the worse psychotic fantasies" (Gubrich-Simitis, 1981, p. 438). The breach of this safety pact between self and other is what constitutes the break of the empathic dyad as described by Dori Laub (Laub, 2005), who views this break the basis of massive traumatizations as in the Holocaust, what I have termed third level of trauma. Moreover, we should keep in mind that security of attachment is the first and major protection towards future traumatizations, both of human agency or of natural cause (for further explanations see Mucci, 2022), and that the trauma of a father or mother is transferred unto the child through the attachment dynamics with a probability up to 82 percent, meaning that if a parent is secure, the child even before birth is expected to be secure with an 82 percent probability (Fonagy et al., 1991). In other words, it is highly unlikely that an insecure or disorganized (meaning traumatized) parent can attend to a child in a modality that creates secure attachment, unless the parent has somehow gone beyond those traumatizations, through therapy or thanks to very positive future love relationships and forms of reparation.

Speaking about intergenerational transmission of trauma, even silence about a topic or a past trauma in the family can contribute to the transferal of hidden traumatic contents between generations. With the blurring of boundaries implied by the very concept of "knowing and not knowing" the trauma, which is how Laub and Auerhahn (1993) described the unrepresentability of traumatization within the self and therefore it is carried through the next generations. Unconsciously or, we should say, implicitly through the amygdala, the trauma, since it is a nonconscious implicit content, nor a repressed content, is carried on. This is what is going to cause the transmission of unconscious material from one generation to the other, and this happens both in massive social trauma and in incest. Survivors often claim that they belong to a secret order that is sworn to silence. They have become the bearers of a secret. By never divulging their stories, they feel that the rest of the world will never come to know the real truth. It becomes a chain, transferred to the next generation, and so on. Giving testimony contributes precisely to the breaking of this pact of silence, inside and outside the survivor. It is also and above all part of a process of dealing with loss and separation. For further development of this point I refer the reader to Laub's writings and to my work in *Beyond Individual and Collective Trauma* (Mucci, 2013) and in my recent *Resilience and Survival. Understanding and Healing Intergenerational Trauma* (Mucci, 2022).

Identification with the Aggressor as the Most Destructive Dynamic of the Second Level of Trauma

The second level of trauma of human agency (in combination with lack of attunement, the first level), adds to the first one, involving nonintentional maltreatment but trauma resulting from disattunement between caregiver and child. The additional stress and dynamic consequences of severe abuse or maltreatment and severe deprivation are deemed to cause a vulnerability towards disorganized attachment in the child and possible dissociative behaviors. This level is particularly visible in the destructive features of personality disorders, in addition to the dysregulation and impulsivity present as a consequence of the first level.

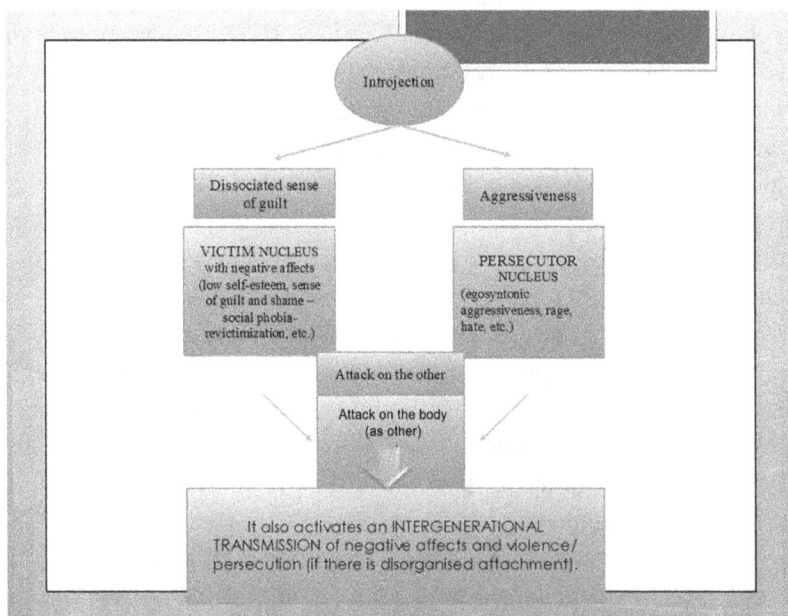

Figure 14.3 Victim-Persecutor Dyad

It creates a split in the personality, a dissociated and internalized dyad with a part of oneself as the victim identified with the victim's affects (low self-esteem, blame, shame, guilt) and a part of oneself identified with an internal persecutor of which the subject is not aware, identified with the affects of the persecutor (violence, hate, aggressiveness – often revolved against one's own body). An identification with the aggressor (Ferenczi, 1988) is used by the personality to adapt in order to survive. The internalized persecutory parts can act against oneself (damaging oneself and one's resources or attacking one's body) or against the other (becoming actually violent against another). I have also assimilated this internalization of a persecutor of traumatic origin to the formation of the alien self as explained by Bateman and Fonagy (2004). Though in my view this alien self that is then externalized through violent behavior and destructiveness is really due not only to lack of mirroring between mother and child (as in Fonagy's theory) but to the real hate and hostility that the mother has felt and has directed against the child, and that the child internalizes. This is a concept to which Ferenczi referred to as the complex of the "ill-received child" (Ferenczi, 1929), which creates destruction and a death drive in the future adult. This is another indication in Ferenczi's theory that aggressiveness is not innate, as in Freud's understanding, but created in a relationship or due to the rejection of the parent. Important towards a rewriting of some tenets of the psychoanalytic theory, it is evident here how the origin of the death drive is not innate for Ferenczi, nor originated by mere chance but the result of an original rejection and violence onto the child, on behalf of the parents or caregivers, in contrast with Freud's theorization of an innate drive and innate aggressiveness. With the internalization of violence in the victim and the subsequent externalization, the male victim more often becomes a persecutor of other victims. In patriarchal and chauvinist societies, in which aggressiveness is considered more acceptable in male children, the identification with the aggressor becomes internalized aggressiveness in the male child/adolescent/adult and is more often directed against the other. The female abused child more often directs that received and internalized aggressiveness against herself, her children, or her own body, in a reversal of dynamics that often leads to depression and self-harming behavior and sometimes also suicidality. In fact 80 percent of borderline patients who self-cut and are suicidal are female; males seem, as far as diagnosis is concerned, to be more often narcissistic or antisocial, with ego-syntonic aggressiveness.

We can see very clearly this typical victim/persecutor internalized dyad at work in severe personality disorders, so common especially in young adults nowadays. Borderline patients cut themselves or try to commit suicide; severe narcissists damage their own resources (including time and intelligence) in order to protect or mask, through the defense of grandiosity and omnipotent control, their own inner fragility and low self-esteem and could also become "malignant narcissists" (a clinical diagnosis not present in DSM but described by Otto Kernberg, 1975). Malignant narcissists, the most severe types of narcissists, behave disruptively against common rules shared by others and enforced by institutions, towards which they feel a sense of entitlement that makes them act beyond the normal constrictions that affect others in society, to the point of behaving against the law and becoming criminals. Research shows more and more consistently how subjects affected by personality disorders have been exposed to levels of traumatizations[1] that sometimes are not consciously recognized as traumatic events because of the dissociation accompanying the personalities and their symptoms, especially when trauma involves attachment relationships, or long-term relationships, creating the symptoms of Complex PTSD. Their psychopathology is expressed through symptoms and destructiveness in various aspects of their lives. Finally, the massive traumatizations created by war, genocides, and political regimes inflicting torture and atrocities on civilian populations leave severe symptoms in the first generations. These symptoms are depression, alexithymia and anedonia, muscular and bone pain, insomnia and nightmares, with aspects of denial and dissociation. Symptoms are also created in the second and third generations of survivors, with the maximum negative effect on the third generations if the traumatic origin is not elaborated and appropriately healed. Often survivors themselves, many clinicians have analyzed in depth the symptoms of the first generation and the dynamics of transpositions of trauma through future generations (for a synthetic overview and a discussion, see Mucci, 2008, 2013, 2022).

Let me stress here that while the first two levels of traumatizations are very often at the basis of the dynamics shown in their destructiveness by people with personality disorders, the third level is not per se conducive to personality disorders (Mucci, 2018). Nonetheless we should keep in mind that parents who have undergone massive traumatization might not be in optimal condition for the special attunement and the enormous emotional and physical work of taking care of offspring, so that they might become uncaring parents or even abusive parents, with lack of emotional attunement or even performing abuse or depriving behavior, what becomes the first and second levels of traumatizations. If we think of the masses of persecuted, displaced, traumatized people who are in this moment migrating or trying to flee war zones, racial or religious persecution, or are trying to relocate in areas of the planet with better land, better climate or improved living conditions, we can imagine the levels of intergenerational transmission that we are going to face on the planet in the next decades. With the additional problem of overpopulated countries and not enough resources (since 20 percent of the rich people consume 80 percent of the global resources), we need to understand, alleviate, and heal the traumatizations of these parents *right now*.

Level III of Trauma of Human Agency: Massive Social Trauma as in War and Genocide

In the last level of trauma of human agency, the third level, both the individual and societies are hit at once, as in war, genocide, extermination, mass political persecutions and torture, and so on. In order for there to be reparation after trauma, there needs to be practices and dynamics that involve individuals as well as communities in society. The thread that links all of the three levels of traumatizations is the transgression and annihilation of the pact among humans that keeps society safe, the pact of empathy and recognition of humanity in the other. This transgression starts with the first blow from one individual to the other, as well represented by Jean Amery (a philosopher who survived Auschwitz but later took his own life), author of *At the Mind's Limits* (Amery, 1980). The first blow received by another human being, as in torture, cancels the entire trust in the human order and becomes an irremediable scar in the human spirit: it is not only the harm received, but the lack of external support and the break of the human pact of trust and safety that is broken by this kind of trauma that devastates the human mind. Cogently Amery writes: "The expectation of help, the certainty of help, is indeed one of the fundamental experiences of human beings, and probably also of animals" (Amery, 1980, p. 28). *Trauma of human agency at all levels breaks and disrupts the fundamental pact among humans, breaking a bond of trust and hope that the other will indeed conserve my life.* The first blow received when in an abusive relationship especially if in a vulnerable position because of age, sex, or powerlessness, breaks the human pact of keeping one's own and the other's bodily boundaries safe and violates the inner belief that the other human will be considerate of my humanity and will see my vulnerability instead of acting as a ferocious enemy. This is the very foundation of human society. Humans as mammals are socially wired towards forming bonds with similar beings and towards the sustenance of solidarity and reciprocity, which supposedly developed for evolutionary aims. As soon as newborns come out of the womb, they begin looking for the connection with the other, showing a pronounced interest in the voice, the face, the breast, the skin, and the gaze of the mother. Newborns seek an immediate connection with the one who has given them life or with whoever is present and available in the environment.

In the same way, young animals seek protection from an older and stronger other and follow them in order to feel safe, setting forth the behavior that has been called attachment. The attachment figures do not need to be biologically related, provided they seem protective and sensitive enough: any adult who is stronger and looks protective and responds with care is a potential candidate as an attachment/protective figure. This attachment model (relational, not biological, even if imprinted in mammals within the right environmental conditions) sets the internal working models for the subject's future capacity to ask for help in the future, to seek protection if necessary, and to find the best strategies to respond and protect their own young from future difficulties. Being capable in the future to fulfill the same duties for the young and vulnerable who seek protection is a cycle that can become what fosters and reinforces good connections and social behaviors or, on the contrary, in case of abuse and deprivation, will enforce violent and destructive behaviors that will also become transferred intergenerationally through attachment. Ideally, societies should work towards ensuring the establishment of further levels of mental and psychological protection, besides ensuring material and economic safety and development. But violence carried out by nations and collectivities often sanctioned by the states or political authority and groups on the contrary breaks the human pact of solidarity between self and others. If providing safety and protection they break the "we" pact, the human expectancy of acceptance and protection by the other. This pact of care and safety is also at the foundation of the human connectedness, a concept I have described in my previous work (Mucci, 2013). Connectedness both relationally and neurobiologically describes the necessity that individual identity cannot be created if not in a pattern of relationships and interventions of others contributing to the development of the self, that is, is no self without another and vice versa, Judith Butler has reminded us of this with her discussion of what makes for a "grievable life," since our identity is all connected to the living beings that have had a mental place and a meaning for us. Loss makes us all aware of how we are defined and shaped by the other, individuals and collectively (Butler, 2004). As Amery shows, break of the expectation about the feeling of protection and security that will preserve my life in a community, damages forever the trust that the other will keep my life (and the boundaries of my body) safe. This has been described as the core of trauma by Laub and Auerhahn, characterized by "the rupture of the empathic dyad" (Laub & Auerhahn, 1989): the assumption that the other human next to me, not necessarily belonging to my family but just as a fellow of my same human kin, will not harm my life and will instead protect me and come to my aid if I am in need. We need the expectation that are created by secure attachment for the subject, a sort of final gift of having received good parenting. When, as in torture, war, or rape, that fundamental trust and safety are violated, there is almost no going back to this mental place of hope and safety. As survivors often say, they feel they don't belong to the world of humans anymore. The encounter with in-humanity erases hope and trust forever (unless there is social and therapeutic intervention). *To rephrase this concept in psychoanalytic terms, the internal good object, which is the symbolic emotional legacy of good attachment and good child rearing, cannot survive under severe interpersonal or massive traumatizations.* This is what Dori Laub describes with the expression that after trauma of this kind no internal witnessing is possible, there is no other (as there is almost no self) (Laub, 1992 in Felman & Laub, 1992), or in other words, "the third is dead," in the expression of Samuel Gerson (2009). In severe trauma of human agency or in interpersonal traumatization, subjectivity itself is fragmented (Ferenczi, 1933), and the personality is split. As a friend who had been raped at 9 has repeatedly told me, "Once the mug is broken, you can glue the pieces back together, but the mug will never be whole again. It is just a collection of pieces glued together." So, the object is lost and damaged forever. Unity stems from integration and integration has been broken and torn to pieces. It is interesting in this connection that several theories nowadays describe identity and the treatment of personality disorders as a matter of integration of past trauma with present restoration and restoration of broken pieces of personality. The restoration (to safety and hope) somehow will have to include that internal and shattered fragility in order for resilience to be born. Resilience will be a gift of tenderness and renewed care experienced and felt even for the damaged and shattered parts inside, instead of being refused and rejected by the victim. Fragility, as pain and mourning, will have to be accepted, embraced and kept with tenderness inside in order to regain a sense of integrity and adaptability to the human realm afterwards. It is similar to Sophocles' idea expressed in the play of the V century B.C., *Philoctetes* (Sophocles, 2014), where the damage is also part of the strength and the resilience of the subject. It is a process that makes the traumatized victim first accepted (see Neottolemus's attitude who wants to save him while Ulysses wants just to use Philoctetes's strength) and then helps the victim regain power and hope and therefore is very capable of forgiving the others. I believe that the restoration process (which we might call "forgiveness" without any religious hint) means the full elaboration and letting go of the internalization of the identification with a part of oneself as victim (with guilt and shame) and a part of oneself with an internalized persecutor, filled with rage and aggressiveness, often revolved against one self and one's own body, as I have explained in *Beyond Individual and Collective Trauma* (Mucci, 2013). Moreover, the body keeps the signs and the remaining scar that hit the body and the human fragility, exposing its limits. The flexibility of the body and the softness of the human flesh, which make our "delicate bodies" ("the body's delicate" is a famous expression of *King Lear* in the scene of the tempest, 4, 3, Shakespeare, 1608, Act 3 scene 4, verse 15).

Therefore our complexity, an extraordinary factor for the mechanisms of our survival and final resilience, is also marked by its fragility. En passant, it is interesting to notice that what artificial intelligence is trying now to infuse into robots is a kind of softness similar to the bodily shell of humans, starting with receptors similar to the softness of the skin sensitive to pain. In addition, the very fragility of the body is also the matrix and site of resilience and resides also paradoxically in the softness and delicacy of the human body, inhabited by pain, mortal threat, and always potentially prey to other animals. Paradoxically, the body of robots because of their lack of softness and tenderness and receptivity is less adaptive therefore, in so far as their body are not rooted or geared towards survival as we are, our fragility or vulnerability is our strength. Philoctetes is the real hero in the Odyssey because his vulnerability is his strength, contrary to the shrewdness and use of tricks and lying without empathy of Ulysses. The security of a living being is characterized by the integrity of the flesh as a guardian to the integrity of the soul. In trauma both have been threatened and severely damaged. When trust and hope are erased and eradicated, the human spirit is dead. Humans become mere bodies reduced to automatic survival, their vulnerability totally exposed and unredeemable. And yet the frailty of the body (and of the emotional life) is one with its potential for resilience and restoration and cure and its fragility resides in the very humanity and empathic source of our being human, resulting in final resilience) (Mucci, 2022, 2023).

Intergenerational Transmittal

I would like to conclude stressing that, though the third level of trauma of human agency does not create personality disorders, it does influence the actual upbringing of future children and, therefore, of the future generations if there is unelaborated trauma and loss, as often is the case in people who had to suffer extermination and were victims of war. It is this difficulty in the future childrearing that can cause or create insecure attachments or even disorganized attachments. I have described these intergenerational dynamics, following not only my clinical observation but also the expertise of eminent psychoanalysts writing on these dynamics, and theoreticians such as Dori Laub, in previous work to which I refer the reader. Dori Laub, a Shoah survivor himself, has defined pivotal points in the traumatogenic intergenerational transmission especially in cases of massive social traumata. Trauma of this interpersonal kind is characterized by dynamics of traumatic "knowing-not knowing," (Laub & Auerhahn, 1993), suggesting that the body is aware at implicit level of the traumatic effects but explicit and declarative knowledge of trauma is impossible precisely for the dissociated or erased aspects of it. Laub and Auerhahn (1989) describe the traumatogenic mechanism as the rupture of the empathic dyad and the impossibility of going back to an internalized good object that gets destroyed in the presence of traumata of human agency. Trauma is therefore characterized by a specific nonfigurability and ineffable status, as if an internal witness had been destroyed, and the possible retrieval of the original traumatization is possible only in the presence of a totally present and fully committed other. This quest for what I call "a testimonial community" for social and individual traumatization and this call for an ethical stance of the psychotherapist position in fact is in coherence with Ferenczi's admonition to the therapist who, in contrast with Freud's cold and neutral stance, should be empathic, fully present and actively committed (Rachman, 1997a, 2018b, 2022). Trauma also follows an internal process of intergenerational transmittance through the identification of the alive with the dead and through the children's stepping into the wishes of the parents and of other relatives, through dynamics of projective identification, dissociative displacements and reversals. According to Laub, there certainly is an unconscious principle of traumatic transmission between and among generations. These transmissions might happen through silent dissociative splits and identification with the split parts of the parents (through attachment, as we have explained and through the limbic system being "downloaded" (Schore's term) between mother and child. In addition, in my own opinion, it is likely that the second generation might "inherit" not only the traumatic content symbolically but a phantasmatic wish to elaborate the traumatizations that the first generation have actually undergone in reality (Mucci, 2013). This explanation is not far from the symbolic and phantasmatic kernel of the trauma inherited by the second generation through the mysterious "crypt" encysted intersubjectively (Abraham & Torok, 1994). Children psychologically "inherit" the problematic themes and issues of the parents, through the porous and labile boundaries of the traumatized parents (who might have dissociated, denied the trauma or might have alexithymically displaced and removed it). Boundary problems are always in the traumatized and as a consequence in the following generations, what is also among the problems of borderline subjects. Moreover, since role reversals are very common in second generations of trauma, these individuals might have the need to care for the parents and repair for them their trauma (as is very often the case in AAI of children whose parents are survivors of massive traumata) (Mucci, 2018).

Symptoms in Trauma Related Disorder

Different studies show a connection between stressful events, especially in childhood and in future pathological responses to life events. Having undergone psychological, physical and/or sexual abuse in childhood individuals develop a higher risk or a vulnerability towards the pathological conditions in adult life (mental disorders, obesity, diabetes, cardiovascular disease).

Given the direct effect of the affective bond on the development of areas and circuits linked to empathy, relationship with others and implicit models of self-other, self-esteem, capacity for self-care and altruism, cognitive, social, affective, and emotional development, people who have been severely deprived or abused are at risk of developing depression, anxiety, dissociation, personality disorders, compulsive disorders, obesity and eating. To conclude, as Schore (2012) writes about attachment trauma patients (whom he defines as personality disorder patients):

> The patient brings into treatment an enduring imprint of attachment trauma: an impaired capacity to regulate stressful affect and an over-reliance on the affect-deadening defense of pathological dissociation [and many others]. Under relational stress this affect disregulation deficit is characterologically expressed in a tendency toward low-threshold, high-intensity, emotional reactions followed by slow return to baseline. Highs and lows are too extreme, too prolonged, or too rapidly cycled and unpredictable. Patients with histories of attachment trauma (i.e. personality disorders) thus contain unconscious insecure working models that automatically trigger right brain stress responses at low thresholds of ruptures of the therapeutic alliance. In addition to their hypersensitivity to even low levels of interpersonal threat (narcissistic injuries), they also frequently experience enduring states of high-intensity negative affect and defensively dissociate at lower levels of stressful arousal.
>
> (p. 164)

I see the bodily attacks and the bodily symptoms of borderline personality disorders, including eating disorders (with the exception of anorexia mostly) and addiction to alcohol, drugs, internet, and compulsive sexual behaviors as forms of traumatic origin sometimes even intergenerationally influenced (Mucci, 2018).

Note

1 The traumatic origin of personality disorders is a very controversial issue, difficult to prove through research but filled with clinical truth. It is the major thesis of *Borderline Bodies* and evident in my personal experience with clinical work with borderline personality disorders. About narcissistic patients, the new book on TFP for narcissistic personality disorders do stress the traumatic origin of the psychopathology (see Diamond, Yeomans, Stern and Kernberg, 2022).

References

Abraham, N. and Torok, M. (1994). *The Shell and the Kernel* (Ed., Trans., and with an introduction by N.T. Rand). Chicago, IL: Chicago University Press (Original work published 1987).

Ainsworth, M. and Eichberg, C. (1991). Effects on infant-mother attachment of mother's unresolved loss of an attachment figure or other traumatic experience. In Marris, P., Stevenson-Hinde, J. and Parkes, C. (Eds.) *Attachment across the Life Cycle*. New York: Routledge, pp. 160–183.

Amery, J. (1980). *At the Mind's Limits: Contemplations by a Survivor on Auschwitz and Its Realities* (S. Rosenfeld and S.P. Rosenfelt, Trans.). Bloomington, IN: Indiana University Press.

Ammaniti, M. and Stern, D.M. (1992). *Attaccamento e psicoanalisi*. Roma-Bari: Laterza.

APA (American Psychiatric Association). (2017). *Diagnostic and Statistical Manual of Mental Disorders* (5th ed., DSM-5). Washington, DC. American Psychiatric Association.

Bateman, A. and Fonagy, P. (2004). Mentalization based treatment of BPD. *Journal of Personality Disorders*. 18(1): 36–51.

Bromberg, P.M. (2011). *The Shadow of the Tsunami and the Growth of the Relational Mind*. New York: Routledge.

Butler, J. (2004). *Precarious Life. The Powers of Mourning and Violence*. London and New York: Verso.

Carlson, E. and Sroufe, L.A. (1995). Contribution of attachment theory to developmental psychopathology. In Cicchetti, D. and Cohen, D.J. (Eds.) *Developmental Psychopathology* (Vol. 1, Issue 25). New York: Wiley, pp. 581–617.

Cozolino, L. (2002). *The Neuroscience of Psychotherapy: Building and Rebuilding the Human Brain (Norton Series on Interpersonal Neurobiology)*. New York: W. W. Norton & Company.

Craig, A.D. (2004). Human feelings: Why are some more aware than others? *Trends in Cognitive Sciences*. 8(6): 239–241.

Diamond, A. and Doar, B. (1989). The performance of human infants on a measure of frontal cortex function, the delayed response task. *Developmental Psychology*. 22(3): 271–294.

Eisenberg, M.A. (1995). The limits of cognition and the limits of contract. *Stanford Law Review*, 211–259.

Felitti, V.J., Anda, R.F., Nordenberg, D., Williamson, D.F., Spitz, A.M., Edwards, V. and Marks, J.S. (1998). Relationship of childhood abuse and household dysfunction to many of the leading causes of death in adults: The Adverse Childhood Experiences (ACE) study. *American Journal of Preventative Medicine*. 14(4): 245–258.

Felman, S. and Laub, D. (1992). *Testimony: Crisis of Witnessing in Literature, Psychoanalysis and History*. New York and London: Routledge.

Ferenczi, S. (1929). The unwelcome child and his death instinct. *International Journal of Psycho-Analysis*. 10: 125–129.

Ferenczi, S. (1933). The Confusion of Tongues between adults and children: The language of tenderness and passion. In Balint, M. (Ed.) *Final Contributions to the Problems and Methods of Psychoanalysis* (E. Moscher, Trans.). New York: Bruner/Mazel, 1980, pp. 156–167.

Ferenczi, S. (1988). *The Clinical Diary of Sándor Ferenczi* (J. Dupont, Ed., M. Balint and N.Z. Jackson, Trans.). Cambridge, MA: Harvard University Press.

Fonagy, P. and Bateman, A.W. (2006). Mechanisms of change in mentalization-based treatment of BPD. *Journal of Clinical Psychology*. 62(4): 411–430.

Fonagy, P., Steele, H. and Steele, M. (1991). Maternal representations of attachment during pregnancy predict the organization of infant mother attachment at one year of age. *Child Development*. 62(5): 891–905.

Fonagy, P., Steele, M., Steele, H., Higgit, A., Target, M. (1992). The theory and practice of resilience. *Journal of Child Psychology and Psychiatry*. 35(2): 231–257.

Fraiberg, S., Adelson, E. and Shapiro, V. (1975). Ghosts in the nursery: A psychoanalytic approach to the problems of impaired mother-infant relationships. *Journal of the American Academy of Child Psychiatry*. 14: 378–421.

Gabbard, G. (2000). *Psychodynamic Psychiatry in Clinical Practice*. New York; Arlington, VA: American Psychiatric Publications.

Gerson, S. (2009). When the third is dead: Memory, mourning, and witnessing in the aftermath of the Holocaust. *The International Journal of Psychoanalysis*. 90(6): 1341–1357.

Green, A. (1993). *Le Travail du négatif*. Paris: Les Éditions de Minuit.

Gubrich-Simitis, I. (1981). Extreme traumatization as cumulative trauma: Psychoanalytic investigation of the effects of concentration camp experiences on survivors and their children. *The Psychoanalytic Study of the Child*. 36: 415–450.

Gunderson, J.G. (2008). *Borderline Personality Disorder: A Clinical Guide*. Washington, DC: American Psychiatric Press.

Henry, J.P. (1993). Psychological and physiological responses to stress: The right hemisphere and the hypothalomo-pituitary-adrenal axis, an inquiry into problems of human bonding. *Integrative Physiological and Behavioral Science*. 28: 369–387.

Hesse, E. and Main, M. (2000). Disorganized infant, child, and adult attachment: Collapse in behavioral and attention strategies. *Journal of the American Psychoanalytic Association*. 48: 1097–1127.

Hesse, E., Main, M., Abrams, K. and Rifkin, A. (2003). Unresolved states regarding loss and abuse can have "second generation" effects: Disorganized, role-inversion and frightening ideation in the offspring of traumatized non-maltreating parents. In Solomon, M.F. and Siegel, D.J. (Eds.) *Healing Trauma: Attachment, Mind, Body and Brain*. New York: W. W. Norton & Company, pp. 57–106.

Hugdahl, K. (1995). Classical conditioning and implicit learning: The right hemisphere hypothesis. In Davidson, R.J. and Hugdahl, K. (Eds.) *Brain Asymmetry*. Cambridge, MA: MIT Press, pp. 235–267.

ICD-11 (2021). *International Classification of Diseases* (11th ed.). Geneva: World Health Organization.

Kernberg, O.F. (1975). *Borderline Conditions and Pathological Narcissism*. New York: Aronson.

Kernberg, O.F. (1976). Technical considerations in the treatment of borderline personality organization. *Journal of the American Psychoanalytic Association.* 24(4): 795–829.

Lanius, R.A., Vermetten, E. and Pain, C. (2010). *The Impact of Early Life Trauma on Health and Disease: The Hidden Epidemic.* Cambridge: Cambridge University Press.

Laub, D. (2005). From speechlessness to narrative: The cases of Holocaust historians and of psychiatrically hospitalized survivors. *Literature and Medicine.* 24: 253–265.

Laub, D. and Auerhahn, N.C. (1989). Failed empathy: A central theme in the survivor's Holocaust experience. *Psychoanalytic Psychology.* 6: 377–400.

Laub, D. and Auerhahn, N.C. (1993). Knowing and not knowing massive psychic trauma: Forms of traumatic memory. *International Journal of Psycho-Analysis.* 74: 287–302.

Lingiardi, V. and McWilliams, N. (Eds.) (2017). *Psychodynamic Diagnostic Manual: PDM-2.* New York: The Guilford Press.

Liotti, G. (1995). Disorganized/disoriented attachment in the psychotherapy of the dissociative disorders.

Liotti, G. and Farina, B. (2011). *Sviluppi traumatici: Eziopatogenesi, clinica e terapia della dimensione dissociativa.* Milan: Raffaello Cortina.

Liotti, G., Intreccialagli, B. and Cerere, F. (1991). Esperienza di lutto nella madre e predisposizione ai disturbi dissociativi nella prole: uno studio caso-controllo. *Rivista di Psichiatria.* 26: 283–291.

Lyons-Ruth, K. and Block, D. (1996). The disturbed caregiving system: Relations among childhood trauma, maternal caregiving, and infant affect and attachment. *Infant Mental Health Journal.* 17: 257–275.

Lyons-Ruth, K., Yellin, C., Melnick, S. and Atwood, G. (2003). Childhood experiences of trauma and loss have different relations to maternal unresolved and hostile-helpless states of mind on the AAI. *Attachment and Human Development.* 5: 330–352.

Main, M. and Hesse, E. (1990). Parents' unresolved traumatic experiences are related to infant disorganized attachment status: Is frightened and/or frightening parental behavior the linking mechanism? In Greenberg, M.T., Cicchetti, D. and Cunnings, E.M. (Eds.) *Attachment in the Preschool Years: Theory, Research, Intervention.* Chicago, IL: University of Chicago Press.

Markowitsch, H.J., Reinkemeier, A., Kessler, J., Koyunciu, A. and Heiss, W.-D. (2000). Right amygdala and temperofrontal activation during autobiographical, but not fictitious, memory retrieval. *Behavioral Neurology.* 12: 181–190.

Modell, A. (1990). *Other Times, Other Realities: Towards a Theory of Psychoanalytic Treatment.* Cambridge, MA: Harvard University Press.

Mucci, C. (2008). *Il dolore estremo: Il trauma da Freud alla Shoah.* Rome: Borla.

Mucci, C. (2013). *Beyond Individual and Collective Trauma: Intergenerational Transmission, Psychoanalytic Treatment, and the Dynamics of Forgiveness.* London: Karnac Books.

Mucci, C. (2017). Ferenczi's revolutionary therapeutic approach. *American Journal of Psychoanalysis*. 77(3): 239–254.

Mucci, C. (2018). *Borderline Bodies: Affect Regulation Therapy for Personality Disorders (Norton Series on Interpersonal Neurobiology)*. New York: W. W Norton & Company.

Mucci, C. (2020). A right-brain dissociative model for right-brain disorders: Dissociation vs repression in borderline and other severe psychopathologies of early traumatic origin. In *The Divided Therapist*. London: Routledge, pp. 202–227.

Mucci, C. (2021). Dissociation vs repression: A new neuropsychoanalytic model for psychopathology. *The American Journal of Psychoanalysis*. 81(1): 82–111.

Mucci, C. (2022). *Resilience and Survival. Understanding and Healing Intergenerational Trauma*. London: Confer Books.

Mucci, C. (2023) *Ereditare la terra. Pratiche per una resilienza politica*. Milano: Raffaello Cortina Editore.

Panskepp, J. (2012). *The Archaeology of Mind. Neuroevolutionary Origins of Human Emotions*. New York: W. W. Norton & Company.

Panskepp, J. and Biven, E. (2012). A meditation on the affective neuroscientific view of human and animalian mind-brains. In Fotopoulou, A., Pfaff, D. and Conway, M.A. (Eds.) *From the Couch to the Lab: Trends in Psychodynamic Neuroscience*, pp. 145–175.

Rachman, A.W. (1994). The Confusion of Tongues theory: Ferenczi's legacy to psychoanalysis. In Haynal, A. and Falzeder, E. (Eds.) *100 Years of Psychoanalysis*. London: Karnac Books, pp. 235–255.

Rachman, A.W. (1997a). *Sándor Ferenczi: The Psychotherapist of Tenderness and Passion*. Northvale, NJ: Jason Aronson.

Rachman, A.W. (1997b). The suppression and censorship of Ferenczi's Confusion of Tongues paper. *Psychoanalytic Inquiry (Psychoanalysis' Favorite Son: The Legacy of Sándor Ferenczi)*. 17(4): 459–485.

Rachman, A.W. (2005). Curing the Confusion of Tongues in adolescent group psychotherapy. *Journal of Counseling and Psychotherapy*. 3.

Rachman, A.W. (2018a). *Elizabeth Severn: The "Evil Genius" of Psychoanalysis*. London: Routledge.

Rachman, A.W. (2018b). Ferenczi's confusion of tongues: A regressive idea conceived by a madman or one of the most important papers in the history of psychoanalysis. *Proposal. International Sándor Ferenczi Conference*. Florence, May 2–6.

Rachman, A.W. (2019a). The psychoanalysis between Sándor Ferenczi and Elizabeth Severn: Mutuality, unconscious communication and the development of countertransference analysis. *Psychoanalytic Inquiry*. 39(3–4): 1–6.

Rachman, A.W. (2019b). The Confusion of Tongues: Sándor and the Budapest School of Psychoanalysis: A revolutionary paradigm shift in psychoanalysis. *Presentation, Irish Psychoanalytic Society*. Dun Laoghaire, May 10.

Rachman, A.W. (2022). *Psychoanalysis and Society's Neglect of Sexual Abuse of Children, Youth, and Adults: Reassessing Freud's Original Theory of Sexual Abuse and Trauma*. London: Routledge Press.

Rachman, A.W. and Klett, S. (2015). *Analysis of the Incest Trauma: Retrieval, Recovery, Renewal*. London: Karnac Books.

Raz, A. (2004). Anatomy of attentional networks. *The Anatomical Record*. 281(1): 21–36.

Sasso, G. (2011). *La nascita della coscienza*. Rome: Astrolabio.

Schiffer, F., Teicher, M. and Papanicolaou, A. (1995). Evoked potentials evidence for right brain activity during recall of traumatic memories. *Journal of Neuropsychiatry and Clinical Neuroscience*. 7: 169–175.

Schore, A.N. (1994). *Affect Regulation and the Origin of the Self: The Neurobiology of Emotional Development*. Mahwah, NJ: Erlbaum.

Schore, A.N. (1997). Early organization of the nonlinear right brain and development of a predisposition to psychiatric disorders. *Development and Psychopathology*. 9(4): 595–631.

Schore. A.N. (2000). Attachment and the regulation of the right brain. *Attachment and Human Development*. 2: 23–47.

Schore, A.N. (2001). The effects of early relational trauma on right brain development, affect regulation and infant mental health. *Infant Mental Health Journal*. 22(1–2): 201–269.

Schore, A.N. (2003a). *Affect Regulation and the Repair of the Self*. New York: W. W. Norton & Company.

Schore, A.N. (2003b). *Affect Dysregulation and Disorders of the Self*. New York: W. W. Norton & Company.

Schore, A.N. (2010). *Relational Trauma and the Developing Right Brain: The Neurobiology of Broken Attachment Bonds*.

Schore, A.N. (2011). The right brain implicit self lies at the core of psychoanalysis. *Psychoanalytic Dialogues*. 21: 75–100.

Schore, A.N. (2012). *The Science of the Art of Psychotherapy (Norton Series on Interpersonal Neurobiology)*. New York: W. W. Norton & Company.

Schore, A.N. (2019a). *The Development of the Unconscious Mind (Norton Series on Interpersonal Neurobiology)*. New York: W. W. Norton & Company.

Schore, A.N. (2019b). *Right Brain Psychotherapy (Norton Series on Interpersonal Neurobiology)*. New York: W. W. Norton & Company.

Schore, A.N. (2000). Attachment and the regulation of the right brain. *Attachment and Human Development*. 2: 23–47.

Shakespeare, W. (1608). *King Lear. The Norton Shakespeare* (S. Greenblatt et al., Ed.). New York: W. W. Norton & Company, 1997.

Siegel, D.J. (1999). *The Relational Mind*. New York: Guilford Press.

Solomon, J. and George, C. (Eds.) (1999). *Attachment Organization*. New York: Guilford Press.

Sophocles (2014). *Philoctetes* (P. Woodruff, Translation and Introduction). Indianapolis, IN: Hackett Publishing Co.

Spitz, R. (1945). Hospitalism: An inquiry into the genesis of psychiatric conditions in early childhood. *Psychoanalytic Study of the Child*. 1: 53–74.

Symonds, M.E., Stephenson, T., Gardner, D.S. and Budge, H. (2006). Long-term effects of nutritional programming of the embryo and fetus: Mechanisms and critical windows. *Reproduction, Fertility and Development*. 19(1): 53–63.

Tronick, E., Als, H., Adamson, L., Wise, S. and Brazelton, T.H. (1978). The infant's response to entrapment between contradictory messages in face-to face interaction. *Academy of Child Psychiatry*. 17(1): 1–13.

Tsakiris, M., Costantini, M. and Haggard, P. (2008). The role of the right termpero-parietal junction in maintaining a coherent sense of one's body. *Neuropsychologia*. 46: 3014–3018.

Tutté, J.C. (2004). The concept of psychological trauma: A bridge in interdisciplinary space. *International Journal of Psycho-Analysis*. 85: 897–921.

Van der Kolk, B. (2014). *The Body Keeps the Score: Mind, Brain and Body in the Transformation of Trauma*. London: Penguin.

Van Ijzendoorn, M.H., Bakermans-Kranenburg, M.J. and Ebstein, R.P. (2011). Methylation matters in child development: Toward developmental behavioral epigenetics. *Child Development Perspectives*. 5(4): 305–310.

van Ijzendorn, M., Palacio, J. et al. (2011). Children in institutional care: delayed development and resilience. *Monograph of the Society for Research in Child Development*. 76(4): 8–30.

Zanarini, M.C., Williams, A.A., Lewis, R.E., et al. (1997). Reported pathological childhood experiences associated with the development of borderline personality disorder. *American Journal of Psychiatry*. 154: 1101–1106.

Chapter 15

Therapy for Trauma of Human Agency

"What Has Been Damaged in a Relationship Needs to be Healed in a Relationship"

Clara Mucci

In a two-person psychology with the theoretical extension of psychoanalysis as we have presented it, following the guidelines of Ferenczi, the analysand is continuously engaged and responding to the ongoing dual communication of the therapeutic process, both consciously and unconsciously. More than trying to resolve repression, in the session with severely traumatized patients there will be patterns of re-enactments of trauma and unconscious material in the here and now, so that dissociated or denied and unreachable parts, unconscious also in the sense explained of unrepressed unconscious (of earlier formation or of dissociative origin) will return in the dual communication of right brain to right brain (see Schore, 2012, 2019a), and these mnestic traces and implicit behaviors may be finally cleared out, thanks also to the momentarily "embodiment" of the emotions of the traumatic core in the therapist (first through bodily perceptions, than through the psychological, mental and verbal expressions that will be received consciously and unconsciously information, as I will explain, in the process of "embodied witnessing"). As Ferenczi writes: "The task of the therapist is to bring the psyche back to life out of these ashes" (April 7, 1932, *Clinical Diary*, Ferenczi, 1988, p. 82). [In addition] "The psyche that has been fragmented or pulverized by trauma feels love, cleansed of all ambivalence, flowing towards it and developing it, as if with a kind of glue: fragments come together into. Larger units; the entire personality may succeed in becoming united (homogeneous)" (January 17, 1932, Ferenczi, 1988, p. 12).

The therapists will empathically attune themselves to receive all information, work through corporeally (even through activation of the polyvagal system, Porges, 2011), as in the cases when the therapists themselves feel pain, headache, stomach-ache or even experience bowel movements and nausea,

DOI: 10.4324/9781003265030-15

as it has often happened to me in highly charged moments of recollections of trauma, especially early or violent interpersonal trauma. The difficulty of the well trained and empathic therapists consists in allowing themselves to be momentarily disregulated and "transformed" in order to tune in and allow expressing at all levels the past experiences encoded in mind and body in the patient. The therapist might feel pain, physical or emotional, to the point of even having tears. Ferenczi recommends not to conceal our emotions:

> Should it even occur, as it does occasionally to me, that experiencing another's and my own suffering brings a tear to my eye. One should not conceal this emotion from the patient, then the tears of doctor and of patient mingle in a sublimated communion, which perhaps finds its analogy only in the mother-child relationship. And this is the healing agent, which, like a kind of glue, binds together permanently the intellectually assembled fragments, surrounding even the personality thus repaired with a new aura of vitality and optimism.
>
> (20 March 1932, Ferenczi, 1988, p. 65)

It is the "glue" of the emotional participation and love that allows the intellectual understanding to be held inside and to become the effective integrative element for the broken pieces.

According to the neuroscientific explanation presented by Allan Schore in his more recent research, dissociation in severe traumatization is primarily a right brain dynamic, while repression seems to be a left brain dynamic, in coherence with the fact that both repression and the left brain are further developments of the human mind and imply a more developed being (Schore, 2019a, 2019b). When carried out by an expert analyst, psychotherapy should allow a mutual regressive movement in which the two unconsciouses (and right hemispheres) will be in contact, in a mutual conversation, both conscious and unconscious, in a process not distant from what Ferenczi had envisioned. This positive or induced regression[1] gives the opportunity to the patient to express the negative emotions buried and unexpressed (in connection with denied or even dissociated parts of consciousness) while at the same time allowing the committed and expert and empathically tuned psychotherapist to observe, name, and validate the emotions of the patient in the process of retrieving or re-experiencing the negative patterns and dysfunctional attitudes towards the self and towards the other, going back to a negative and traumatic imprinting. The therapy needs to move on towards a more positive imprinting of a new relationship, since "abreaction," to echo Ferenczi, is not enough. Rachman (2018, 2022) explains very cogently the necessity for noninterpretive measures. It is the necessity for the use of an empathic clinical nurturing attitude, not a matter of intellectually "coming to know" what went wrong in the past when clarifying or decoding the confusion and the unelaborated emotions. Intellectual and interpretative practices are imbued with the power of those who really presume to know (as happens unfortunately in many therapeutic encounters), imposing a kind for truth onto the other subject, considered more vulnerable, weaker, fragile and therefore not capable of knowing or expressing their own truth.

The patient needs to reappropriate, emotionally and through the encoding of a new meaning in the dyadic experience – both in the sense that the relationship of the past referred to a child or a helpless being, while now the subject has a different awareness and power, and in the sense that the new relationship of trust and care with the therapist allows a rewriting and reappropriation of the emotional truth of the past – the pieces of the story that have been deleted because of shame, guilt, anger, dissociation due to extreme stress and overwhelming emotions. This is possible within the stability and safety of the long-term therapeutic work, thanks to the emotional, availability, attunement and ethical attitude of the committed therapist, sensitively involved but capable of going very deeply in the involvement without losing boundaries or control of the emotions involved in both. In this two-person psychoanalysis, a path that Ferenczi opened with his clinical practice and his writings, the therapist is in the place of a real committed other, which was missing in the past, a witness to the traumatizations of the past as they are reenacted in the here and now of the psychoanalytic process. It is through this new relational positive experience, inscribing a new trace even in the neurobiological and mental circuits, that healing is achieved, self-esteem restored through the regained integrity of pieces and parts of one's own story with the awareness of what has actually happened but can now be taken in, cleared out of the negative emotional and dysregulating impact. It is not the Freudian common view of "making conscious the unconscious" because we are not speaking of a repressed unconscious for severe borderline patients but rather of the unrepressed unconscious, something that was primary and earlier than the repressed unconscious and also something that could not be repressed because of extreme traumatization and dissociation, while repression is a further developmental defense. The analytic movement needs to be in tune with these primary or earlier or underdeveloped parts of emotional experience. Dissociation is first and foremost a way of casting out of the process of identity formation unacceptable truths and contents. Therefore it is not a matter of making conscious what was repressed but of regaining emotional integrity of displaced dissociated parts. I strongly agree with Liotti and Farina (2011) when they write:

> It is worth stressing that the purpose of treating traumatic memories is not to help the surfacing of repressed content, rather, to reconstruct the lived events in their integrity, to associate the different fragmented components (emotional, sensorial motorial, cinestesic, cognitive), to assimilate them and to enable their integration into the autobiographical narration for the patient, in order to avoid or to reduce their disorganizing effect.
>
> (Liotti & Farina, 2011, p. 181, translation from the Italian for this edition)

As Ferenczi warns us, if everything remains on the intellectual level, the patient remains in his distorted conviction: "It cannot be true that all this is happening to me, or someone would come to my aid" and the patient prefers to doubt his own judgment rather than believe in our coldness, or lack of intelligence, or in simpler terms, our stupidity and nastiness" (Ferenczi, 1988, p. 25).

A committed and empathic other is the only one capable of redeeming the pain of the past and restituting the truth that has been erased or canceled. Differently from Freud's "hypocrisy" as Ferenczi called his analyst's attitude, a committed and empathic witness, as Ferenczi wrote. It allows a repetition "with difference," repeating the phrase of Joel Fineman (1989, p.108). This refers to the retrieval of the dissociated and missing parts that are nonetheless distorting the behavior and the consciousness, distorting even the cognition of what has really happened. The importance of this committed other holding an empathic attitude in order for the past wounds to be healed is unmistakable in this famous passage by Ferenczi and is so much in advance of his time:

> It appears that patients cannot believe that an event really took place, or cannot fully believe it, if the analyst, as the *sole witness* of the events, persists in his cool, unemotional, and as patients are fond of

stating, purely intellectual attitude, while the events are of a kind that must evoke, in anyone present, emotions of revulsion, anxiety, terror, vengeance, grief, and the urge to render immediate help. . . . One therefore has a choice: to take really seriously the role one assumes, of *the benevolent and helpful observer*, that is, actually to transport oneself with the patient into that period of the past (a practice Freud reproached me for, as being not permissible), with the result that we ourselves and the patient believe in its reality, which has not momentarily transposed into the past.

(Ferenczi, 1988, p. 24)

The therapist works as a benevolent and helpful witness to past traumatic events which have inscribed distorted and destructive visions of self and other. This is the basis of a kind of mind-body-therapy for the survival of interpersonal trauma and violence that I have defined "embodied witnessing," since analysts first and foremost has to take part in the dual relationship with all of their conscious, unconscious and bodily presence and commitment. I describe this process in my previous work devoted to clinical cases (Mucci, 2018) whose etiopathogenesis is based in interpersonal trauma and dissociation, therefore they suffer from the consequences of complex PTDS, not PTSD as in the DSM, and have consequently developed personality disorders.

Briefly, the presence of a committed other, empathically connected and ethically present, physically engaged with mind, body, voice, gaze, and so on, creates the space for an internal other who can witness the emotionally unbearable contents of the events while at the same time helping to reconstruct a sensitive, internal object that is benign and caring. The presence of that emotionally tuned in and caring other renders that reconnection internal and external, physical and psychical, neurobiological and spiritual, a sort of sacred event, creating a sacred human space of retrieval, memory, going through and a possible road towards acceptance and finally forgiving, intrapsychically and possibly interpersonally (Mucci, 2013). In contrast to Freud's view of a neutral (verging on, hypocritical) therapeutic attitude, Ferenczi in his *Clinical Diary* expressed the necessity of making the therapeutic exchange a kind of testimony, where the therapist is able to testify to the patient's life experiences, restoring life and truth through the therapist's own benevolent, complete, and committed presence:

The analyst is able, for the first time, to link emotions with the above primal event and thus endow that event with the feeling of a real experience. Simultaneously the patient succeeds in gaining insight, far more penetrating than before, into the reality of these events that have been repeated so often on an intellectual level.

(Ferenczi, 1988, pp. 13–14)

In his *Clinical Diary* and in his article "Confusion of Tongues" (1933), Ferenczi, before the horrible experiences of the Second World War and the new understanding of traumatization that came about both in theory and in practice after that event, shows a surprisingly modern understanding of emotional tuning, testimony, and bodily participation on the part of the therapist, in which it is through the emotions of the therapist and his or her active participation (right hemisphere) that the patients finally gets in touch with his or her own disconnected parts. The work of the analyst through their embodied participation, as the integration of right-brain theory, polyvagal theory, and Ferenczi's understanding have shown, is such that not only does it give back to the patient a restored sense of emotional truth of what has happened in early experiences, but also, through the therapist's role as witness, emotional truth is acknowledged and recognized – or finally "known" if we use the model of the "knowing–not knowing" reality typical of trauma, according to Laub and Auerhahn (1993) – instead of being acted out in destructiveness and symptomatic actions.

The Body in the Two-Person Psychoanalysis

Through neuroscience, neurophysiology, and interpersonal neurobiology, we now understand why the body can be considered the second channel of information in the therapeutic communication (as Kernberg states in the treatment he devised for personality disorders, Clarkin et al., 1998). Countertransference can be a channel for the reception of the total emotions between two bodies–mind–brain entities in therapy and through the exchange taking place by way of the right brain. Nonverbal communication in therapy was also first analyzed and commented on by Ferenczi (Rachman, 1997). The way the patients position their body during the session and in various meaningful moments is of great importance, as it is the result of a complex functioning and interrelation of the cortical, subcortical, and neural innervation that constitutes the base of the self and the maintenance of self-esteem. The position of the body and what the body in its polyvagal interaction conveys constitute one of the three channels of communication, as Otto Kernberg explains, and is a major instrument in therapy for obtaining information about the continual transference–countertransference tuning of the two protagonists of the dyadic exchange. As Kernberg points out in considering the value of body information, the voice might recount one thing, and the body will confirm or deny what is being said. The patient might express one emotion, for instance, hiding resentment or even hostility, but the body speaks another language, sometimes in opposition to it, and might take a defiant or withdrawn and hostile pose. We lose a great deal of important information if we do not have the patient in front of us available and visible in the interaction as the therapeutic exchange takes place. It is not only a verbal interaction but also a bodily, face-to-face, interchange, in addition to the fact that fundamental movements for dyadic regulation that the therapy can provide would be partially lacking or greatly depleted and diminished. With nonneurotic patients, it is necessary to construct a language that allows "corporality to speak" (Lombardi, 2016), precisely because the severe nonneurotic patient has fewer "symbolic levels of expression to bring into therapy: not only might the language be less metaphoric, but also the bulk of the information might be precisely in the behavior – in the attitude and posture of the body and in the corporeal quality of the exchange (with psychotic patients, even the peculiar odor of the body becomes a means of communication).

This is also what Bucci (1997) refers to when she talks about the emotional and embodied communication in the therapeutic relationship, especially with severe, nonneurotic patients, who represent the great majority of the persons seeking treatment at present. Therapy at its best allows the expression and the recognition and acceptance of sub-symbolic, corporeal, and sensorial modalities of expression that constitute a new imprinting in the body–mind–brain system and are reinforced constantly by the rhythmic cadence of the therapy and the regularity of the scheduled encounters of the treatment. For severe personality disordered patients, this regular rhythm and established bond of trust (even with the difficulties that a disorganized or at least insecure attachment will necessarily posit in the first few months of treatment) is the major instrument towards the beginning of the formation of a continuity of internalized good objects, a basis for a structured and harmonious self.

The Neuroscience of the Face-To-Face Technique for Severe Personality Disorders

Ferenczi's *Clinical Diary* (Ferenczi, 1988) and his controversial article "Confusion of the Tongues" (Ferenczi, 1933) have paved the way for a relational move in psychoanalysis and for the two-person psychology that is our theoretical basis today. Therefore, the new paradigm shift in psychoanalysis implies a going back to Ferenczi (Mucci, 2013; Rachman, 2019). He demonstrated a surprisingly modern understanding of emotional tuning, clinical empathy, testimony, and bodily participation on the part of the therapist, in which it is through the emotions of the therapist and their active participation (right hemisphere) that the patients finally get in touch with their own disconnected parts. It is the affective participation of the analyst that allows the retrieval of the hidden disguised repressed or dissociated parts and allows to resolve the fragmentation of the personality. Fragmentation, in fact, is what Ferenczi highlights as the result of the assault on the child by people of trust or attachment figures, what we now understand as dissociation, followed, in his own words, by a "permanent split in the personality" (Ferenczi, 1988). On March 25, 1932 ("Psychic Bandage"), Ferenczi describes how the painful experience from the environment leaves a permanent mark, a "split in the personality" as a form of adaptation, "a change in their behavior":

> From the moment when bitter experience teaches us to lose faith in the benevolence of the environment, a permanent split in the personality occurs. . . . Actual trauma is experienced by children in situations where no immediate remedy is provided and where adaptation, that is, a change in their own behaviour, is forced on them – the first step towards establishing the differentiation between inner and outer world, subject and object. From then on, neither subjective nor objective experience alone will be perceived as an integral emotional unit.
>
> (Ferenczi, 1988, p. 69)

This last excerpt clarifies how the effect of trauma and the split of the self-experiencing it, which has to fragment itself in order to survive, results in a blurring of boundaries between reality and nonreality, about what is real and what comes to be believed as truth, and about what is perceived as internal and what is external. This is to say, in terms of Freud that "the essence of a traumatic situation is an experience of helplessness

[Hilflosichkeit] on the part of the ego in the face of accumulation of excitation, whether of external or internal origin", and it implies a distinction that is not possible for the traumatized self. We have already seen with the concept of identification with the aggressor in Ferenczi theory more a kind of incorporation, rather than a defense (as it was for Anna Freud) that something external becomes internalized.

This blurring of boundaries between self and other implies a second consequence of the damages of trauma for the self, that is, the impossibility for the subject to clearly ascertain the truth, which might result in a permanent distortion of reality. We clearly see this behavior in the borderline patients, for instance, where reality testing in theory is retained but where the distortions of reality are very severe and impair the patient's capacity to live a fulfilling life. This kind of personality disorder with distortion of truth and blurring of boundaries between inside and outside, self and other, is typical of abuse, both psychological and physical or sexual, the main example of this being incest. As Ruth Leys (2004) has written, more fundamental than any other traumatogenic factor, including the actual sexual assault to which Ferenczi gave rightly so much weight: "was the lie and the hypocrisy of adults that, forcing the child to doubt her own judgment about the reality of her experience, fragmented and hystericized her" (p. 153) and, I would add, condemned her to silence and compliance. I would rephrase this in other words, saying simply that what the child is deprived of is their own truth in connection with her experience of an event that is, at its core relational, and the implication of this is that the distortion is going to be repeated, without the child's being aware of it, in future relationships including the analytic one. As Lewis Kirshner (1993) writes, "trauma impairs the child's capacity to evaluate reality, a tendency which may subsequently be re-enacted in psychoanalytic treatment where the patient may conform to his analyst's authoritarian interpretations"; he continues: "Unless the analyst actively establishes a different kind of relationship with her patient in which acceptance and equality are manifested, she has little chance of helping the analysand discover the historical truth of his traumatized past" (pp. 221–222).

This is the source of the harsh criticism of Ferenczi against the hypocrisy or insensitivity of the traditional analyst such as Freud himself. Returning now to how the cure needs to make a difference and how abreaction and repetition alone, as Freud seems to imply in his practice, will not provoke a change, is fundamental to break the chain of identification with the aggressor as Ferenczi wrote (Ferenczi, 1933, 1988). Identification with the aggressor and with aggressive affects and behaviors will intensify sadomasochistic patterns and sadistic aspects of the super-ego (Blum, 1986, p. 20).

Expressing their criticism towards Freud's theory, Laub and Auerhahn very cogently write:

> Freud labels as "hysterical fantasies" what we would now understand as a re-enactment of childhood trauma in dissociative states. . . . It is the nature of trauma to elude our knowledge, because of both defense and deceit. . . . During massive trauma, . . . this blurring of boundaries between reality and fantasy conjures up affects so violent that it exceeds the ego's capacity for regulation . . . in this form of traumatic memory, the centre of experience is no longer in the experiencing "1." Events happen somewhere, but are no longer connected with the conscious Subject. The self is fragmented into a "me" and a "not-me" and any connection between the two has been severed. What the survivor manifests is a painful state of concurrent awareness of a depleted self and of an intense experience that is disconnected and "forgotten," but nevertheless affectively permeates and compromises life strategies of adaptation and defense. This double state of knowing and not knowing leaves the survivor in grief not only for his dead loved ones but also for his lost memories. That lack of knowledge prevents the revival of despair that would accompany mourning, but leaves the survivor alone and unknown to himself. . . . This double status of knowing and not knowing depends on the fact that trauma disrupts the link between self and nurturing other, the very fabric of psychic life.
>
> (Laub & Auerhahn, 1993, pp. 287–291)

This discontinuity between states of the mind, of traumatic origin, masterfully elaborated on and clinically described by Philip Bromberg (2011) has been further studied in its neuroscientific research by Allan Schore (1994, 2001, 2003a, 2003b).

The consequence of this dissociative state of knowing and not knowing in my mind is that the reconstruction of the "real fact" cannot take place if the emotional integration – which helps in reconstituting eventually what the meaning of the event is for the patient – is not facilitated by the therapist. *If trauma is precisely the rupture of the fundamental link of trust and hope between self and other, only in the reconstruction of that link can meaning be recuperated and reconnection with the other beings and life be re-established.* As Ferenczi wrote:

> What is fundamentally significant in all this is the fact that an abre-action of quantities of the trauma is not enough; the situation must be different from the actually traumatic one in order to make possible a different, favorable outcome. The most essential aspect of the altered repetition is the relinquishing of one's own rigid authority and the hostility hidden in it. The relief that is obtained thereby is then not transient, and the convictions derived in this way are also more deeply rooted.
>
> (Ferenczi, 1988, p. 108)

Therefore, splits in consciousness and, what we would nowadays call "personality disorders," distortions of truth and the condemnation to a pact of silence in the implicit identification with the aggressor (with all the consequences that have been identified with this Ferenczian construct) are among the psychic sequelae of incest trauma. Silence in particular, together with the blurring of boundaries we mentioned in our discussion of the knowing and not knowing of trauma, is what is going to cause the transmission of unconscious material from one generation to the other (and this happens both in massive social trauma and in incest). Survivors often claim that they belong to "a secret order" that is sworn to silence. They have become the "bearers of a secret." By never divulging their stories, they feel that the rest of the world will never come to know the real truth. It becomes a chain, transferred to the next generation, and so on. Giving testimony contributes precisely to the breaking of this pact of silence, inside and outside the survivor. It is also and above all part of a process of dealing with loss and separation (see also Mucci, 2023, in Barnea-Astrog and Becker eds, 2023).

The conviction, introduced by Freud and present in psychoanalytic thought for quite a long time, that it is psychical reality which is the decisive kind, leads to the view that what is reconstructed in analysis is a narrative, whose truth is not necessarily veritable and, which, in any case, is never the object of attempts at verification. This becomes problematic when, in the words of two contemporary psychoanalysts, Peter Fonagy and Mary Target, we conclude with a statement like this: "there can be only psychic reality behind a recovered memory – whether there is historical truth and historical reality is not our business as psychoanalysts and psychotherapists" (Fonagy & Target, 1997, p. 216). It is an extremely delicate, complex, and also an important ethical point; we are well aware of the consequences of extreme positions held in the context of what goes under the rubric of "the recovered memory debate," with real trials going on in several English-speaking countries in the '80s and '90s. But the question at issue here seems to me a very problematic one. Although we agree that the kind of knowledge the psychoanalyst is looking for is not, and should never be treated as if it were, on the level of a deposition in a court of law, it is nonetheless important to stress the responsibility (civil/ ethical) that the therapist has, especially in cases of victims of domestic violence, wars, political persecution, massacres and racial cleansing, to make sure that the victims are not surrounded by that silence that Ferenczi described as part of the tragic secondary aspect of trauma, creating in turn a vicarious traumatization. In other words, the analyst should never be in the position of the third term in the family, a potential witness who refused to see and negated reality.

This is where trauma, from being a private issue, acquires a social and political aspect with consequences for the community and collectivity. And this is how I believe the practice of psychoanalysis cannot but have an effect on collectivity if it concerns itself with restoring a word of truth into the world. "Repression, dissociation, and denial are phenomena of social as well as individual consciousness," writes Judith Herman (1992, p. 9) and is echoed by Laub and Lee when they equate this mechanism of denial to another sign of the death instinct at work: "We want to emphasize that it is not the lie itself, but the continual communal acceptance of the lie, that indicates the operation of the death instinct. This constant and relentless opposition to knowing compromises the ability to see and recognize the truth. Indeed, we believe, it was death instinct – induced resistance to knowing that enabled Holocaust to proceed further as if unnoticed" (Laub & Lee, 2003, p. 439). The responsibility in psychoanalytic practice is always two-sided: towards the individual and towards the social group. The individual asks that her sufferings be understood and that her history be faithfully reconstructed with attention, sensitivity and care. The social group asks that the chain of repetition be interrupted so that the "not knowing about the trauma" cannot go on causing damage. I agree with Judith Herman when she writes in her simple but extremely profound language:

"Survivors also understand that those who forget the past are condemned to repeat it. It is for this reason that public truth-telling is the common denominator of all social action" (Herman, 1992, p. 208) and, I would emphasize, telling lies about the trauma is an extremely serious individual and social violence. The problem of whether the recovered memory is true or reconstructed through fantasy might exceed psychoanalytic theoretical discussion; but as Paul-Claude Racamier argues in L'Incest et l'Incestual, without disavowing the very premises from which psychoanalysis stems, it is important to question also what happens when the event has in fact taken place, not only when it has been fantasied (Racamier, 1995). Speaking to this concern, Werner Bohleber underlines: "Psychoanalysis, originally undertaken in order to discover repressed childhood memories, is now in danger of becoming a treatment technique that actually fades out history" (2010, p. 109). In fact, if there is a feature characteristic of psychoanalysis throughout its developmental phases over the years, it is its contribution to the discovery of a kind of disguised or repressed truth, therefore, an ethical commitment that lies at the core of the psychoanalytic practice: psychoanalysis both in theory and in practice cannot but be a contributor to the restoration of truth in the individual and in society. I therefore fully agree with Ilse Grubrich-Simitis when she states that, when working with severely traumatized patients:

> The analyst has to resist not only his natural need to protect himself but also the tendency, reinforced by his training, to bypass reality and to devote his attention, from the beginning, to the patient's fantasies. It is only to the extent that the historical reality is ascertained that the patient will be able to approach his own inner and outer reality.
> (Gubrich-Simitis, 1981, p. 440), italics added)

After the Holocaust and the occurrence of post-war disorders in the survivors, disorders that sometimes came to the attention of psychoanalysts very late, as much as 25 years later, it was no longer possible to accept the idea that trauma and reality are not necessarily linked together. The fantasy aspect might be what emerges more in the second or third generations of traumatized persons, not in the first one; but not to acknowledge this difference becomes to my mind an act of hypocrisy or a denial of truth.

In psychoanalytic practice, the recuperation of historical facts is fundamental, in opposition to something that has been and still is fashionable in psychoanalysis nowadays, that is, what is called "narrative truth" or narrativity, as was advocated by Donald Spence (Spence, 1984) and currently supported by Antonino Ferro (2003). In fact, the use of symbolic techniques in therapy – verbal narrative reconstruction on the part of the patient whenever possible, artistic expression and rendering of the emotions linked to the event, if suitable – remains a fundamental tool towards the recovery of the missing elements, that is the split-off elements that escape consciousness while at the same time haunting it with uncanny returns (symptoms, split images, sensations). But the reconstruction of truth should not remain vague and undetermined, thereby leaving the responsibility of others in the shadows. Symbolic means are necessary as a way for the subject to go deeper into her emotional life, but the final result needs to be a kind of historical, definite truth, attributing meaning and responsibility.

If, on the level of the technique, in order to reconstruct a symbolic truth for the patient, some levels of uncertainty are inescapable in certain moments of the therapy, nonetheless this <u>should not give license to analysts to state that symbolic truth and real events are the same thing; it contradicts the ethics of the profession</u>. In acknowledging and retrieving the truth of the event, <u>the therapist becomes a witness to what the patient has experienced</u>. At the same time, we should not disclaim the experience of the patient that, when the truth of an historical event is ascertained, remembers something different from what reality attests to, while retaining the emotional validity of it. The therapist should gently work towards the re-establishment of the truth, granting that that piece of memory was a sort of emotional bridge towards her own experience and the reclaiming of her own truth (which is one of the final goals of therapy).

Working Through Enactments, or Relational Psychic Encounters

Implicit traumatic memories thus encoded and encysted in the right brain, in connection with amygdala activation more than cortical awareness, have to find a path towards explicit consciousness and verbal expression, which in turn means that a Self with wider awareness has been restored to reality. This is the route of psychotherapy. Psychotherapy that is fine-tuned between patient and therapist through the right brain, in any case, is particularly useful for this kind of (traumatized, right brain lateralized) patient. Narrational processes seem to be able to perform the neuronal integration that is missing or poor in traumatized minds.

Psychotherapy will work on the implicit, bodily imprints, the traces of internalized representations of past relationships, starting from attachment traces. When implicit memory is retrieved, the neural net profiles that are reactivated involve circuits on the brain that are a fundamental part of our everyday experience of life: behaviors, emotions, and images that are encoded in nonverbal operational models of the mind are there in the here and now of the session. Destructive patterns are there repeated and enacted in moments of one-to-one exchanges in which both participants in the dialogue rehearse a right-brain-implicit model that has been interiorized (but the therapist can make use of left strategies as well through language and interpretation, too). Especially severe patients, like the borderline ones, prone as they are to a mass of unregulated emotions and massive primitive defenses, will enact a flood of unstable and violent affects that is mostly unconscious in the sense that they cannot be cortically controlled and balanced. Any occasion in the limits of setting of the therapy will re-enhance and reactivate the emotional *Sturm und Drang* they are subject to: the continuous storm of enactments will on one hand enable the repetition of what has not been dominated and understood consciously, on the other hand will be the object of the exploration and the exchange with the on-going dialogic mental and bodily process of the therapeutic encounter: it is the process that guides the content, this is why content per se and interpretation per se will not affect the process. Moreover, as Laub has argued, language has to be understood and will be understood within a relational process in which Freudian abreaction is not enough (as Ferenczi had stated as early as 1932) and a real change in the implicit interiorized representation of experience has to be reinscribed.

And this is why, as Rachman (2016) recommends, it is not interpretation and interpretive measure that these patients need but empathic presence and a relationship of trust and safety that enables them to repeat and repair past abusive experiences where their truth was not listened to and their feelings were not validated. As Laub and Auerhahn (1989) argue in "Failed empathy," a point I strongly underline,

> since the traumatic state cannot be represented it cannot be modified by interpretation . . . and what is initially requested by the therapy is

not the elucidation of the conflict but the restructuring of a new relationship and a new connection between self and other (p. 392).

I totally agree with Lyons-Ruth (1999) and colleagues of the Boston
Change Process Study Group, when they affirm that

> If clinical process is affect-guided rather than cognition guided, [then]
> therapeutic change is a process that leads to the emergence of new forms
> of relational organization. New experiences emerge but they are not cre-
> ated by the therapist for the benefit of the patient. Instead, they emerge
> somewhat unpredictably from the mutual searching of patient and thera-
> pist for new forms of recognition, or new forms of recognition, or new
> forms of fitting together of initiatives in the interaction between them.
>   (Lyons-Ruth, 1999, p. 17, in Dell & O' Neill, 2009, p. 647)

In this kind of treatment, enactments play an important role (see the fundamental text on enactments. that is Schore, 2012). As "affectively driven
repetition of converging emotional scenarios from the patient's and the
analyst's lives" (Maroda, 1998, p. 520). Right brain patterns of interaction
based on their own implicit and unconscious representations and enactments are fundamental tools in the therapeutic process. They are not only
repetitions but active reinscriptions of different models of relationships
that provide "a new opportunity for awareness and integration" (Maroda,
ibid). I have described in *Borderline Bodies* (Mucci, 2018) how in some
cases with severe borderline disorders, dissociative states come back in
the therapy room in moments of enactments. It is important to stress how
the repetition of this dissociated content cannot happen if unsolicited by
the therapist's mind, in the sense that the mind of the therapist needs to
be open flexible and strong enough to actually accept the return of deeply
disturbing feelings, emotions and even visions (in a case I described in
the book, the presence of the "devil" was an embodiment of an incestuous father. The therapeutic movement is from unconscious cognition
to unconscious emotion and self-regulatory processes. Affect regulation
therapy is linked to intersubjectivity and implicit-procedural processes.
Following Schore's neuroscientific explanation and Bromberg relational
description, we could say that enactments are right-brain to right brain
transference countertransference communications, interactions occurring
between the patient's relational unconscious and the therapist's relational

unconscious (Mucci, 2020). From Freud's univocal and intrapsychic perception (corresponding to a neutral, one-sided and according to Ferenczi, hypocritical and cold therapeutic process) we have therefore arrived at an intersubjective, relational unconscious that is right-brain based. To conclude enactments, very common in psychotherapy with borderline patients as I demonstrated in the case of Dorothy in *Borderline Bodies* (Mucci, 2018), are extremely powerful instruments for the unconscious communication between patient and therapist and allow the therapist to have access to the window of disregulation (or the disorganized and anguished or dissociated states of mind) of the patient, becoming an instrument for new affect regulation, and potential reorganization of cortical (i.e., orbitofrontal) – subcortical (i.e., amygdala) connectivity.

This is why I see the practice of "embodied witnessing" (Mucci, 2018), with the presence of the committed analyst at all levels of self, mind and body as the most apt for the reparation of what has been damaged in previous attachment relationship. I would conclude with these affirmations by Judith Herman, the author of the excellent book *Trauma and Recovery*:

> The moral stance of the therapist is of enormous importance. . . . It is not enough to be neutral or non judgmental. It is necessary to affirm a position of moral solidarity with the survivor. Throughout the exploration of the trauma story, the therapist is called upon to provide a context that is at once cognitive, emotional, and moral. The therapist normalizes the patients's responses, facilitates naming and the use of language, and shares the emotional burden of the trauma. She also contributes to constructing a new interpretation of the traumatic experience that affirms the dignity and value of the survivor.
>
> (Herman, 1992, pp. 178–179)

And finally: "[S]urvivors also understand that those who forget the past are condemned to repeat it. It is for this reason that public truth-telling is the common denominator of all social action" (Herman, 1992, p. 208 italics added)

Note

1 This mutual regression is for Allan Schore "induced" or facilitated by the therapist; in my mind, it is a mutual "contamination" of the minds where the therapist allows himself/herself/themselves to be partially and momentarily

dysregulated but the affect dysregulation, dissociative process and unconscious of both self and other.

References

Blum, H. (1986). The concept of the reconstruction of trauma. In Rothstein, A. (Ed.) *The Reconstruction of Trauma: Its Significance in Clinical Work*. Madison, CT: International Universities Press, pp. 7–27.

Bohleber, W. (2010). *Destructiveness, Intersubjectivity, and Trauma: The Identity Crisis of Modern Psychoanalysis*. London: Karnac Books.

Bromberg, P.M. (2011). *The Shadow of the Tsunami and the Growth of the Relational Mind*. New York: Routledge.

Bucci, W. (1997). Symptoms and symbols: A multiple code theory of somatization. *Psychoanalytic Inquiry*. 17(2): 151–172.

Clarkin, J., Yeomans, F.E. and Kernberg, O.F. (1998). *Psychotherapy for Borderline Personality*. New York: Wiley.

Dell, P.F. and O'Neill, J.A. (Eds.) (2009). *Dissociation and the Dissociative Disorders. DSM-V and Beyond*. New York: Routledge.

Ferenczi, S. (1933). The Confusion of Tongues between adults and children: The language of tenderness and passion. In Balint, M. (Ed.) *Final Contributions to the Problems and Methods of Psychoanalysis* (E. Moscher, Trans.). New York: Bruner/Mazel, 1980, pp. 156–167.

Ferenczi, S. (1988). *The Clinical Diary of Sándor Ferenczi* (J. Dupont, Ed., M. Balint and N.Z. Jackson, Trans.). Cambridge, MA: Harvard University Press.

Ferro, A. (2003). *Il lavoro clinico*. Milano: Cortina.

Fineman, J. (1989). *Shakespeare's Will: The Temporality of Rape*. Berkeley, CA: University of California Press, pp. 25–76.

Fonagy, P. and Target, M. (1997). Attachment and reflective function: Their role in self-organization. *Development and Psychopathology*. 9: 679–700.

Gubrich-Simitis, I. (1981). Extreme traumatization as cumulative trauma: Psychoanalytic investigation of the effects of concentration camp experiences on survivors and their children. *The Psychoanalytic Study of the Child*. 36: 415–450.

Herman, J.L. (1992). *Trauma and Recovery: The Aftermath of Violence – From Domestic Abuse to Political Terror*. New York: Basic Books.

Kirshner, L.A. (1993). Concepts of reality and psychic reality in psychoanalysis as illustrated by the disagreement between Freud and Ferenczi. *International Journal of Psycho-Analysis*. 74: 219–230.

Laub, D. and Auerhahn, N.C. (1989). Failed empathy: A central theme in the survivor's Holocaust experience. *Psychoanalytic Psychology*. 6: 377–400.

Laub, D. and Auerhahn, N.C. (1993). Knowing and not knowing massive psychic trauma: Forms of traumatic memory. *International Journal of Psycho-Analysis*. 74: 287–302.

Laub, D. and Lee, S. (2003). Thanatos and massive psychic trauma: The impact of the dead instinct on knowing, remembering and forgetting. *Journal of the American Psychoanalytic Association.* 51(2): 433–463.

Leys, R. (2004). Traumatic cures: Shell shock, Janet, and the question of memory. *Critical Inquiry.* 20: 623–662.

Liotti, G. and Farina, B. (2011). *Sviluppi traumatici: Eziopatogenesi, clinica e terapia della dimensione dissociativa.* Milan: Raffaello Cortina.

Lombardi, M. (2016). *Il terrorismo del nuovo millennio.* Milan: Vita e pensiero, pp. 1–106.

Lyons-Ruth, K. (1999). The two-person unconscious: Intersubjective dialogue, enactive relational representation, and the emergence of the new forms of relational organization. In Aron, L. and Harris, A. (Eds.) *Relational Psychoanalysis: Innovation and Expansion* (Vol. 2). Hillsdale, NJ: Analytic Press, pp. 311–349.

Mahler, M., Pine, F. and Bergman, A. (1995). *The Psychological Birth of the Human Infant.* New York: Basic Books.

Maroda, K.J. (1998). Enactment: When the patient's and the analyst's past converge. *Psychoanalytic Psychology.* 15: 517–535.

Mucci, C. (2013). *Beyond Individual and Collective Trauma: Intergenerational Transmission, Psychoanalytic Treatment, and the Dynamics of Forgiveness.* London: Karnac Books.

Mucci, C. (2018). *Borderline Bodies: Affect Regulation Therapy for Personality Disorders (Norton Series on Interpersonal Neurobiology).* New York: W. W Norton & Company.

Mucci, C. (2020). A right-brain dissociative model for right-brain disorders: Dissociation vs repression in borderline and other severe psychopathologies of early traumatic origin. In *The Divided Therapist.* London: Routledge, pp. 202–227.

Mucci, C. (2023). In Barnea-Astrog, M. and M. Becker (Eds.) *Relational Conversations on Meeting and Becoming. The Birth of a True Other.* London and New York: Routledge.

Porges, S. (2011). *The Polyvagal Theory: Neurophysiological Foundations of Emotions, Attachment, Communication, and Self Regulation.* New York: W. W. Norton & Company.

Racamier, P.C. (1995). *L'inceste et l'incestual.* Paris: Éditions du Collège.

Rachman, A.W. (1997). *Sándor Ferenczi: The Psychotherapist of Tenderness and Passion.* Northvale, NJ: Jason Aronson.

Rachman, A.W. (2016). *The Budapest School of Psychoanalysis.* London: Routledge.

Rachman, A.W. (2018). *Elizabeth Severn, The "Evil Genius" of Psychoanalysis.* London: Routledge, pp. 246–248.

Rachman, A.W. (2019). The Confusion of Tongues: Sándor and the Budapest School of Psychoanalysis: A revolutionary paradigm shift in psychoanalysis. *Presentation, Irish Psychoanalytic Society.* Dun Laoghaire, May 10.

Rachman, A.W. (2022). *Psychoanalysis and Society's Neglect of Sexual Abuse of Children, Youth, and Adults: Reassessing Freud's Original Theory of Sexual Abuse and Trauma*. London: Routledge Press.

Schore, A.N. (1994). *Affect Regulation and the Origin of the Self: The Neurobiology of Emotional Development*. Mahwah, NJ: Erlbaum.

Schore, A.N. (2001). The effects of early relational trauma on right brain development, affect regulation and infant mental health. *Infant Mental Health Journal.* 22(1–2): 201–269.

Schore, A.N. (2003a). *Affect Regulation and the Repair of the Self*. New York: W. W. Norton & Company.

Schore, A.N. (2003b). *Affect Dysregulation and Disorders of the Self*. New York: W. W. Norton & Company.

Schore, A.N. (2019a). *The Development of the Unconscious Mind (Norton Series on Interpersonal Neurobiology)*. New York: W. W. Norton & Company.

Schore, A.N. (2019b). *Right Brain Psychotherapy (Norton Series on Interpersonal Neurobiology)*. New York: W. W. Norton & Company.

Spence, D. (1984). A linguistic mode of psychotherapeutic listening. *The Journal of Psychotherapy Practice and Research.* 3(1): 37–43.

Chapter 16

The Analysis Between Sigmund Freud and Anna Freud

A Confusion of Tongues

Freud's Intellectual Genius and His Human Condition

There is a taboo which has been developed in the psychoanalytic community against analyzing Freud's personal functioning. This attitude had created an aura surrounding Freud as an infallible God-like figure. With this attitude, psychoanalysts have welcomed what he has done, said, or written as the truth, to be accepted, but not to be analyzed. Two prime examples of what can be called a hero-worship attitude has been established by Ernest Jones, Freud's biographer (Jones, 1953, 1955, 1957) as well as Kurt Eissler's book on his defending Freud's abandoning his seduction theory (Eissler, 2001). Both publications dramatically established that, through the hero-worship attitude, Freud was a genius and infallible figure who was to be accepted as having the truth about human behavior. Their attitude suggests that analyzing Freud's ideas or personal functioning would lessen his theories as containing the truth. As Fromm (1959) discussed, Freud surrounded himself with so-called company men, psychoanalysts who would protect his ideas and his functioning. Freud's dramatic conflict with Ferenczi, when he believed his student was deviating from his standard of theory and technique, demonstrated his need to have his students, colleagues and friends adhere to a standard which he established (Rachman, 2018b; see chapter three). He did not maintain an open dialogue with Ferenczi when he thought his student had gone beyond what he considered the acceptable boundaries of psychoanlysis. Rather he cut off contact with Ferenczi, then denounced him and finally encouraged a campaign to silence Ferenczi and remove his influence from the psychoanalytic community (Rachman, 1997b, 1999, 2018a). We should celebrate Freud's intellectual genius, which made him a pioneering scholar who deserved

DOI: 10.4324/9781003265030-16

the Nobel Prize for his discovery of the sexual abuse of children by their parents, which he outlined in his Seduction Theory. This discovery was the original concept on which psychoanalysis was developed (Freud, 1954). The discovery of sexual abuse of children by their parents, establishes childhood sexual abuse as a source of traumatic disorder. This discovery which Freud later abandoned for the Oedipal complex theory, was revived and expanded in Ferenczi's Confusion of Tongues idea (Rachman, 1994). Freud's original discovery of psychoanalysis as a method of understanding human behavior, treating emotional disorder, and discovering the significance of childhood sexual abuse as a dynamic in a trauma disorder was worthy of a Nobel Prize. The first Nobel Prize was awarded in 1901, five years after Freud's discovery of childhood sexual seduction. Freud was never nominated, nor awarded a Nobel Prize for medicine. The first medal in medicine went to a German physiologist and microbiologist, Emil von Behring. He developed an antitoxin to treat diphtheria, until then causing thousands of deaths each year. Freud's discovery that psychological disorder can be caused by childhood sexual abuse within familial interaction was a groundbreaking event, which contributed greatly to understanding human behavior. This deserved a Nobel Prize because it contributed to a significant human health problem by changing the false assumption that sexual abuse of children was perpetrated by strangers, criminal individuals who molest children in shady places like back alleys. Freud's discovery that child sexual abuse actually took place in middle class families rather than with strangers, was also an important discovery. We have seen in the last 119 years that this groundbreaking discovery occurs in contemporary society in epidemic proportions (Rachman, 2022). Freud was prophetic in making this discovery as he pointed the way to our need to understand childhood sexual abuse as a mental health issue of epidemic proportions. As we shall see, Ferenczi verified Freud's findings, which he reported in the Confusion of Tongues paper (Ferenczi, 1933). Freud, as he became preoccupied with verifying his Oedipal theory, lost interest in the sexual abuse of children. He favored a unitary theory of psychoanalysis where the unconscious was the primary focus. When Ferenczi wrote his basic findings on sexual abuse as a psychodynamic in human behavior (Ferenczi, 1933, 1988), Freud thought Ferenczi was trying to push psychoanalysis back into the past. Freud's idea of Ferenczi regressing theoretically and clinically to the beginning of psychoanalysis was totally untrue. Ferenczi and the Confusion of Tongues idea was offered as an attempt to bring psychoanalysis forward into a new era where trauma disorder is recognized as a significant dimension of human behavior.

Silencing the Confusion of Tongues

In discussions of the Confusion of Tongues paper, there are attempts to silence the controversy that surrounds this paper (Blum, 1994; Jacobson, 1992; Modell, 1991). These authors who neglect the intense controversy between Freud and Ferenczi about the Confusion of Tongues idea also act as if this contribution of Ferenczi was fully accepted by mainstream psychoanalysis. They also act as if this idea became part of the analytic community after it was presented. The silence of contemporary analysts about the campaign to remove the Confusion of Tongues from psychoanalysis can be understood as part of the continuation of the Totschweigen campaign initiated by Freud and Jones (see chapter four) to silence and remove Ferenczi's contributions from psychoanalysis (Rachman, 2018a, 2022).

Freud's Analysis of Anna

Freud's capacity to easily criticize Ferenczi's personal functioning did not apply to examining his own personal functioning. A dramatic example of Freud being unattuned to his own personal functioning, or his emotional blindness is his analysis of his daughter Anna. We can speculate that Freud's analysis of his daughter may have been a sign of affection. He wanted to give Anna the best of what he had to give, namely, he wanted to use his genius intellect, his skill as a clinician, and love for her, to help his daughter with her emotional disturbance. We can grant Freud was a loving father who desired to help his daughter in the best way he could, to give of himself. His daughter, who idolized him, felt it was an honor to be analyzed by the founder of psychoanalysis. What is more, she was so emotionally attached to him, she could not refuse his offer to analyze her. Should she have turned him down for his offer to analyze her? As difficult as that may have been for her, she needed to think through his offer and tell him it presented an emotional dilemma for her. Freud's desire to analyze his daughter has inherent limitations. Analyzing a family member has always been considered a limitation because familial attachment contaminates the transference. The analysis does not begin without established emotional reactions between analyst and analysand. The analyst is not free

to respond without an already established emotional reaction to the analysand. When the family member is the analyst's child, the limitations for a
meaningful analysis are attenuated. How is it possible for Freud to analyze
Anna's Oedipal complex, which would mean he would be exploring his
daughter's sexual feelings towards him to her? In the analysis, she would
need to fully express her sexual feelings to him. The possibility of this
kind of openness is not likely. But, even if such self-disclosure did exist,
father and daughter exploring their sexual feelings with each other constitutes sexual abuse. Every child should be granted the emotional privilege
to maintain the privacy of having their so-called Oedipal feelings without
sharing them with their parents. Such privacy maintains the unconscious
space for such feelings and thoughts of the individual to be experienced
and work on and through in a safe psychological space. Freud's severe
criticism of Ferenczi's clinical behavior (see Chapter Three) for alleged,
and unfounded sexual behavior (Rachman, 1993a) indicated Freud's problem with sexuality. He was actually _emotionally blind_ to what can be considered sexually seductive behavior in analyzing his daughter. He never
questioned analyzing his daughter. In fact, when he was contacted by the
Italian psychoanalyst, Edoardo Weiss, he said that his analysis of Anna
was a success (Stewart-Steinberg, 2012). If we use Freud's definitions
of a successful analysis, _To Love, To Work_ (Erikson, 1950), how do we
evaluate Anna's functioning after her analysis with her father? Using his
criteria for analytic success, she had great success in her work, as she was
a pioneer in child analysis. But how do we evaluate Freud's criteria of,
"To Love," in Anna's case. She did not have a heterosexual relationship
or become part of a traditional marriage, which was Freud's standard for
heterosexual primacy. Anna did have a long-term, live-in relationship with
Dorothy Tiffany Burlingham (Young-Bruehl, 1988), which is open to discussion as to whether it was a Boston Marriage or a lesbian union.

Boston Marriage or a Lesbian Union

The term Boston Marriage began to be used after Henry James's book,
The Bostonians (James, 1886), when he detailed a marriage-like relationship between two women. They were women who were independent of
male support, not married, and self-supporting. Whether these were lesbian relationships is debatable. The likelihood is that some were, some
weren't. Today, the term _Boston Marriage_ is sometimes used for lesbian

relationships – two women living together – which may be sexual, but, usually romantic and sometimes erotic. They might be called domestic partnerships (Rothblum & Brehony, 1993). In my discussions with Elizabeth Young-Bruehl, Anna Freud's biographer (Young-Bruehl, 1988), I asked her if she thought Anna Freud was a lesbian. She said that when she was researching her book on Ms. Freud, she had the fantasy that she would discover that Anna Freud would be one of the great lesbians of all time. But she could not conclude from any material she examined that Anna Freud was a practicing lesbian. With Young-Bruehl's report, one could conclude Anna Freud was involved in a Boston Marriage with Dorothy Burlingham.

Dorothy Trimble Tiffany Burlingham – (October 11, 1891-November 19, 1979)

Dorothy Burlingham was an American child psychoanalyst and educator. A lifelong friend and partner of Anna Freud. Burlingham is known for her joint work with A. Freud on the analysis of children. She was the last of four children born to Louis Comfort Tiffany, the artist and creator of stain glass lamps and decorations. She married Robert Burlingham in 1914 and had four children, before separating from her husband in 1921. Dorothy Burlingham arrived in Vienna in 1925 to have Anna Freud analyze her 10-year-old son Bob, and her 8-year-old daughter Mabbie. Dorothy also began her first analysis with Theodore Reik. Then she was with Sigmund Freud for 12 years. The therapeutic relationship between the Freuds and the Burlinghams was implemented by a personal relationship between Anna and Dorothy. Anna became the "analytic stepparent" for the Burlingham family. Coffey (2015) a scientific novelist had written a novel about Anna Freud, describing her own ideas about Anna and Dorothy Burlingham. Rebecca Coffey said she read everything she could lay her hands on in order to understand Anna Freud. This meant she read Freud's published works, official and unofficial biographies, Freudian criticisms, and Freud's available diary. She believed doing this enabled her to become sure of the events and individuals in Anna's life. She felt she was able to connect the dots in Anna's life, integrating the facts with her own imagination. Coffey reached many conclusions based on her research and formed many intellectual speculations about her subject. Many analysts called Anna a "vestal virgin." Clearly, the analytic community wondered whether Anna had a sexual life, with either a male or female. The use of such a designation implied that she was so dedicated to her father and psychoanalysis, that she had not time or interest in sex. She could also be characterized as a nun of psychoanalysis. People wondered about Anna's sexuality because, as mentioned, the mandate to discuss the personal life of Freud and Anna was a taboo subject, not to be discussed or analyzed.

Coffey also noted Dorothy Burlingham's name was associated with Anna Freud. Once again, there was no information available about their relationship because of the taboo regarding the investigation of the personal functioning of the Freud family. People close to the Freud family made vague proud references to men Anna could have married but somehow never got around to dating. The general sentiment expressed was poor, lonely Anna was too devoted to her Papa to live a full life. As we shall discuss in the sections to come, there is some meaningful speculation that Freud's personal history and his analysis of his daughter can explain her sexuality.

Freud's Problematic Clinical Interaction with Anna

A belief in a scholarly examination of Freud's unusual clinical behavior with his daughter, Anna, is long overdue and will help lift the taboo that has existed in our field ever since the analysis occurred in the early 1920s. The desire to enter into an extraparental relationship with one's child has occurred in science before and after Freud's analysis of his daughter, Anna.

There have also been scientists who have used them as research tools. Darwin's studies of his first son; Piaget's observations of his children's cognitive development; it is possible that Roentgen conducted experiments on his children. A distinction can be made between Freud's desire to analyze his daughter Anna, and his actually performing the analysis. It can be an act of love to entertain the fantasy to help your child by offering your expertise. It is not an act of love to actually analyze your child, no matter how well intentioned you are. Freud's analysis of his daughter, although well intentioned, was born of a desire to fulfill narcissistic needs. Freud seemed blinded to the possibility that in analyzing his daughter her was involved in a form of emotional seduction that had decided sexual overtones (Klein & Tribich, 1981). This analysis occurred even though there were other very qualified psychoanalysts who could perform the clinical task. Freud could have referred Anna to his friend and favorite pupil,

Sándor Ferenczi, for whom Anna had positive feelings. There are many issues to examine in the analytic experience between Sigmund and Anna Freud. Was Freud's willingness to analyze his daughter an indication of an emotional blindness to the issue of seduction in theory and method? Was Freud's vehement and mean-spirited objections to Ferenczi's courageous attempts to reformulate the seduction theory, especially in Ferenczi's "Confusion of Tongues" paper (Ferenczi, 1933) and his clinical diary (Ferenczi, 1988), also partially fueled by his emotional blindness to the issue of seduction? In fact, was Freud's campaign to suppress and censor Ferenczi's "Confusion of Tongues" paper, one of psychoanalysis' dirty little secrets (as was the secret of Anna Freud's real analyst)? In a series of letters and telegrams, it is clear that Freud – along with Jones, Eitingon, Rivère, and others in his orthodox circle, prevented Ferenczi's "Confusion of Tongues" paper from being published (Rachman, 1997a, 1997b), through the practice of Totschweigen (Rachman, 1999).

Freud, in an amazing statement, suggested that the analyst cannot traumatize, corrupt, or seduce a child by introducing sexual material into their discussion (Rachman & Mattick, 2012). Consequently, he freely introduced sexual interpretations into the analysis of Dora (Freud, 1905), because the presence of her "hysterical" symptom meant Dora had sexual thoughts. The symptom is the expression of a sexual wish. A hysteric is like a repressed pervert: They have sexual feelings and ideas they don't sublimate, but they repress and turn the desire into symptoms. Freud, therefore, felt fully justified to say sexual things to Dora – such as that she had the fantasy of wanting to have oral sex with her father – when there is no evidence to support this approach (Rachman & Mattick, 2012), or to analyze his daughter without concern of emotionally seducing her. Freud's statement about seduction in the analytic situation, as stated in the case of Dora, was as follows:

> There is never any danger of corrupting an inexperienced girl. For where there is no knowledge of sexual process even in the unconscious, no hysterical symptom will arise; and where hysteria is found there can no longer be any question of "innocence of mind" in the sense in which parents and educators use the phrase. With children of ten, or twelve, or fourteen, with boys and girls alike, I have satisfied myself that the truth of this statement can be invariably relied upon.
>
> (Freud, 1905, p. 42)

If Ferenczi knew of Freud's analysis of Anna, he could think of it as an example of the Confusion of Tongues. Freud's analysis of his daughter inherently created an emotionally seductive experience, using an understanding of the Confusion of Tongues theory (Rachman, 1989, 1994, 1997a, 2003; Rachman & Mattick, 2002). Anna wanted tenderness, affection, and love from her father in submitting herself to being analyzed by him. Did she approach him for an analysis or did Freud volunteer? Did either of them question the wisdom of their decision? The issues of seduction, intrusion and betrayal must be considered as factors in the analysis of one's child. In Freud's analysis of his daughter, Anna, the issue of emotional seduction must be raised. Freud's Oedipal theory clearly suggests that the child's need to fantasize about sexuality must be protected. A child, according to the Oedipal theory, needs to have the opportunity to desire the parent sexually in the privacy of his or her unconscious. This Oedipal fantasy needs to be protected from parental intrusion in order to be maintained at the level of fantasy. Any discussion of it with the actual parent contaminates the experience as a wish and could initiate the idea of acting upon it. The parent, in pointing out the sexual desire of the child for him, sexualizes the interaction. He creates the situation that sex is the central topic, but then disavows that he has an interest in being in such an interaction. This creates a classical Confusion of Tongues. He takes a situation, which is not explicitly defined as sexual and defines it as a sexual one. But he does not admit he is so defining the situation. It is his daughter's wish to seduce him. The seducer became the seduced. The technique of the seducer is to ascribe the technique of seduction to the other person. The child experiences some negative interaction with the parent, which is denied and projected onto the child. Confusion as to what has transpired in the relationship ensues. The child does not trust his or her own sense of reality and begins to accept the parental version of the drama. This is where identification with the aggressor becomes a significant mechanism.

In agreeing to analyze Anna, Freud created an expectation that he would be able to be a full transferential figure. He led her to believe he would be a container for all her feelings, whether sexual, dependent, or aggressive. In essence, he would contain all of her psychopathology. What father could hear his daughter's masochistic fantasies (Freud, 1923) for example, her beating fantasies – as Freud did (Freud, 1919), and maintain a neutral, objective, therapeutic stance? It seem so easy to be over-concerned, to want to intervene so as to soothe her hurt before one heard and explored the full extent and meaning of the subjective experience of wanting to be beaten as a stimulus to masturbation. Was Freud the exceptional father-scientist, that he could hear Anna's masochistic fantasies and treat her like a female stranger who needed his detached objectivity? If he plays the scientist, is he being a good father by not soothing his daughter? If he soothes his daughter, however, he is not being the scientist and following his method. But can one's own child experience the father in the role of objective analyst as warm, caring, responsive, and affectionate? Anna is placed in an emotional compromise. She must not ask for soothing, to be the good analysand. So to be a good daughter, she must not disappoint him and be an inadequate analysand. She can't, therefore, require him to be a good father. If Anna wanted a nonanalytic response, Freud would be obligated to not give a transference interpretation. "Both Freud and his daughter located the origin of post-Oedipal beating fantasies in the repression of the 'love fantasy' a child has for his or her father" (Young-Bruehl, 1988, p. 109). Anna would be obligated to accept this interpretation. The result of this interaction would have been that Freud had encouraged his daughter to say she had sexual feelings for him Imagine the emotional impact this could have on his daughter: If she accepts this interpretation, she is responsible for her sexual feelings towards him. He is not responsible for creating any sexual stimulation in their interaction. He is only uncovering the truth. As in the Dora case, Freud does not feel responsible for the sexualized interaction.

As we can see from Ferenczi's work during the period when Anna was undergoing her analysis, roughly 1918–1924, some analysands reacted negatively to the interpretative analyst, feeling they were being retraumatized by the cold, distant, detached observer who exerted his power, control, and status over them with sexual interpretations (Ferenczi, 1988). Balint (1968), Winnicott (1965), and Kohut (1984), were to confirm these findings as they brought Ferenczi's original observations into psychoanalysis' modern era. Needing warmth, affection, and responsiveness, Anna settled for interpretation. What kind of interpretation did Freud offer to his daughter when she told him of her beating fantasies? The connection between Sigmund Freud's paper, "A Child Is Being Beaten" (Freud, 1919), with Anna's paper, "Beating Fantasies and Daydreams" (Freud, 1923) has been made:

This fifth patient sounds very much like Anna Freud. . . . But the sixth patient is not directly described at all, and this may signal that Freud protected his daughter's privacy with silence. Beating Fantasies and Daydreams [A. Freud's paper] was modeled – in general, if not in complete detail – on her own case, and her essay's descriptive framework is identical with the one that applies to two if the female cases in Freud's essay.

(Young-Bruehl, 1988, p. 104)

Interpretation, if Freud was true to his method, was his gift to his daughter. Is interpretation sufficient to encourage the child to feel loved and attended to in an analysis? To be a good girl – to be "daddy's good girl," accepting interpretations – was her duty. As Young-Bruehl (1988) has indicated, "he [S. Freud] certainly knew the degree to which her fantasy life was susceptible to regression and her intellectual energies to inhibition" (p. 108). Could Anna Freud reject an interpretation by her father? Could one imagine her saying to the founder of psychoanalysis, "That is an interesting interpretation you have offered me, but I don't think it applies to my case" Could Anna have followed Dora in not only rejecting his sexual interpretations by also terminating her analysis? How, then, did the necessary phenomenon of resistance emerge and develop in this analysis? Resistance, although conceptualized as the enemy of change, was nevertheless the necessary impetus for growth, and the emergence of the self-striving to metabolize the insights of the doctor who was the enemy of neurosis. Was Sigmund Freud able to challenge an analysand to express her negative transferential feelings directly to him, as was his pupil Sándor Ferenczi? Ferenczi complained of his analysis with Freud, which occurred before Anna's, in that his analyst would not enter into a dialogue about their relationship (Ferenczi, 1988). Freud remained aloof, as he had done earlier with Jung, refusing to relinquish his position of authority by making associations to a dream he had told Ferenczi and Jung on their joint crossing of the Atlantic on the way to the Clark lectures (Rosenzweig, 1992). Had Freud changed this behavior by the 1920s? Did he behave differently with his daughter?

Freud's problematic analysis of his daughter Anna cannot be considered a traditional psychoanalysis because it did not adhere to the clinical methodology Freud used as the standard for an analytic encounter.

What is more, we are suggesting that rather than it being a therapeutic experience, it can be considered to be a traumatic one. Freud created an experience where his daughter was encouraged to talk about her thoughts, feelings, and sexual fantasies about her father, with her father. Her emotional safety was intruded upon. He seemed to be more emotionally connected to analyzing his daughter as a way to help her with her neurosis than being attuned to whether his daughter was having emotional difficulty with examining her Oedipal thoughts and feelings about him. Since Freud did not practice a two-person clinical interaction, he was focused on his behavior with Anna, not her experience with him. In such a one-person experience, Freud concentrated on correctly interpreting Anna's Oedipal associations. She was focused on being a good analysand by accepting her father's interpretations. What happened between them, when she had associations which were disturbing and didn't want to share with her father? Did he tell her she was in resistance? Did she respond to his analysis of her resistance? Freud's analysis of his daughter, Anna, raises many questions, all of which need discussion. In this chapter we attempt to raise the issue of Freud's neglect of the importance of sexual trauma on Anna's personality development. We believe Freud neglected and suppressed Ferenczi's Confusion of Tongues theory of trauma due to sexual abuse by a parent to their child. We raise the issue as to whether Freud analyzing his daughter, Anna, while arranged with the best of intentions, can be considered an example of "emotional abuse." He was "emotionally blind" and neglected the emotional trauma caused to Anna by asking her to self-disclose and analyze her sexual feelings about her father, thus, intruding into the sanctity of the unconscious. This experience is an example of "emotional seduction." The nature of this interaction, of a father/analyst analyzing his daughter's Oedipal thoughts and feelings about him, is by definition, a sexually-traumatic experience. As Freud described it in his theory of psychosexual stages of development it is a child's feelings of desire for his or her opposite-sex parent and jealousy and anger towards his or her same-sex parent. Essentially, a girl feels that she is competing with her mother for her father's affections. The Oedipal stage for girls is known as the Electra complex in which girls feel desire for their fathers and jealousy of their mothers. The term Electra complex was introduced by Carl Jung to describe how this complex manifests in girls. In order to develop into a successful adult with a healthy identity, the child must identify with the same-sex parent in order to resolve the conflict of the phallic stage. If the conflict is not resolved, a fixation at that point in development can result. Girls who do not deal with this conflict effectively become "father fix-ated." An unresolved Oedipus complex can lead to challenges in achieving mature adult romantic relationships (Freud, 1905, pp. 123–246). The Oedipus Complex, according to Anna Freud, became the cornerstone of psychoanalysis, which her father felt must remain the analytic standard (Masson, 1984).

References

Balint, M. (1968). The disagreement between Freud and Ferenczi and its reper-cussions. In *The Basic Fault: Therapeutic Aspects of Regression*. London: Tavistock Publications, pp. 149–156.

Blum, H.P. (1994). The Confusion of Tongues and psychic trauma. *International Journal of Psychoanalysis*. 75: 871–882.

Coffey R. (2015). The elephant in Sigmund Freud's consulting room: Anna Freud's gay conversion therapy. *Psychology Today*.

Eissler, K. (2001). *Freud and the Seduction Theory*. New York: International Uni-versities Press.

Erikson, E.H. (1950). *Childhood and Society*. New York: W. W. Norton.

Ferenczi, S. (1933). The Confusion of Tongues between adults and children: The language of tenderness and passion. In Balint, M. (Ed.) *Final Contributions to the Problems and Methods of Psychoanalysis* (E. Moscher, Trans.). New York: Bruner/Mazel, 1980, pp. 156–167.

Ferenczi, S. (1988). *The Clinical Diary of Sándor Ferenczi* (J. Dupont, Ed., M. Balint and N.Z. Jackson, Trans.). Cambridge, MA: Harvard University Press.

Freud, A. (1923). Beating fantasies and daydreams. In *The Writings of Anna Freud* (Vol. I). New York: International Universities Press, pp. 135–157.

Freud, S. (1905). *Standard Edition*. 7: 1–122 (London: Hogarth Press).

Freud, S. (1919). A child is being beaten: A contribution to the study of the origin of sexual perversions. *Standard Edition*. 17: 175–204.

Freud, S. (1954). *The Origins of Psychoanalysis: Letters to Wilhelm Fliess, Drafts and Notes, 1887–1902* (M. Bonaparte, A. Freud and E. Kris, Eds., Mosbacker and J. Strachey, Trans.). New York: Basic Books.

Fromm, E. (1959). *Sigmund Freud's Mission*. New York: Harper & Row.

James, H. (1886). *The Bostonians*. London: Macmillan and Co.

Jones, E. (1953). *The Life and Work of Sigmund Freud, Vol I.: The Formative Years and Great Discoveries*. New York: Basic Books.

Jones, E. (1955). *The Life and Work of Sigmund Freud, Vol II.: Years of Maturity. 1901–1919*. New York: Basic Books.

Jones, E. (1957). *The Life and Work of Sigmund Freud, Vol. III: The Last Phase 1919–1939*. New York: Basic Books.

Klein, M. L. and Tribich, C. (1981). Freud's blindness to the damaging influence of parent's personalities. *New York Academy of Sciences.* 22(8): 14–20.

Kohut, H. (1984). *How Does Analysis Cure?* (A. Goldberg and P.E. Stepansky, Eds). Chicago, IL: University of Chicago Press.

Masson, J.M. (1984). *The Assault on Truth.* New York: Farrar, Straus, and Giroux.

Modell, A. (1991). A Confusion of Tongues or whose reality is it? *Psychoanalytic Quarterly.* 60: 227–244.

Rachman, A.W. (1989). Confusion of Tongues: The Ferenczian metaphor for childhood seduction and emotional trauma. *Journal of the American Academy of Psychoanalysis.* 17(2): 182–205.

Rachman, A.W. (1993a). Ferenczi and sexuality. In Aron, L. and Harris, A. (Eds.) *The Theoretical and Clinical Contributions of Sándor Ferenczi.* Hillsdale, NJ: Analytic Press, pp. 81–100.

Rachman, A.W. (1993b). *The Abusive Parental Transference in Group Analysis of the Incest Trauma* (Presentation). San Diego, CA: American Groups Psychotherapy Association.

Rachman, A.W. (1994). The Confusion of Tongues theory: Ferenczi's legacy to psychoanalysis. In Haynal, A. and Falzeder, E. (Eds.) *100 Years of Psychoanalysis.* London: Karnac Books, pp. 235–255.

Rachman, A.W. (1997a). *Sándor Ferenczi: The Psychotherapist of Tenderness and Passion.* Northvale, NJ: Jason Aronson.

Rachman, A.W. (1997b). The suppression and censorship of Ferenczi's Confusion of Tongues paper. *Psychoanalytic Inquiry (Psychoanalysis' Favorite Son: The Legacy of Sándor Ferenczi).* 17(4): 459–485.

Rachman, A.W. (1997b). The suppression and censorship of Ferenczi's Confusion of Tongues paper. *Psychoanalytic Inquiry (Psychoanalysis' Favorite Son: The Legacy of Sándor Ferenczi).* 17(4): 459–485.

Rachman, A.W. (1999). Death by silence (Totschweigen): The traditional method of silencing the dissident in psychoanalysis. In Prince, R.M. (Ed.) *The Death of Psychoanalysis: Murder, Suicide, or Rumor Greatly Exaggerated?* Northvale, NJ: Jason Aronson, pp. 154–164.

Rachman, A.W. (2000). Ferenczi's Confusion of Tongues theory and the analysis of the incest trauma. *Psychoanalytic Social Work.* 7(1): 27–53.

Rachman, A.W. (2003). Freud's analysis of his daughter Anna: A Confusion of Tongues. In A. Roland, B. Manov, & C. Barbe (Eds.), *Creative Dissent: Psychoanalysis in Evolution.* Westport, CT: Praeger, pp. 59–72.

Rachman, A.W. (2012). Confusion of Tongues between Sándor Ferenczi and Elizabeth Severn. *Presentation. International Sándor Ferenczi Congress — "Faces of Trauma."* Budapest, Hungary, June 3rd

Rachman, A.W. (2018a). *Elizabeth Severn: The "Evil Genius" of Psychoanalysis.* London: Routledge.

Rachman, A.W. (2018b). Ferenczi's confusion of tongues: A regressive idea conceived by a madman or one of the most important papers in the history of psychoanalysis. *Proposal. International Sándor Ferenczi Conference.* Florence, May 2–6.

Rachman, A.W. (2022). *Psychoanalysis and Society's Neglect of Sexual Abuse of Children, Youth, and Adults: Reassessing Freud's Original Theory of Sexual Abuse and Trauma*. London: Routledge Press.

Rachman, A.W. and Mattick, P. (2012). The confusion of tongues in the psychoanalytic relationship. *Psychoanalytic Social Work*. 19(1–2): 167–190.

Rosenzweig, S. (1992). *Freud, Jung, and Hall the King-Maker*. St. Louis, MO: Ranna House Press.

Rothblum, E.D. and Brehony, K.A. (1993) *Boston Marriages: Romantic but Asexual Relationships Among Contemproary Lesbians*. Amherst: University of Massachusetts Press.

Stewart-Steinberg, S. (2012). *Impious Fidelity: Anna Freud, Psychoanalysis, Politics*. Ithaca, NY: Cornell University Press.

Winnicott, D.W. (1965). *The Maturational Process and the Facilitating Environment*. New York: International Universities Press.

Young-Bruehl, E. (1988). *Anna Freud: A Bibliography*. New York: Summit Books.

Chapter 17

The Confusion of Tongues of Mrs. Mary Rowlandson

A First-Person Account of Captivity and Trauma in Colonial America

King Phillip's War: The First Indian War

The King Phillip's War, which is the background conflict which framed the captivity of Mrs. Mary Rowlandson, was an armed conflict between Native American inhabitants of present-day New England and English colonists and their Native American allies in 1675–1678. The war is named after the main leader of the Native American side, Metacomet, known to the English is "King Phillip" (Lepore, 1999). Major Benjamin Church emerged as the Puritan hero of the war; it was his company of Puritan Rangers and Native Americans that finally hunted down and killed King Phillip on August 12, 1676 (Gould, 1996). The war continued in northern New England (primarily in Maine at the New England and Acadia border) until a treaty was signed at Casco Bay in April 1678 (Norton, 2002). The King Phillip's War was the single greatest calamity to occur in 17th-century Puritan New England, and is considered by many to be the deadliest war in American history (Drake, 2000). In the space of little more than a year, twelve of the region's towns were destroyed and many more damaged, the colony's economy was all but ruined, and its population was decimated, losing one-tenth of all men available for military service. The losses were 600 out of the 80,000 English colonists (1.5 percent), and 3,000 out of 10,000 Native Americans (30 percent) lost their lives due to the war (Gould, 1996; Schultz & Touglas, 2000). Throughout the winter of 1675–1676, Native Americans attacked and destroyed more frontier settlements in their effort to expel the English Colonists. Attacks were made at Andover, Bridgewater, Chelmsford, Groton, Lancaster, Marlborough, Medfield, Medford, Millis, Portland, Providence, Rehoboth, Scituate, Seekonk, Sunsbury, Sudbury, Suffield, Warwick, Weymouth, and Wrentham, including what is modern-day Plainville. The famous account written and

DOI: 10.4324/9781003265030-17

published by Mary Rowlandson after the war gives a subjective, first-person colonial captive's perspective of the conflict (Rowlandson, 2009).

Mary Rowlandson was Taken Hostage

The value of the Confusion of Tongues theory is also valuable in its capacity to understand the psychology of psychohistorical events. An example of using the concept of the Confusion of Tongues to understand the psychology of trauma are contained in a remarkable event dating back to Colonial America, where there is a heritage of trauma in cases of individuals being taken hostage by Native Americans (Rowlandson, 2009).

Mary Rowlandson described the Native Americans overtaking her family:

> On the tenth of February 1675, came the Indians with great numbers upon Lancaster . . . hearing the noise of some guns, we looked out, several houses were burning, and the smoke ascending to heaven. There were five persons taken in one house; the father, the mother, and a suckling child they knocked on the head; the other two they took and carried away alive.
>
> (Rowlandson, 2009, p. 3)

She went on to describe the atrocities that were carried out on the other Colonials, including being killed by blows to the head, being stripped naked, being disemboweled, and being shot to death. Rowlandson then went on describe the attack on her house:

> About two hours . . . they have been about the house before they prevailed to fire it. . . . Some in our hour house were fighting for their lives, others wallowing in their blood, the house on fire over our heads, and the bloody heathen ready to knock us on the head, if we stirred out. Now might we hear mothers and children crying out for themselves and one another. . . . But out we must go, the fire increasing, and coming along behind us, roaring, and the Indians gaping before us with their guns, spears, and hatchets to devour us. . . . No sooner were we out of the house, but my brother-in-law fell down dead . . . . the bullets flying thick, one went through my side and . . . though the bowels and hand of my dear child in my arms. . . . Thus were we <u>butchered by this</u>

<u>merciless heathen</u>, standing amazed with the blood running down our heels.

(Rowlandson, 2009, pp. 1–2)

This description indicated the savage attack by the Native Americas on an innocent white family of New England in Colonial Times. Mary Rowlandson's narrative clearly notes her horror and emotional disturbance at the trauma of being brutalized by the attack by Narragansett Wampanoag and Nashaway Native Americans, whom she saw as savages, wild animal-like people. After the butchering of the Colonials, Mary Rowlandson tell of being taken as a hostage:

the Indians laid hold of us, pulling me one way and the children another, and said, "Come go along with us"; I told them they would kill me: they answered, if I were willing to do along with them, they would not hurt me.

(Rowlandson, 2009, p. 4)

She began to speak in traumatic terms of the barbaric attack that had transpired:

It is a solemn sight to see so many Christians lying in their blood, . . . like a company of sheep torn by wolves, all of them stripped naked by a company of hell-hounds, roaring, singing, ranting, and insulting, as it they would have torn our very hearts out; yet the lord by His almighty power preserved a number of us from death, for there were twenty-four of us taken alive and carried captive.

(Rowlandson, 2009, p. 4)

Mary Rowlandson admitted she wanted to remain alive:

I had often before this said that if the Indians should come, I should choose rather to be killed by them than taken alive, but when it came to the trial my mind changed; their glittering weapons so daunted my spirit, that <u>I chose rather to go along with those</u> . . . <u>ravenous beasts</u>, than that moment to end my days; and that I may the better declare what happened to me during that grievous captivity.

(Rowlandson, 2009, p. 4)

My Life was Gone

Mary Rowlandson described the aftermath of being a captive of the Indians as being filled with grief, mournfulness and sadness:

> Oh the roaring, and singing and dancing, and yelling of those black creatures of the night, which made the place a lively resemblance of hell . . . our merciless enemies, who were joyful enough, though we were disconsolate . . . my thoughts ran upon my losses and sad bereaved condition. <u>All was gone, my husband gone . . . my children gone, my relations and friends gone, our house and home . . . all gone . . . all was gone (except my life), and I knew not but the next moment that I might go too. There remained nothing to me but one poor wounded babe, and it seemed a present worse than death that it was in such a pitiful condition.</u>
>
> (Rowlandson, 2009, p. 4)

Mary Rowlandson described her emotional sense of loss as she was removed from her town, family, relatives and friends, that is, from her life. This was a moment of great despair and the feeling she had nothing to live for.

> the next morning, and travel with them into the vast and desolate wilderness. . . .. It is not my tongue, or pen, can express the sorrows of my heart and bitterness of my spirit that I had at this departure. . . . One of the Indians carried my poor wounded babe upon a horse. . . . I went on foot after it, with sorrow that cannot be expressed . . . carried it in my arms till my strength failed and fell down with it . . . <u>like inhumane creatures laughed, and rejoiced to see it, though I thought we should they have ended our days, as overcome with so many difficulties.</u> . . . My body would also grow so stiff that I could scarce sit down or rise up. . . . I must sit all this cold winter night upon the cold snowy ground, with my sick child in my arms, looking that every hour would be the last of his life; and having no Christian friend near me, either to comfort or help me" (Rowlandson, 2009, p. 5). . . . Thus nine days I sat upon my knees with my babe in my lap, till my flesh was raw again, my child being ever ready to depart this sorrowful world. . . . About two hours in the night, my sweet baby like a lamb departed this life on Feb. 18, 1675. It being about six years and five months old. I went

to take up my dead child in my arms to carry it with me, but they bid me let it alone; there was no resisting but go I must and leave it (Rowlandson, 2009, p. 6). The first week of my being among them I hardly ate anything; the second week I found my stomach grew very faint for want of something, and yet it was very hard to get down their filthy trash,; but the third week, though I could have formerly my stomach would turn against this or that, and I could starve and die before I could eat such things, yet they were sweet and savory to my taste.

(Rowlandson, 2009, p. 9)

Mary Rowlandson suffered the trauma of being abducted by Indians; her family being separated from her; having a child die in her arms; having to let the "savages" take it away from her; and being starved until she was in danger of losing her health and consciousness. She was also on the verge of despair, losing hope she would live and return home and be reunited with her family.

Mary Rowlandson's Religious Belief Contributed to Her Emotional Survival

Mary Rowlandson began her narrative of her captivity and restoration declaring her belief in God. As a hostage she witnessed unbelievable atrocities by what she called "savages," "inhumane creatures," "merciless heathen," "the infidels," which caused her horrific trauma, despair, and a profound sense of loss. She clearly indicated in her first-person narrative that her religious belief and the presence of God in her life was a source of her capacity to endure the trauma and have faith she would survive the nightmare:

> The sovereignty and goodness of GOD, together with the faithfulness of his promises displayed . . . commended to her, to all that desires to know the Lord's doings to, and dealings with her.

She also quotes the bible, Deuteronomy 32:39:

> See now that I, even I am he, and there is no god with me, I kill and I make alive, I would and I heal, neither is there any can deliver out of my hand.

(Rowlandson, 2009, pp. 2–3)

At every dark moment of her traumatic experiences, she turned toward God, by reading her bible. When she was captured and had to leave her home and town and was thrown into the wilderness, she said the following in her narrative to help her with the beginnings of her trauma.

> but God was with me in a wonderful manner, carrying me along, and bearing my spirit.
>
> (Rowlandson, 2009, p. 5)

She suffered a wound in her abduction which became worse, to which she said:

> Oh, I may see the wonderful power of God, that my Spirit did not utterly sink under my affliction.
>
> (Rowlandson, 2009, p. 5)

One of her children had died, and one was in the wilderness, and a third she did not know where it was. She walked on her journey in the wilderness, as a captive, searching for her children, thinking of the biblical verse:

> Me (as he said) have bereaved of my children, Joseph is not, and Simeon is not, and ye will take Benjamin also, all these things are against me. . . . And indeed quickly the lord answered, in some measure, my poor prayers; for as I was going up and down mourning and lamenting my condition, my son came to me and asked me how I did. I had not seen him before, since the destruction of the town, and I knew not where he was, till I was informed by himself.
>
> (Rowlandson, 2009, p. 7)

A woman named Joslen, who was among the captives said she wanted to run away. Mary did not want her to run away. Mary opened her Bible and asked they read it together:

> We opened the Bible and lighted on Psalm 27, in which we especially took notice. . .: "Wait on the lord, Be of good courage, and he shall strengthen thine Heart, wait I say on the lord.
>
> (Rowlandson, 2009, p. 8)

As her heart ached with the thoughts of there being scattered among the wild beast heathens in the forest, her mind became overwhelmed with negativity, turning to the bible to find comfort and hope:

> the lord brought that precious Scripture to me: ". . . refrain thy voice from weeping, and thine eyes from tears, for thy work shall be rewarded, and they shall come again from the land of the enemy" ([Jeremiah 31:16]).
>
> Rowlandson, 2009, p. 8)

When Mary Rowlandson needed to be revived emotionally; needed comfort and searched for hope, she turned to her bible whose words helped her. Mary Rowlandson did develop a Confusion of Tongues Trauma, becoming emotionally disturbed as to why the authority, God, which she believed and turned towards for comfort, emotional nourishment and hope for survival, would help the savages, the wild beasts of the forest, . . . when they did not help her and the colonial captives. It is an emotional confusion that every abused and traumatized individual experiences when they believed the authority who they loved and depended upon for nourishment and affection does not help them:

> I cannot by take notice of the strange providence of God in preserving the heathen.
>
> (Rowlandson, 2009, p. 9)

Positive Interaction with the Indians

One of the first positive interactions with the Indians was described by Mary Rowlandson. She had traveled by canoe, all night, when they came ashore, the Indians laughed and celebrated their victory, while she wept. When they asked her why she was crying because they would kill her, they answered:

> No . . . none will hurt you. Then came one of them and gave me two spoonfuls of mead to comfort me, and another gave me half a pint of peas; which was worth more than many bushels at another time.
>
> (Rowlandson, 2009, p. 11)

Shortly afterwards, another important positive interaction occurred. . . . She was asked to make a cap for the . . . chieftain's son. She was invited to have dinner, then

> he gave me a pancake, about as big as two fingers. It was made of parched wheat, beaten, and fried in bear's grease, but I thought I never tasted pleasanter meat in my life. There was a squaw who spoke to me to make a shirt. . ., for which she gave me a piece of a bear.
>
> (Rowlandson, 2009, p. 11)

Mary Rowlandson was able to use her capacity for resilience to establish a positive interaction with her captors. As she began to survive, she was able to establish a meaningful relationship with them:

> going among the wigwams, I went into one and there found a squaw who showed herself very kind to me, and gave me a piece of bear. I asked her to let me boil my piece of bear in her kettle which she did, and gave me some ground nuts to eat with it; and I cannot but think how pleasant it was to me.
>
> (Rowlandson, 2009, p. 13)

Her resilience and capacity to form meaningful relationships . . . helped her to work through some aspects of her trauma. As her captors were kind, she sought them out for empathy. From her captivity, she only expected brutality as she originally saw them as savages. Yet, there were those who were kind to her. Emotionally, she was then able to integrate their kindness, which lessened her Confusion of Tongues trauma:

> One bitter cold day I could find no more room to sit down before the fire, I went out, and could not tell what to do, but I went in to another wigwam, where they were also sitting around the fire, but the squaw laid a kin for me, and beg me to sit down, and gave me some ground nuts, and bade me come again.
>
> (Rowlandson, 2009, p. 13)

Mary Rowlandson developed a sense of empathy with her Indian Master, which lead to a reduction in her Confusion of Tongues trauma:

My son being now a mile from me, I asked liberty to go and see him; they bade me go, and away I went, . . . I was gone from home, and met with all sorts of Indians . . . yet not one of them offered the least imaginable miscarriage to me, I turned homeward again, and met with my master. He showed me the way to my son.

(Rowlandson, 2009, p. 13)

References

Drake, J.D. (2000). *King Phillips War: Civil War in New England*. Amherst, MA: University of Massachusetts Press.

Gould, P. (1996). Reinventing Benjamin. Church, virtue, citizenship, and the history of King Phillips War. *Journal of the Early Republic*. 16: 645–657.

Lepore, J. (1999). *The Name of War: King Phillip's War and the Origins of American Identity*. New York: Vintage.

Norton, M. B. (2002). *In the Devil's snare: The Salem witchcraft crisis of 1692*. New York: Vintage Books.

Rowlandson, M. (2009). *A Narrative of the Captivity and Restoration of Mrs. Mary Rowlandson*. Librivox: Audiobook.

Chapter 18

The Confusion of Tongues of an Abducted Child

The Case of Elizabeth Smart

In June of 2002, a Mormon youth of fourteen, Elizabeth Smart was abducted from a tightly knit religious family living in a Utah suburb in the United States. Elizabeth was taken from her own bed, by Brian David Mitchell, when he broke into their house in a suburb of Salt Lake City, Utah. He was looking for a sexual partner. Mitchell forced Elizabeth to come with him by threatening to kill Elizabeth and her family if she resisted (Rachman, 2016). Sexual abuse was a primary focus of Elizabeth Smart's experience with Brian David Mitchell. He used religious beliefs to manipulate and control Elizabeth. She, however, was not taken in by Mitchell's attempts to manipulate her to have sex with him. She succumbed to his sexual desires not because she was fulfilling God's desires, but because she didn't want to die in her captive's hands. She was raped on a regular basis. Her normal assertive personality was altered by her captor. By his giving her alcohol, drugs, and showing her pornography Elizabeth was forced to give her body to her captor, but she never gave him her spirit.

Sexual, emotional, and physical trauma was the factor in the transformation of Elizabeth from a beautiful, happy, and responsive teenager into a bizarre-looking, reticent, zombie-like pseudo-adult.

Elizabeth Took on a New Persona

During her captivity Elizabeth's face and figure was covered from head to toe in a pseudo-hippie outfit made of gauze. She was forced to wear a veil over her face, and a hood covering her head. Her captors were dressed in a similar fashion. Together they appeared to be a New Age hippie trio. They became a pseudo-family. At no time did Elizabeth try to escape. As in the case of Mary Rowlandson, the abductee, she became bound to her

DOI: 10.4324/9781003265030-18

captors through the influence of the Confusion of Tongues trauma. The abductee forms a bond with the abuser through the "terrorism of suffering" (Ferenczi, 1933). The victim uses the defense mechanisms which the Confusion of Tongues triggers (see Chapter Seven) in order to maintain a sense of self-cohesion in the light of experiencing the suffering of abuse and continuing trauma.

Nine months after the abduction of Elizabeth Smart, she was found alive, in the company of her kidnappers in the town of Sandy, Utah, about 18 miles from her home. She was approached by a very intelligent and perceptive policewoman who remembered the police reports and media publicity about Elizabeth's kidnapping. Noticing the pseudo-family trio, dressed in hippie-like outfits, the policewoman approached the youngest of the group, asking her if she was Elizabeth Smart. At first, Elizabeth didn't answer. The policewoman watched Elizabeth walk around, then asked her again. Elizabeth's silence when first asked can be explained as her being in a dissociative phase of the Confusion of Tongues trauma. Making contact, for the first time in almost a year, with a nonabusive positive adult broke through the dissociation. Elizabeth was dissociated, but not psychiatrically separated from reality. One could assume the policewoman's voice and demeanor suggested concern and possibly empathy. The second time the policewoman asked her if she was Elizabeth Smart, the young lady identified herself. The policewoman then acted in the psychologically assertive manner that was necessary for the situation, immediately separating Elizabeth from her captors. By correctly separating Elizabeth from her traumagenic kidnappers, the policewoman became a psychological hero. Her behavior demonstrated the need for a therapeutic intervention when a Confusion of Tongues trauma is operative. The policewoman had the courage, intelligence, assertiveness, and compassion to intervene in a social situation to literally save the life of an abused child with concern for the child's welfare. But correctly, she did not use police aggression. This kind of intervention by police should stand as a model for training and intervention in emotionally traumatic situations.

Elizabeth Smart's Confusion of Tongues Trauma

The psychodynamics of Elizabeth Smart's trauma as an abducted child is a Confusion of Tongues experience can be described in the following way:

1. The child is psychologically disoriented when they are abducted and removed from the safety of their home and the love of their parents. Such an experience disorients and destabilizes the individual so that they lose their orientation to the world and themselves. They become dependent upon their captors for affirmation, affection, a sense of reality, and safety. Such vulnerability develops a bond of trauma between the abused and the abuser.

2. A profound sense of abandonment develops as captivity endures. The child loses hope that they will ever again see their parents. Even more profoundly, the child can come to believe their parents no longer care or love them. The captor uses a lack of parental contact as proof to the child of the parental abandonment. The loss of a belief in parental care and love is devastating. The child is unhinged from their sense of security, safety, object consistency, and belief in their parents as protectors and nurturers. The trauma encourages dependency on the captor. Elizabeth Smart, even with her constant belief in her parents' and sister's love and a belief that God was looking after her, fell under the psychological domination of her captor, Brian David Mitchell.

3. The abuser isolates the child from interpersonal and communal contact. Emotional and interpersonal contact occurs exclusively with the abuser. The captor has every desire to replace the child's parent. To survive, the child must depend upon their captor to satisfy their survival and developmental needs. As Ferenczi first suggested, the child in the throes of a Confusion of Tongues experience identifies with the aggressor (the abuser) (Ferenczi, 1933). The child's developmental needs are dependent upon the whims of the abuser, whose narcissismdetermines their response. Such emotional need creates a need to please the abuser to receive need fulfillment. <u>This creates a diabolic psychodynamic, which the abuser can use to manipulate, control, and overpower the child</u>.

4. The captor creates a vacuum of affection, love, empathy, and safety which makes the child susceptible to the abuser so that they can lose their own capacity to test reality. The individual can lose their capacity to discern their own reality from the reality of the captor.

Recovery of Elizabeth Smart

Elizabeth Smart's emotional recovery, like Mary Rowlandson, both from abduction, which caused a Confusion of Tongues trauma is very important for psychoanalysts to understand. All psychoanalysts would probably say that recovery from severe trauma necessitates some long-term intensive psychotherapy or psychoanalysis. Of course, in colonial times, counseling, psychotherapy, and psychoanalysis was unknown, so Mary Rowlandson did not have therapy available to her. Elizabeth Smart did have all of the contemporary treatment options available to her. For the early days of 2003, when Elizabeth returned to her family, there was no evidence from any sources that she received any professional help. Her parents offered therapy to their daughter. We have now Elizabeth Smart's experience, described in her own words (Smart & Stewart, 2013):

> I always get asked the same questions, "How did you survive?" and "How did you overcome what happened to you?" The answer to the first question is pretty simple. The main reason I was able to survive is because of my God, my family, and my community . . . some [people] . . . might think, <u>given the fact that I haven't received any professional counseling</u>, that something must still be wrong with me, that I'm hiding my wounds or putting on a happy face . . . that there are certain things that I'm not ready to face.
>
> (Smart & Stewart, 2013, p. 297)

Elizabeth's path to recovery involved her Mormon faith, belief in God, contemplation and self-reflection, conversations with her immediate family, as well as regular participation in the activities of horseback riding and playing the harp. It does not mean that Elizabeth rejected therapy as much as it means she had developed, as a child and adolescent, her own meaningful way of dealing with feelings and emotional disturbance. Two significant relationships, one with her grandfather and one with her mother, as well as horseback riding and playing the harp were Elizabeth's avenues for therapeutic recovery. Her grandfather and her riding horseback provided her with silence, contemplation, the enjoyable presence of her grandfather, and being with animals and nature. Elizabeth's mother provided her with the words that would help her to put her trauma to rest. Her mother's words helped her:

> At the end of the day, God is our ultimate judge. He will make up to you every pain and loss that you have suffered. And if it turn out that these wicked people are not punished here on Earth, it doesn't

matter. . . . If you go and feel sorry for yourself, or if you dwell on what happened, if you hold on to your pain, that is allowing him to steal more of your life away. . . . Don't let him! Not one more second for yourself. . . . It's been ten years since my mother said those words. The years have proven she was right.

(Smart & Stewart, 2013, p. 286)

After returning to her family and being free of the trauma of abduction, Elizabeth returned to high school and graduated from Brigham Young University in Provo, Utah. After announcing a January 2011 engagement, Elizabeth Smart and Matthew Gilmour were married in a Mormon ceremony in Hawaii. She agreed to help the United States Department of Justice put together a sixty-three-page guide for survivors of kidnapping (Hunt, 2008). On July 7, 2011, Elizabeth Smart was hired as an ABC news correspondent (Carter, 2017). Also in 2011, she founded the Elizabeth Smart Foundation, which supports the Internet Crimes Against Children Task Force, and educates children about violent and sexual crime. As has been cited, in 2013, she wrote a book about her abduction trauma. She testified in February 2014 before the Utah State House of Representatives in favor of a bill that would create a nonmandated curriculum for use in Utah schools to provide training on child abuse prevention.

References

Carter, N. (2017) *Elizabeth Smart's Incredible Story: From Kidnapped Teen to Survivor and Married Mom.* https://people.com/crime/elizabeth-smart-abduction-rescue-and-marriage/

Ferenczi, S. (1933). The Confusion of Tongues between adults and children: The language of tenderness and passion. In Balint, M. (Ed.) *Final Contributions to the Problems and Methods of Psychoanalysis* (E. Moscher, Trans.). New York: Bruner/Mazel, 1980, pp. 156–167.

Hunt, S. (2008). Kidnap victim offers advice in survival guide. *Salt Lake Tribune,* May 21. https://archive.vcstar.com/news/kidnap-victim-offers-advice-in-survival-guide-ep-373734663-352564691.html/

Smart, E. and Stewart, C. (2013). *My Story, Elizabeth Smart.* New York: St. Martin's Press.

Chapter 19

The Confusion of Tongues Trauma Between Franz Kafka and His Father

Family and Work

Franz Kafka was born on July 3, 1883, in Prague, the capital of what is now the Czech Republic He grew up in an upper middle-class Jewish family as the surviving eldest son of six children. He had a difficult relationship with both of his parents. His mother, Julie, was a devoted homemaker who was thought to lack the intellectual depth to understand her son's dreams to become a writer (Brod, 1960). Kafka's father, Hermann, had a forceful personality that often overwhelmed his son. He was a successful business-man selling men and women's clothing. The father had a profound impact on both Kafka's life and writing. For much of his adult life, Kafka lived in physical and emotional close proximity to his parents (Brod, 1960). Kafka was a smart child who did well in school. He earned the respect of his teachers at an academic elite high school; he chafed under their and the school's control of his life. After high school, he earned a law degree from the Ferdinand University of Prague in 1906. He began a lengthy experi-ence in 1907 with the Workers' Accident Insurance Institute for the King-dom of Bohemia. He worked well in his capacity as his boss' right-hand man completing the company's annual report. He was seen as a popular employee, easy to socialize with and having a good sense of humor. Kafka remained with the company until 1917 when he was forced to take a sick leave because of tuberculosis, eventually returning in 1922 (Brod, 1960).

Personal Life

Kafka's relationship with women was filled with difficulties and inse-curities. He never married. Kafka was tortured by sexual desire (Hawes, 2008). His life was full of womanizing, and he was filled with a fear of

DOI: 10.4324/9781003265030-19

sexual failure (Stach, 2007). Kafka visited brothels for most of his adult life (Hawes, 2008; Stach, 2017). However, he did have close relationships with women during his lifetime. Felice Bauer, a relative of Max Brod, his best friend and literary executor, communicated with him through letters for over five years. They met occasionally and were engaged twice. They separated in 1917. He was engaged for a third time to Julie Wohayzek, and although they set a wedding date, they did not marry (Hawes, 2008; Stach, 2017). Mélena Jesenská was a Czech journalist who translated one of his short stories. Her letter to him began an intense and passionate correspondence. They only met twice. Kafka broke off the relationship because Mélena was unable to leave her husband. Mélena, it is likely, was Kafka's most fervent love object, yet his most unfulfilled. This emotional tragedy left a lingering sense of darkness in his mind and soul (Brod, 1960).

His Literature

While it seems unusual, even incongruous, for such a literary giant as Kafka to spend his adult life working in an insurance company as a high-level clerk, he was dedicated to earning a living. His best friend, Max Brod, was vital in supporting and preserving his literary work, both during his life and for generations afterward. In fact, the world owes Brod an enormous debt for saving Kafka's oeuvre after his death. Before his death, Kafka asked his friend to destroy his works. The world can thank Brod for going against his friend's wishes, saving the work of one of the giants of 20th century literature for the world to enjoy and study. Kafka's celebrity as a writer only came after his death. During his lifetime, he published a fraction of his overall work. His most popular and best-selling work was the short story, *The Metamorphosis* (Kafka, 1996), published in 1915 in Leipzig. This story will be discussed in Section IV when Kafka's traumatic relationship with his father will be analyzed.

The term Kafkaesque, derived from Kafka's work, is used to describe concepts and situations which were developed from the emotional and interpersonal climate of his work. The description refers to instances in which bureaucracies overpower people, often in a surreal, nightmarish milieu which evokes feelings of senselessness, disorientation, and helplessness. Characters in a Kafkaesque setting often lack a clear course of action to escape a labyrinthine situation. The term has transcended the literary to apply to real-life occurrences and situations that are incomprehensibly complex, bizarre, or illogical (Strelka, 1984).

Illness

Kafka was diagnosed with tuberculosis in August 1917, and moved for a few months to the Bohemian village in Zürau. He felt comfortable there and later described this time as perhaps the best period of his life, probably because he had no responsibilities. For many years, even before he contracted tuberculosis, Kafka had not been well. Constantly strained and stressed, he suffered from migraines, boils, depression, anxiety, and insomnia. In an attempt to overcome his tuberculosis, he traveled to Vienna for treatment at a sanatorium. He died in Kierling, Austria on June 3, 1924. He was buried with his parents in Prague's New Jewish Cemetery in Olsake (Gelman, 1995).

II. The Tradition of Obedience in a Jewish Father/Son Relationship: The Akedah Yitchak – The Binding of Isaac

The iconic tale from the Old Testament, The Akedah Yitchak, The Binding of Isaac, can be seen as standard for a traditional Jewish father's relationship with his son. In Genesis 22, Abraham, The Father of the Jews, is asked to go through a harrowing experience with his son Isaac in order to test his loyalty and devotion to God. The experience centers on a disturbing idea of infanticide. The story appears in the Rosh Hashanah liturgy, the celebration of the Jewish New Year. The actual tale will be presented first, then its meaning for the understanding of the father/son relationship between Herman and Franz Kafka will be discussed.

Genesis 22: The Akedah: The Binding of Isaac

22:1   "Sometime afterward God put Abraham to the test. He said to him, 'Abraham', and he answered, 'Here I am'.

22:2   And he said, 'Take your son, your favored one, Isaac, whom you love, to the land of Hariah, and offer him there as a burnt offering, and set out for the place of which God had told him.

22:3   So early the next morning Abraham saddled his ass and took with him two of his servants and his Isaac. He split the wood for the burnt offering, and he set out for the place of which God had told him.

22:4   On the third day, Abraham looked up and saw the place from afar.

22:5   Then Abraham said to his servants, 'You stay here with the ass The boy and I will go there; we will worship and we will return to you'.

22:6   Abraham took the wood for the burnt offering and put it on his son Isaac. He himself took the firestone and the knife; and the two walked off together.

22:7   Then Isaac said to his father Abraham, 'Father'! And he answered, 'Yes, my son', and he said, 'Here are the firestone and wood; but where is the sheep for the burnt offering'?

22:8   And Abraham said, 'God will see to the sheep for his burnt offering, my son.' And the two of them walked on together.

22:9   They arrived at the place of which God had told him. Abraham built an altar there, he laid out the wood; he bound his son Isaac; he laid him on the altar, on top of the wood.

22:10   And Abraham picked up the knife to slay his son.

22:11   Then an angel of the LORD called to him from heaven: 'Abraham! Abraham'! and he answered, 'Here I am.'

22:12   And he said, 'Do not raise your hand against the boy, or do anything to him. For now I know that you fear God, since you have not withheld your son, your favored one, from Me.'

22:13   When Abraham looked up, his eye fell on a ram, caught in the thicket by its horns. So Abraham went and took the ram and offered it up as a burnt offering in place of his son.

22:14   And Abraham named that side Adonai-yireh (the Lord), whence the present saying, 'On the mount of the Lord, there is vision.'

22:15   The angel of the LORD called to Abraham a second time from heaven.

22:16   And said, 'By Myself', I swear the LORD declares: 'because you have done this and have not withheld your son, your favored one'.

22:17   'I will bestow Myself upon you and make your descendants as numerous as the stars of the heavens and the sands of the seashore; and your descendants shall seize the gates of your foes.'

22:18   'All the nations of the earth shall bless themselves by your descendants, because you have obeyed my command.'

22:19   Abraham then returned to his servants, and they departed together for Beersheba; and Abraham stayed in Beersheba."

(Jastrow, McCardy, Jastrow, & Ginsberg, 2012)

The harrowing story of how Abraham nearly sacrificed his son, Isaac on Mount Moriah is troubling and has raised fundamental questions as to the meaning of the Genesis story. Two fundamental questions that the Akedah raises are: How could God demand that Abraham kill his son? How could a virtuous person be willing to kill a child? (Levenson, 1993). Religious and biblical scholars have concluded that the Akedah is God's testing the loyalty of Abraham, the Father of the Jews, in his willingness to sacrifice his son. What is more, these commentaries also emphasize that God never intended to have Abraham be involved in infanticide. The idea of child sacrifice was the strongest test of loyalty, not the manifestation of an angry loveless God. Another meaning which can be extracted from the Akedah is the traditional nature of a father/son relationship assigned to a Jewish father and his son by God. In analyzing the statements contained in the Old Testament, the Book of Genesis 22 verses 1–19, we discern that God, with no explanation offered, demanded Abraham to obey his request to make a sacrifice of his son on Mount Moriah. Abraham assumed the sacrifice God is asking him to make is a kosher animal sacrifice, described and commanded in the Torah (the law of God as revealed to Moses and recorded in the first five books of the Hebrew scriptures). The sacrifice was a bull, sheep, goat, grain, meal, wine or incense. Offerings were often cooked and most of it eaten by the offerer, with parts given to the Kohen priests (High Priests), and small parts burned on the altar of the Temple in Jerusalem (Jastrow et al., 2012).

Abraham does not question God's request, consequently bringing his son Isaac along to execute the burnt offering is taken for granted. When God asked Abraham to bind his son, Isaac to the area where the fire will be made, Abraham once again does not question God's disturbing request to offer up Isaac as the burnt offering. What it more, Abraham does not voice an objection to God's outrageous demand for infanticide. An angel emerged in the tale to prevent Abraham from igniting the fire. Why didn't God stop Abraham from sacrificing his son? Finally,

Abraham returns home, after the emotional trauma of The Binding of Isaac, in a state of denial and dissociation. He behaves as if nothing of significance has happened to him or his son. What is more, he had nothing of concern to say to God after the trauma. With these considerations in mind, the Akedah can be understood as the prototype of a Jewish father asking the son for total obedience to his requests. God, the father, Abraham, the father. Their relationship is characterized by the father having power, control, and status over the son. Mutual and democratic ideals are not dimensions of such a relationship. God and Abraham and Isaac's prototypical relationship will be compared to the relationship between Franz and Herman Kafka, a Jewish father and son in modern times whose traumatic relationship can be understood by the Confusion of Tongues paradigm.

III. The Jewishness of Franz Kafka

Freud commented on what he considered the essence of Jewishness:

> We Jews have always known how to respect spiritual values. We preserved our unity though ideas and because of them we have survived to this day. The fact that Rabbi Jochana ben Zakkai, immediately after the destruction of the Temple, obtained from the conqueror permission to establish the first academy for Jewish knowledge in Yavneh was, for me, always one of the most significant manifestations in our history.
>
> (Richards, 2010, p. 3)

Franz Kafka's sense of Jewishness was manifested, in the same manner as Freud's statement about the essence of Judaism, as being intellectuality and morality. As we shall see in our discussion, Franz's view of Judaism was in stark contrast to his father's, Hermann Kafka. The difference in outlook marked the emotional struggle in which they were imprisoned and contributed to the trauma that enveloped Franz during his lifetime. Kafka was well aware of his Jewish heritage:

> In Hebrew, I am called Amschel like my mother's maternal grandfather, whom my mother remembers as a very devout and learned man with a long white beard.
>
> (Bauer, 1971, p. 184)

With few exceptions, there is little overt references to Jews and Jewishness in Kafka's literature. It would be a mistake, however, to conclude that Jewishness did not matter to him, or it did not have any import for his writing. From his biography, diaries, and letters we know he was indifferent in his youth to Jewishness and Judaism. Beginning from 1911 on, when Kafka was 28, his Jewishness began to matter very much. From that time on, he began to be intensely interested in Jewish history, Jewish tradition, and Jewish lore and culture. This interest was sustainable and constant until his death in 1924 at the age of 40. It is significant for his writing that Kafka's turn to Judaism was preceded by less than one year in what he called his breakthrough. This is the work of his maturity, to the kind of writing that established his posthumous fame and for which the adjective Kafkaesque has been coined. There is a connection between the nature of Kafka's later writing and his discovery of what he considered to be authentic Judaism. He had deep regrets about not knowing of this connection earlier in his life (Sokel, 1999).

Kafka discovering his Jewishness has more than one dimension. It is necessary to present the complexity of Kafka's early disconnect from Judaism. We need to understand the Zeitgeist of the Jews of Prague in Kafka's time, to view his Jewishness. The fact was that his family were minimally observant German-speaking Jews. Kafka's parents probably spoke a German influenced by Yiddish. As the German language was considered the vehicle of social mobility, they encouraged their children to speak standard German (Hawes, 2008). German became Kafka's first language. In fact, despite the Czech background and Jewish roots, Kafka's identity favored German culture. Julie and Hermann Kafka were a typical Jewish couple of Eastern Europe of the early part of the 20th century. Their thinking and behavior reflected the assimilation of the Jewish bourgeoisie. The Zeitgeist of Eastern European society was deceptive. On the surface, the Jewish middle class was striving for economic and social assimilation, but Jews were not enjoying integration and acceptance. Franz Kafka, being an intellectually gifted and emotionally sensitive child and adolescent, was aware there was a profound discrepancy between the appearance of assimilation, solidity, and the reality of alienation. He struggled with the subjective experience of feeling the family and society in which he lived and worked presented a menace to the individual. Authority presented a threat to the individual. He did not believe his family and society were providing solid ground that allowed the individual to feel secure, safe and hopeful. A profound psychodynamic which influenced Kafka's sense of Jewishness was the disturbed relationship with his father.

Kafka's View of His Father's Jewishness

Hermann Kafka demanded that his son observe Judaism in his way: to accompany him to the synagogue, sit next to him, and join him in the recitation of the liturgy. His father's expression of power, control, and status over his son to be Jewish like him became a dimension of the emotional trauma that developed between them. Kafka's disinterest in joining his father in the synagogue was not a sign of angry defiance, but his struggle to maintain his independence and sense of self:

> I found little escape from you in Judaism . . . it would have been thinkable that we might both have found each other in Judaism or that we might have begun from there in harmony. But what sort of Judaism was it I got from you?
>
> (Heller, 1979, p. 215)

In a remarkable literary and psychological exposition of their relationship, *The Letter to His Father* (1919), Kafka spelled out three areas of conflict between himself and his father about Judaism:

1. As a child I reproached myself . . . for not going to the synagogue often enough, for fasting . . . I thought that in this way I was doing a wrong not to myself but to you and I was penetrated by a sense of guilt. (Kafka, 1919, p. 215)
2. Later, as a young man, I could not understand how, with the insignificant scrap of Judaism you yourself possessed, you could reproach me for not making an effort (for the sake of piety at least, as you put it) to cling to a similar insignificant scrap. It was . . . a mere nothing . . . not even a joke. Four days a year, you went to the synagogue . . . closer to the indifferent than to those who took it seriously . . . went through the prayers as a formality . . . it was also very frightening for me there, . . . because you once mentioned . . . that I might be called to the Torah. That was something I dreaded for years. . . . It was impossible to make a child acutely observant from sheer nervousness, understand that the few flimsy gestures you performed in the name of Judaism. . . . For

you they had meaning . . . you could do this through persuasion or threat. (Kafka, 1919, pp. 215–226)

3. Had your Judaism been stronger, your example would have been more compelling, too; that I was taking more interest in Jewish matter . . . Through my interventions, Judaism became abhorrent to you, Jewish writing unreadable; they "nauseated" you. This may have meant you insisted that only that Judaism which you had shown me in my childhood was the righteous, and beyond it there was nothing. . . . But then the "nausea" (apart from the fact it was directly primarily not against Judaism but against me personally) could only mean that unconsciously you did acknowledge the weakness of your Judaism and my Jewish upbringing, and did not wish to be reminded of it in any way, and reacted to any reminder with frank hatred.

(Kafka, 1919, p. 219)

The quotations from The Letter to His Father (Heller, 1979), dramatically illustrates Kafka's subjective experience of his father's hypocrisy regarding his Jewishness. Hermann Kafka was not a model of being a faithful and a devoted religious Jew. What he expressed in his interaction with his son was his need for power, control, and status in their relationship. Hermann did not pass down the meaning of being Jewish as Freud described it: respect for spiritual values; values of study, and intellectual knowledge. Nor did his father transmit a love of the Jewish Culture, the preservation of the Yiddish language, the admiration and connection to Jewish sages and secular heroes. It was not until Franz Kafka emotionally separated from his father that he discovered his Jewish heritage. In his struggle for self-definition, he lost connection with Judaism because it was defined by his authoritarian father. He was finally able to connect with his intellectual, spiritual, and cultural heritage when he became less dependent and needy for his father's affirmation. At that point, he could investigate and integrate his own understanding of Jewish belief and culture.

IV. Franz Hermann Kafka's Relationship: An Oedipal Complex or Traumatic Disorder

Kafka, as did Shakespeare before him, communicated a narrative which exposed the phenomenological experience of human relations: the hurt and pain in familial and love relationships; the individual's journey to understanding of their inner emotional state. In Kafka's contribution to the study of the father/son relationship, he was redefining Freud's idea of an Oedipal complex, the gripping unconscious drama between father and son for the love of the mother. But Kafka's father/son drama is made of a different cloth than the biologically driven Oedipal drama. Kafka's father/son drama rises from actual disturbed relational interaction in the here and now of their relationship. His father, as he was described by his son, was a domineering, physically overpowering, mean-spirited, emotionally and physically abusive, neglectful individual with a frail, emotionally sensitive, and traumatized son. The Kafka drama is not a matter of the son being a player in a biologically driven family romance. The primary psychodynamic was not a struggle with unconscious longings for his mother and fearing the wrath and punishment from his father. Kafka was describing in his The Letter to His Father (Kafka, 1919) a trauma disorder (Rachman & Klett, 2015). Kafka was struggling with a father who was actually hurting him; it was not an unconscious, fantasy experience. Kafka offered a relational perspective understanding for neurotic interaction which predated Sándor Ferenczi's introduction of a relational framework for trauma and psychoanalysis (Ferenczi, 1933; Rachman, 2022; Rachman & Mucci, 2023 [this volume]). Kafka's mother was a loving emotionally responsive presence, helping him to develop a sense of self in order to use his creativity to develop the capacity to love. But the mother did not protect her family from the tyrannical, abusive father. She became a model of emotional suffering. Kafka was identified with his mother's silent, weak suffering self. The good wife taught her son to be a good child. It was only through his literature that he found his voice. Kafka in Prague, Ferenczi in Budapest were weaving a tapestry in literature and psychoanalysis which illuminated the phenomenology of the inner experience of a parent/child relational trauma (Rachman & Mucci, 2023 [this volume]).

Franz Kafka was an icon of dark existentialist and absurdist literature, who frequently wrote about the themes of isolation, alienation, authoritarianism, and oppression. He had a complex experience while living at home because he suffered from hypersensitivity to noise and a yearning for solitude. His father, Hermann Kafka, was verbally, physically, and emotionally abusive to his son, a truth revealed in Kafka's written work. Franz never rebelled openly against his father. He did, however, express his feelings and emotions about the relationship he had with his father. Hermann

Kafka was a major influence in his life, loud, impulsive, and authoritarian. We will explore the emotional relationship between Franz and Hermann Kafka as it is revealed in two literary works. The aforementioned, Letter to His Father (Kafka, 1919) and The Metamorphosis (Kafka, 1996). The Letter to His Father is Franz Kafka's emotional confession of the trauma he suffered in childhood by his abusive and neglectful father and, on the other hand, his attempt to emotionally separate from his traumatogenic father. The Metamorphosis is a symbolic narrative illustrating the phenomenology of Kafka's subjective experience of severe trauma, where he disclosed his deepest sense of vulnerability and feelings of a loss of self. His trauma caused dissociation of his personality and fragmentation of sense of self. The present discussion has attempted to establish that Franz Kafka suffered from a trauma disorder originating in his disturbing emotional relationship with his father. His father often verbally abused him, did not provide him with affirmation in a meaningful human way, withheld affection and love, was relentlessly critical and demeaning, expressed disappointment in his son's performance and career, and had no interest in the literature he created. As mentioned, Kafka never did rebel openly against his father, but his literature was the vehicle for expressing his feelings of abuse by his father. The literature presented a description of the psychology of abuse in the disturbed relationship to authority, feelings of isolation, loneliness, rejection, and self-disintegration. Two of his iconic literary productions are vehicles for Kafka to express himself about his relationship with his father. The Metamorphosis symbolically expresses the emotional damage he suffered from the abuse of his relationship with his father. As has been outlined, Ferenczi introduced a paradigm shift in psychoanalytic theory with the Confusion of Tongues theory of trauma (Rachman, 1994, 2018, 2022; Rachman & Klett, 2015; Chapter Seven of this volume). Kafka's two literary products add to the phenomenology of the relational trauma experience.

The pathological confusion which arises from parental abuse is that parent and child speak different languages which leads to emotional disturbance. The child speaks the language of tenderness, affection, and love, which it needs for emotional development and personal growth. When a parent speaks the language of passion and sexuality, he/she interjects their narcissistic need for their self-fulfillment onto the child, creating an abusive experience. This Confusion of Tongues experience damages the child. It produces a host of psychopathology which arrests personality development and produces a trauma disorder (Ferenczi, 1933; Chapter Seven, this volume). Parental abuse can take the form of physical, sexual, emotional, and interpersonal abuse. The child, if subjected to repeated and/ or intensive abuse, can become emotionally bound to their abuser, losing their own sense of self as they repeatedly try to gain the love and the nurture they need from the traumatogenic object. This childhood Confusion of Tongues trauma created a vulnerability which lead to Kafka's traumatic experience and self-damaging thoughts and feelings as an adult (Rachman & Klett, 2015). Ferenczi's formulation of the Confusion of Tongues, as we shall see, helps understand Franz Kafka's traumatic relationship with his father.

The Letter to His Father: Transforming Literature into Psychological Insight About Relational Trauma

On November 10, 1919, Franz Kafka wrote a 45-page letter to his father, Hermann Kafka. It was a "lawyer's letter," he told his friend and lover, Milena Jesenká. But it was the furthest from a legal brief that anyone has ever written. It is a disturbing document specifying Kafka's traumatic experience with his father, which began in childhood and continued throughout his adult lifetime. It is, at the same time, a remarkable literary piece as well as a psychological treatise. The Letter to His Father as a narrative has the capacity to elevate simple declarative sentences to the level of searing insights, piercing the inner space of the human psyche. What he says in this journey to the center of his psyche is a phenomenological study of trauma. The Letter remains today, 101 years after it was written, a unique piece of psychological literature. This is so because Kafka's self disclosures about his relationship with his father were intensely emotionally open, coarsely self disclosing, and emotionally searing. He documented his childhood humiliations suffered at his father's hands, writing as a 36-year-old man, but sounding like an injured child. According to Max Brod, Kafka actually gave the letter to his mother to hand to his father. His mother never delivered the letter but returned it to her son. The original letter, 45 pages long, was typewritten by Kafka and corrected by hand (Brod, 1960). There are a series of issues contained in this remarkable document, which detailed how disturbed the relationship between Franz and Hermann Kafka was, and how the son's sense of self was diminished by the father's relentless emotional abuse. The

Letter began with a passage that illuminates dramatically a child's experience of parental abuse and the subsequent formation of trauma:

> You asked me recently why I maintain that I am afraid of you. As usual, I was unable to think of any answer . . . for the very reason that I am afraid of you . . . the fear and its consequences hamper me in relation to you.
>
> (Kafka, 1919; p. 186)

Kafka goes on to describe the trauma more fully:

> You would trample me underfoot so that nothing was left of me (p. 189).
> [You were] completely tied to the business scarcely able to be with me even once a day.
>
> (Kafka, 1919, p. 190)

Kafka described an experience of childhood which lodged into his psyche, producing a traumatic memory which influenced his personality development:

> One night I kept whimpering for water . . . after several vigorous threats has failed to have any effect, you took me out of bed, carried me out onto the pavlatche (courtyard balcony), and left me there alone for a while in my nightshirt, outside the shut door. . . . I was quite obedient afterwards . . . it did me inner harm . . . the extraordinary terror of being carried outside. Even years afterward, I suffered from the tormenting fancy that the huge man, my father, the ultimate authority would come almost for no reason at all, and take me out of bed in the night and carry me out onto the pavlatche, and that meant I was a mere nothing to him.
>
> (Kafka, 1919, p. 190)

Kafka used the trauma of the pavlatche experience to understand how his father's abusive behavior interfered with his development:

> this sense of nothingness that often dominates me. What I would have needed a little encouragement, a little friendliness . . . you really only

encourage me in anything when you yourself are involved in it, when what is at stake is your own sense of self-importance.

(Kafka, 1919, p. 191)

In a passage that evokes his damaged sense of self, Kafka described in The Metamorphosis:

I was . . . weighed down by your more physical presence . . . how we often undressed in the same bathing hut. There was I, skinny, weakly, slight; you strong, tall, broad. Even inside the hut I feel a miserable specimen, and whats more, not only in your eyes but in the eyes of the world.

(Kafka, 1919, pp. 191–192)

The Metamorphosis Kafka's Narrative for Psychological Disturbance

In The Metamorphosis (Kafka, 1996) described Gregor Smasa, a traveling salesman who awakes one day to find himself transformed into a giant insect. Gregor has a new body as an insect that struggles to get out of bed. The door to his bedroom is locked. Gregor says he is ill, but will attempt to go to work. Gregor's father and others drive him back into his room as they are repulsed by him. As time passes, Gregor's family members become accustomed to living with Gregor as less than a human being. His sister Grete is the only family member who has the courage to enter his room. When Gregor leaves his room weeks later, his mother becomes distraught and his father forces him back into his room by throwing apples at him. Gregor is injured by this attack and suffers a lonely convalescence. He is neglected by his family. They invade his living space by storing items in his room in order to make room for three lodgers who are taken in to supplement their income. Commenting on the revolting conditions of the household, the boarders threaten to depart. Gregor's sister realizes they must get rid of the insect, which she no longer experiences as her brother. The following morning, the charwoman who was hired to keep the household clean enters Gregor's room and finds him dead. When the lodgers appear for breakfast, Ms. Samsa sends them away. The charwoman, who is giggling, reports she has disposed of Gregor's body. The story ends as

Gregor's parents exhibit optimism for the future. They express no concern for their deceased son. Gregor's parents focus on their daughter's positive qualities, realizing she has grown into a woman.

The Metamorphosis: Trauma, Alienation, and Self-Disintegration

The Metamorphosis can be seen as the phenomenological description of Kafka's subjective experience of his traumatic experience with his father and the damage he suffered as a result of the abuse. Scholarly thematic evaluations of his work have involved psychoanalytic, symbolic, or allegorical natures of the story. Themes which have been suggested are social and emotional; alienation from society; familial alienation; and disturbance and disintegration. As the theme of this volume indicates, Metamorphosis can be analyzed from a psychologically relational-trauma perspective (Rachman, 1994, 1997a, 1997b, 1998, 2012, 2018, 2022; Rachman & Mucci, 2023 [this volume]). Both Letter to His Father and The Metamorphosis are literary expressions characteristic of Kafka's gifts, his powerful and searing narratives, which provided insight into the subjective experience of human beings traumatized by disturbing relational interaction with family, authority, and societal institutions. The Metamorphosis has been called a fantasy or a dream. Kafka's depiction of an insect/human being is the unconscious expression of Kafka's subjective experience of his own identity as a neglected human being by his father. Consequently, he interjected his family's treatment of him as being less than a human being, more like an animal, a "monstrous vermin."

The experience of Gregor Samsa embedded in The Metamorphosis is of an individual who has transformed from a human into a giant insect as a result of damaging abuse from his family, particularly his father. The father is alienated, emotionally neglectful, and physically hurtful to his son. I am suggesting that Gregor being transformed from a human being into an animal is Kafka's literary narrative for his emotionally disturbing relationship between himself and his father, which is the origin of the psychological transformation. Gregor could no longer tolerate the abuse which produced his unlivable trauma. His personality became so fragmented and dissociated that he lived in a delusional state, experiencing himself as an insect. His dissociation enabled him to become nonhuman and separate himself from his family and father. But separation and believing he was an insect was a journey towards leaving his unbearable traumatic world. The delusion of the metamorphosis was a death wish, to leave his traumatic early existence behind and end his intolerable suffering.

VII. Franz Kafka's Journey into Inner Space: The Phenomenology of Personal Trauma

At a time when psychoanalysis was attempting to chart a universal schematic for human experience defined by an understanding of the unconscious mind, Franz Kafka sat alone in his garret, office cubicle, synagogue bench, or hospital bed silently confronting his own inner psychological sense of self. He also wrote, weaving his thoughts, feelings, and experience into a unique literature. His closest friend and literary executor, Max Brod, knew Kafka was producing a treasure chest of literature. Brod became the caretaker of this treasure of personal statements, penetrating insights, and searing observations on relationships, authority, bureaucracy, government, ethnicity, and religious belief. Freud, in the first two decades of the 20th century, established his psychology of human neurosis with the belief in the universality of the Oedipal complex, establishing psychoanalysis as the study of the unconscious. Psychological disturbance was defined by what transpired in the unconscious zone of the human mind. Kafka, in the same time period, established a different trajectory. He offered the psychology of trauma, expressing his insights about human beings suffering from the oppression of authority. Trauma needs to be understood as a personal and societal issue. The intellectual climate in the sister cities of Vienna, Budapest, and Prague, during the first decades of the 20th century, produced three brilliant contributors, Sigmund Freud, the founder of psychoanalysis, Sándor Ferenczi, the analyst who pioneered trauma analysis, and Franz Kafka, the literary giant who presented us with his phenomenological description of trauma caused by authoritarianism.

References

Bauer, J. (1971). *Kafka and Prague*. New York: Praeger.

Brod, M. (1960). *Franz Kafka: A Biography*. New York: Schocken Books.

Ferenczi, S. (1933). The Confusion of Tongues between adults and children: The language of tenderness and passion. In Balint, M. (Ed.) *Final Contributions to the Problems and Methods of Psychoanalysis* (E. Moscher, Trans.). New York: Bruner/Mazel, 1980, pp. 156–167.

Gelman, S.L. (1995). *The Jewish Patient*. London: Routledge.

Hawes, J. (2008). *Excavating Kafka*. London: Quercus.

Heller, E. (1979). *Franz Kafka*. New York: Vintage Books.

Jastrow, M., Jr., McCardy, J., Jastrow, M. and Ginsberg, L. (2012). *The Jewish Encyclopedia: A Descriptive Record of the History, Religion, Literature, and Customs of the Jewish People from the Earliest Times to the Present Day*. Leicester: Forgotten Books.

Kafka, F. (1919). Letter to his father. In *Dearest Father: Stories and Other Writings* (E. Kaiser and E. Wilkins, Trans.). New York: Schocken Books, 1954.

Kafka, F. (1996). *The Metamorphosis*. New York: W. W. Norton & Company.

Levenson, J.D. (1993). *The Death and Resurrection of the Beloved Son*. New Haven, CT: Yale University Press.

Rachman, A.W. (1994). The Confusion of Tongues theory: Ferenczi's legacy to psychoanalysis. In Haynal, A. and Falzeder, E. (Eds.) *100 Years of Psychoanalysis*. London: Karnac Books, pp. 235–255.

Rachman, A.W. (1997a). *Sándor Ferenczi: The Psychotherapist of Tenderness and Passion*. Northvale, NJ: Jason Aronson.

Rachman, A.W. (1997b). The suppression and censorship of Ferenczi's Confusion of Tongues paper. *Psychoanalytic Inquiry* (*Psychoanalysis' Favorite Son: The Legacy of Sándor Ferenczi*). 17(4): 459–485.

Rachman, A.W. (1998). Ferenczi's "relaxation-principle" and the contemporary clinical practice of psychoanalysis. *American Journal of Psychoanalysis*. 58(1): 63–81.

Rachman, A.W. (2012). Confusion of tongues between Sándor Ferenczi and Elizabeth Severn. *Presentation. International Sándor Ferenczi Congress – "Faces of Trauma."* Budapest, June 3.

Rachman, A.W. (2022). *Psychoanalysis and Society's Neglect of Sexual Abuse of Children, Youth, and Adults: Reassessing Freud's Original Theory of Sexual Abuse and Trauma*. London: Routledge Press.

Rachman, A.W. and Klett, S. (2015). *Analysis of the Incest Trauma: Retrieval, Recovery, Renewal*. London: Karnac Books.

Richards, A.D. (Ed.) (2010). *The Jewish World of Sigmund Freud*. Jefferson, NC: McFarland.

Sokel, W.H. (1999). Kafka as a Jew. *New Literary History*. 30(4): 837–853.

Stach, R. (2007). *Kafka: The Early Years: The Early Years*. Princeton, NJ: Princeton University Press.

Strelka, J.P. (1984). Kafkaesque elements in Kafka's novels and in contemporary narrative prose. *Comparative Literature Studies*. 21(4): 434–444.

Index

psychoanalysis: analysis for analysts 84–85; analyst/analysand relationship 99–100, 108–109; body in dyadic psychoanalysis 175–183; developmental 118; dyadic experience 172; erotic/sexual contact 85–86; expanded role of analyst 67–73; face-to-face technique 177–183; limitations with family members 192–193, 195–201; mutual analysis 71; role of therapist 170–172; training institutes 105; as two-person partnership 4, 20, 37–42, 67, 118–121, 123–124, 170–172, 176
Psychoanalytic Society of Vienna 19
psychoneurosis 21–22
psychopathology: rooted in maltreatment/abuse and disorganized attachment 145–150; severe 123
Psychopathology of Everyday Life, The (Freud) 24
PTSD (post-traumatic stress disorders) 116–117; Complex PTSD 135, 136–137, 156

Racamier, Paul-Claude 182
Rachman, Arnold W. 13, 34, 112, 116–117, 120, 125–126, 136, 147, 149–152, 172, 184
Rank, Otto 104–105
regression, induced 171
Reik, Theodore 194
relational psychic encounters 183–186
repression 114, 132, 172–173
resilience 138, 160, 211–212; in recovery from trauma 55–60
Resilience and Survival (Mucci) 154
right brain/left brain dynamics 124, 126, 127, 136, 140, 149, 170–171, 183
right brain patterns of interaction 183–186
Riviere, Joan 32, 33, 62
Roazen, Paul 20, 66–67
Rowlandson, Mary 204–212

Schore, Allan 118, 121–124, 126, 133, 135, 139–141, 150, 163, 171, 179, 185
Searles, Harold 54
secrets 153, 180
Seduction Hypothesis (Freud) 3, 21–22, 92, 191
self-analysis 19–21, 24, 25, 84–85

Severn, Elizabeth 12–14, 27, 64, 66, 67, 68, 71; origins of Confusion of Tongues paradigm 104–110
sexuality, language of 75–80
sexual trauma theory 81–88
Siegel, Dan 118
Sigmund Freud's Mission (Fromm) 39
Smart, Elizabeth 213–217
social trauma 157–161, 175
Society of Rings 27, 29, 39
Sophocles 160
Spence, Donald 183
Spitz, René 123, 144
splitting of personality 50–51, 134, 135–136, 149, 155, 159, 177
Studies on Hysteria (Breuer & Freud) 96, 114
suicide 97–99

"talking cure" 101
Target, Mary 180–181
tenderness: and attachment, need for 150–151; confused with sexuality 76–77, 79; tender mothering 65–67, 87
terrorism of suffering 54, 214
therapeutic relationships, presence of an other 25
therapeutic touch 42
Thompson, Clara 15, 27–28, 34, 40–42, 62–63
Three Essays on the Theory of Sexuality (Freud) 96
Tiffany, Louis Comfort 194
Totschweigen campaign against Confusion of Tongues 27–35
touch: nurturing contrasted with erotic 47, 53; therapeutic 42
Tower of Babel and Confusion of Tongues paradigm 1–4
trance state techniques 13, 109
transference: abusive parental transference 87; countertransference 70–71, 73, 102, 106, 175; love 85–86
transgender individuals 96–97
trauma: and captivity, Elizabeth Smart's case 213–217; and captivity, Mary Rowlandson's case 204–212; and developmental arrest 66; early relational trauma 133–134; iatrogenic trauma 86; freezing response 147–148; healing from 179–180; human agency trauma 122–123, 135–136; identification with aggressor 52–53, 54–55, 136–137,

For Product Safety Concerns and Information please contact our EU
representative GPSR@taylorandfrancis.com
Taylor & Francis Verlag GmbH, Kaufingerstraße 24, 80331 München, Germany

9 7 8 1 0 3 2 2 0 7 4 7 6